NORMANDY
GOLD

TITAN
COMICS

NORMANDY **GOLD**

TITAN COMICS

EDITOR: TOM WILLIAMS
DESIGNER: OZ BROWNE

Senior Editor Andrew James
Titan Comics Editorial Jonathan Stevenson,
Lauren McPhee, Amoona Saohin
Senior Production Controller Jackie Flook
Production Supervisor Maria Pearson
Production Controller Peter James
Production Assistant Natalie Bolger
Art Director Oz Browne
Senior Sales Manager Steve Tothill
Press Officer Will O'Mullane
Marketing Manager Ricky Claydon
Commercial Manager Michelle Fairlamb
Head of Rights Jenny Boyce
Publishing Manager Darryl Tothill
Publishing Director Chris Teather
Operations Director Leigh Baulch
Executive Director Vivian Cheung
Publisher Nick Landau

WWW.TITAN-COMICS.COM

NORMANDY GOLD
9781785858642
Published by Titan Comics
A division of Titan Publishing Group Ltd.
144 Southwark Street, London, SE1 0UP

10 9 8 7 6 5 4 3 2 1
First Published April 2018
Printed in Spain

Become a fan on
Facebook.com/comicstitan

Follow us on
Twitter @comicstitan
For information on advertising, contact adinfo@titanemail.com or call **+44 20 7620 0200**
For rights information contact jenny.boyce@titanemail.com

NORMANDY
GOLD

WRITTEN BY
MEGAN ABBOTT &
ALISON GAYLIN

ARTWORK BY
STEVE SCOTT & RODNEY RAMOS

COLORS BY
LOVERN KINDZIERSKI

LETTERING BY
COMICRAFT

CONSULTING EDITOR
CHARLES ARDAI

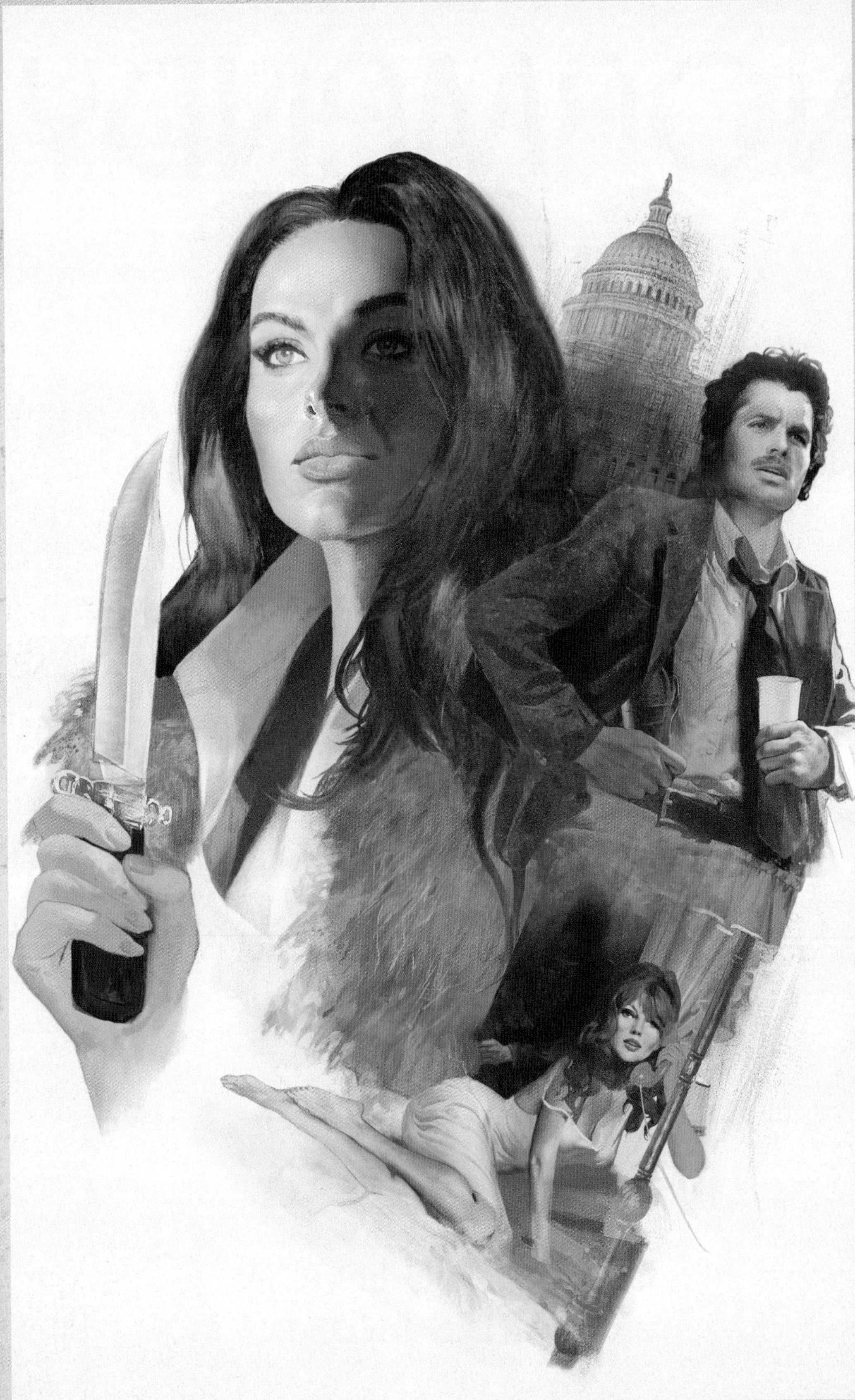

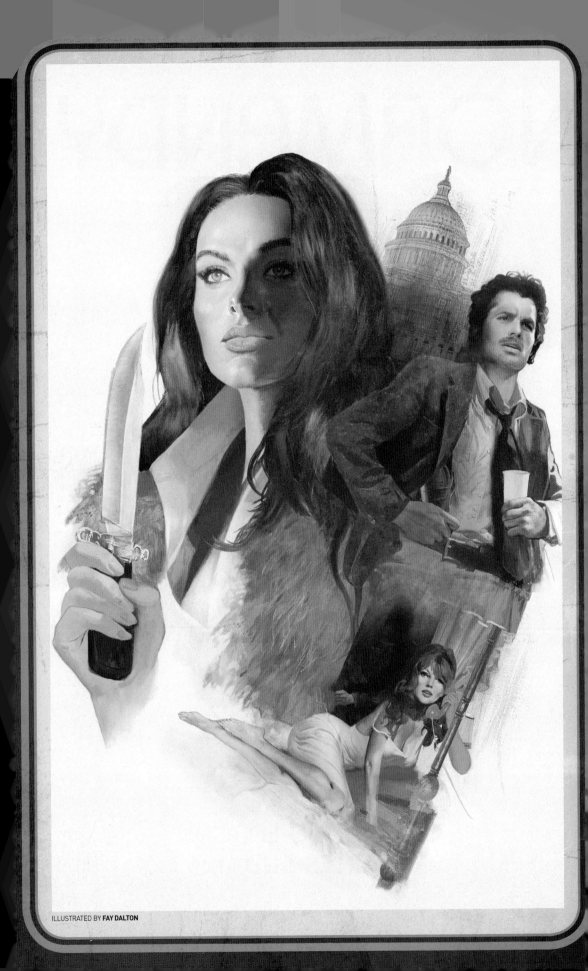

ILLUSTRATED BY **FAY DALTON**

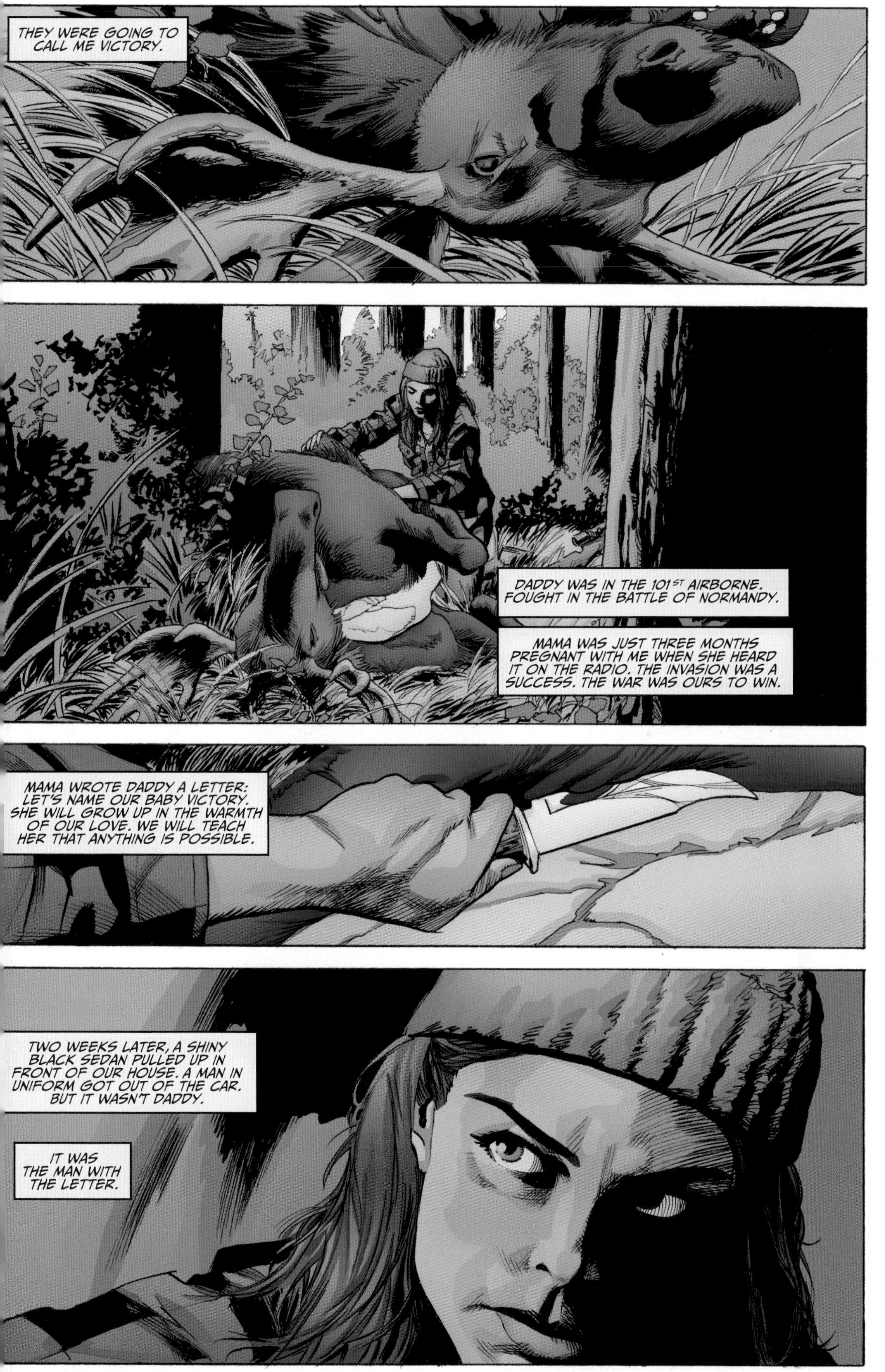
THEY WERE GOING TO CALL ME VICTORY.
DADDY WAS IN THE 101ST AIRBORNE. FOUGHT IN THE BATTLE OF NORMANDY.
MAMA WAS JUST THREE MONTHS PREGNANT WITH ME WHEN SHE HEARD IT ON THE RADIO. THE INVASION WAS A SUCCESS. THE WAR WAS OURS TO WIN.
MAMA WROTE DADDY A LETTER: LET'S NAME OUR BABY VICTORY. SHE WILL GROW UP IN THE WARMTH OF OUR LOVE. WE WILL TEACH HER THAT ANYTHING IS POSSIBLE.
TWO WEEKS LATER, A SHINY BLACK SEDAN PULLED UP IN FRONT OF OUR HOUSE. A MAN IN UNIFORM GOT OUT OF THE CAR. BUT IT WASN'T DADDY.
IT WAS THE MAN WITH THE LETTER.

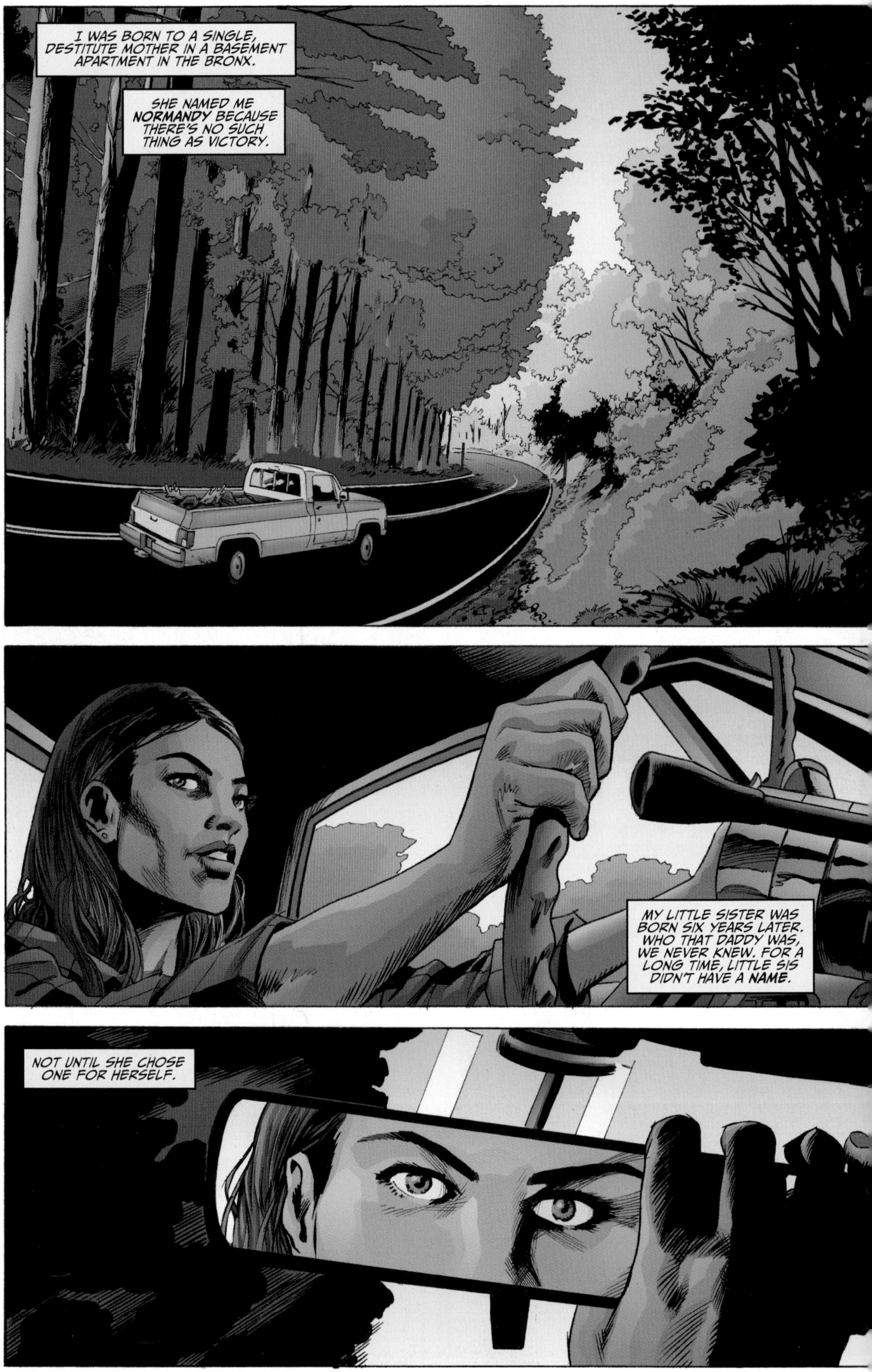
I WAS BORN TO A SINGLE, DESTITUTE MOTHER IN A BASEMENT APARTMENT IN THE BRONX.
SHE NAMED ME **NORMANDY** BECAUSE THERE'S NO SUCH THING AS VICTORY.
MY LITTLE SISTER WAS BORN SIX YEARS LATER. WHO THAT DADDY WAS, WE NEVER KNEW. FOR A LONG TIME, LITTLE SIS DIDN'T HAVE A **NAME**.
NOT UNTIL SHE CHOSE ONE FOR HERSELF.

NORMANDY? IT'S SO GOOD TO HEAR YOUR VOICE.

LILA? LILA, IS THAT YOU?

LIKE SO MUCH IN LIFE, IT STARTED WITH A PHONE CALL.

I'D BARELY SPOKEN TO DELILAH IN THE 12 YEARS SINCE I RAN AWAY FROM HOME, LEAVING HER WITH MAMA.

IT FELT LIKE YESTERDAY. IT FELT LIKE FOREVER.

LILA, ARE YOU OKAY?

BETTER THAN OKAY, SIS. I'M IN LOVE WITH A WONDERFUL MAN. HE'S MARRIED, BUT HE'S LEAVING HIS WIFE FOR ME AND...

... AND WE'RE GOING TO GET MARRIED. I'VE NEVER BEEN SO HAPPY IN MY—

LILA, WHERE ARE YOU?

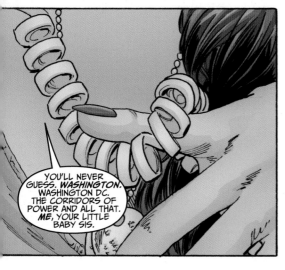

YOU'LL NEVER GUESS. WASHINGTON. WASHINGTON DC. THE CORRIDORS OF POWER AND ALL THAT. ME, YOUR LITTLE BABY SIS.

I ... I DIDN'T FORGET YOU, LILA.

I KNOW YOU DIDN'T. AND I NEVER BLAMED YOU FOR LEAVING HOME. NOT EVEN FOR A SECOND.

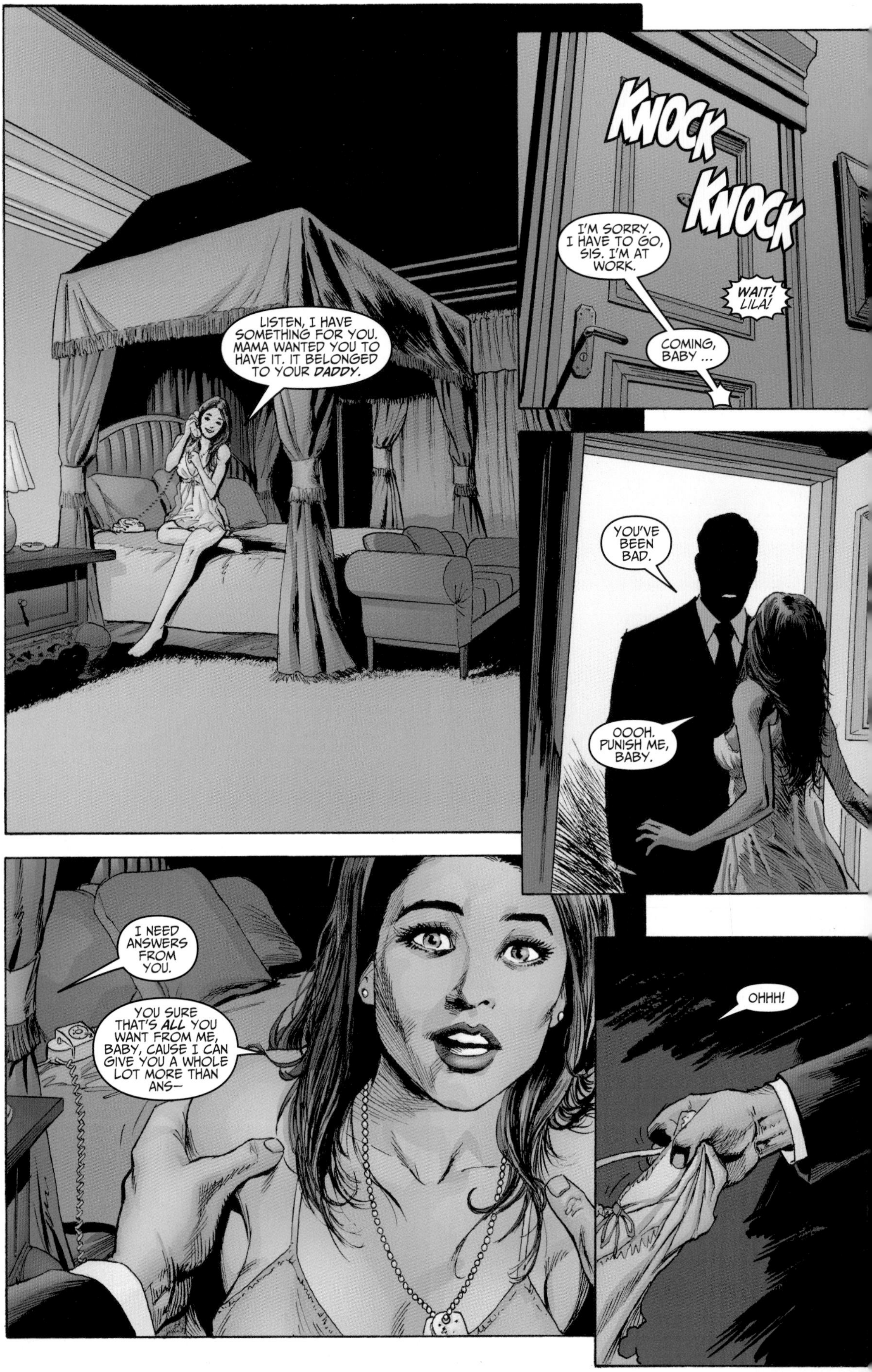
LISTEN, I HAVE SOMETHING FOR YOU. MAMA WANTED YOU TO HAVE IT. IT BELONGED TO YOUR DADDY.
KNOCK
KNOCK
I'M SORRY. I HAVE TO GO, SIS. I'M AT WORK.
WAIT! LILA!
COMING, BABY ...
YOU'VE BEEN BAD.
OOOH. PUNISH ME, BABY.
I NEED ANSWERS FROM YOU.
YOU SURE THAT'S ALL YOU WANT FROM ME, BABY, CAUSE I CAN GIVE YOU A WHOLE LOT MORE THAN ANS—
OHHH!

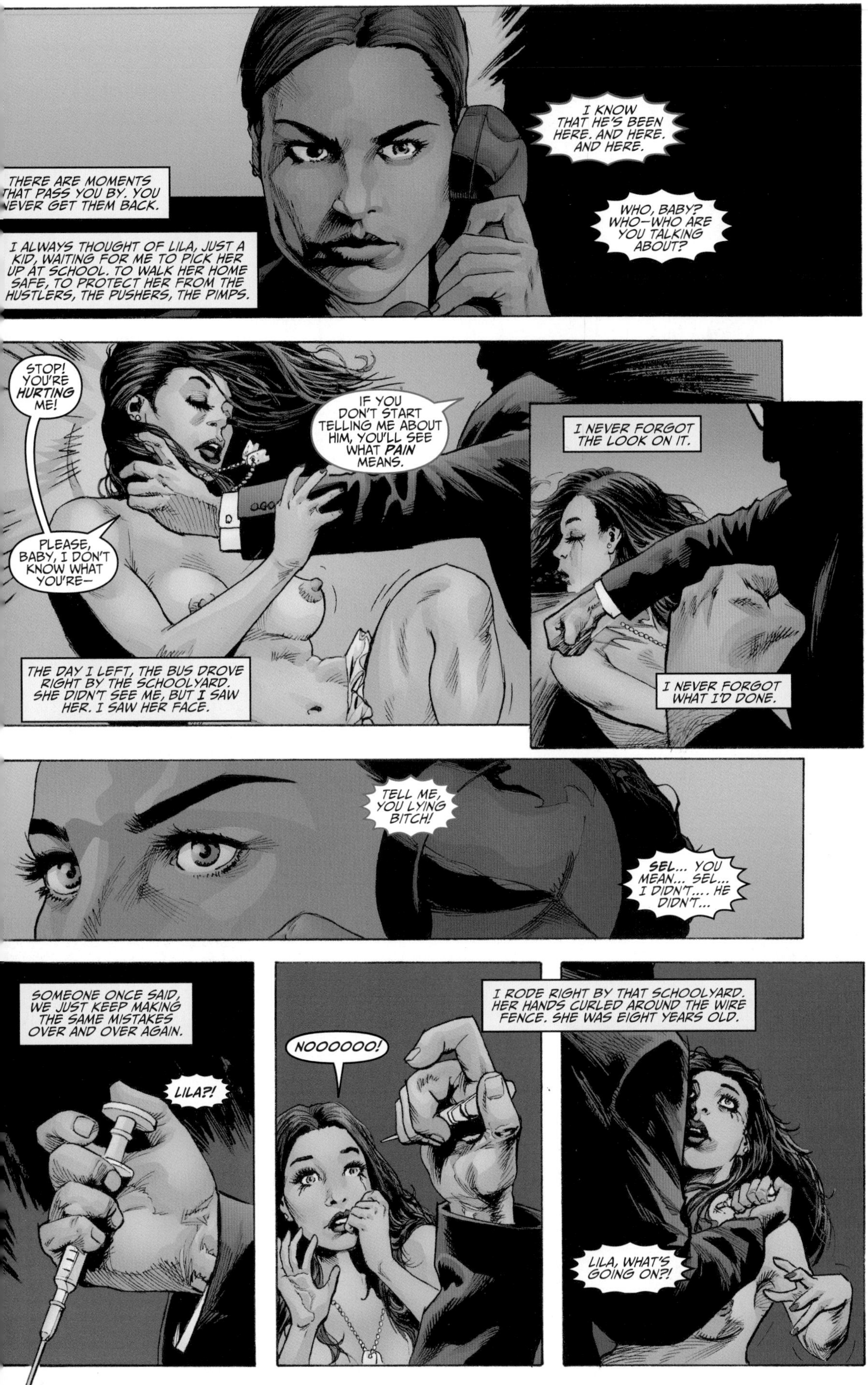
THERE ARE MOMENTS THAT PASS YOU BY. YOU NEVER GET THEM BACK.
I ALWAYS THOUGHT OF LILA, JUST A KID, WAITING FOR ME TO PICK HER UP AT SCHOOL. TO WALK HER HOME SAFE, TO PROTECT HER FROM THE HUSTLERS, THE PUSHERS, THE PIMPS.
I KNOW THAT HE'S BEEN HERE. AND HERE. AND HERE.
WHO, BABY? WHO—WHO ARE YOU TALKING ABOUT?
STOP! YOU'RE HURTING ME!
IF YOU DON'T START TELLING ME ABOUT HIM, YOU'LL SEE WHAT PAIN MEANS.
PLEASE, BABY, I DON'T KNOW WHAT YOU'RE—
THE DAY I LEFT, THE BUS DROVE RIGHT BY THE SCHOOLYARD. SHE DIDN'T SEE ME, BUT I SAW HER. I SAW HER FACE.
I NEVER FORGOT THE LOOK ON IT.
I NEVER FORGOT WHAT I'D DONE.
TELL ME, YOU LYING BITCH!
SEL... YOU MEAN... SEL... I DIDN'T.... HE DIDN'T...
SOMEONE ONCE SAID, WE JUST KEEP MAKING THE SAME MISTAKES OVER AND OVER AGAIN.
LILA?!
NOOOOOO!
I RODE RIGHT BY THAT SCHOOLYARD. HER HANDS CURLED AROUND THE WIRE FENCE. SHE WAS EIGHT YEARS OLD.
LILA, WHAT'S GOING ON?!

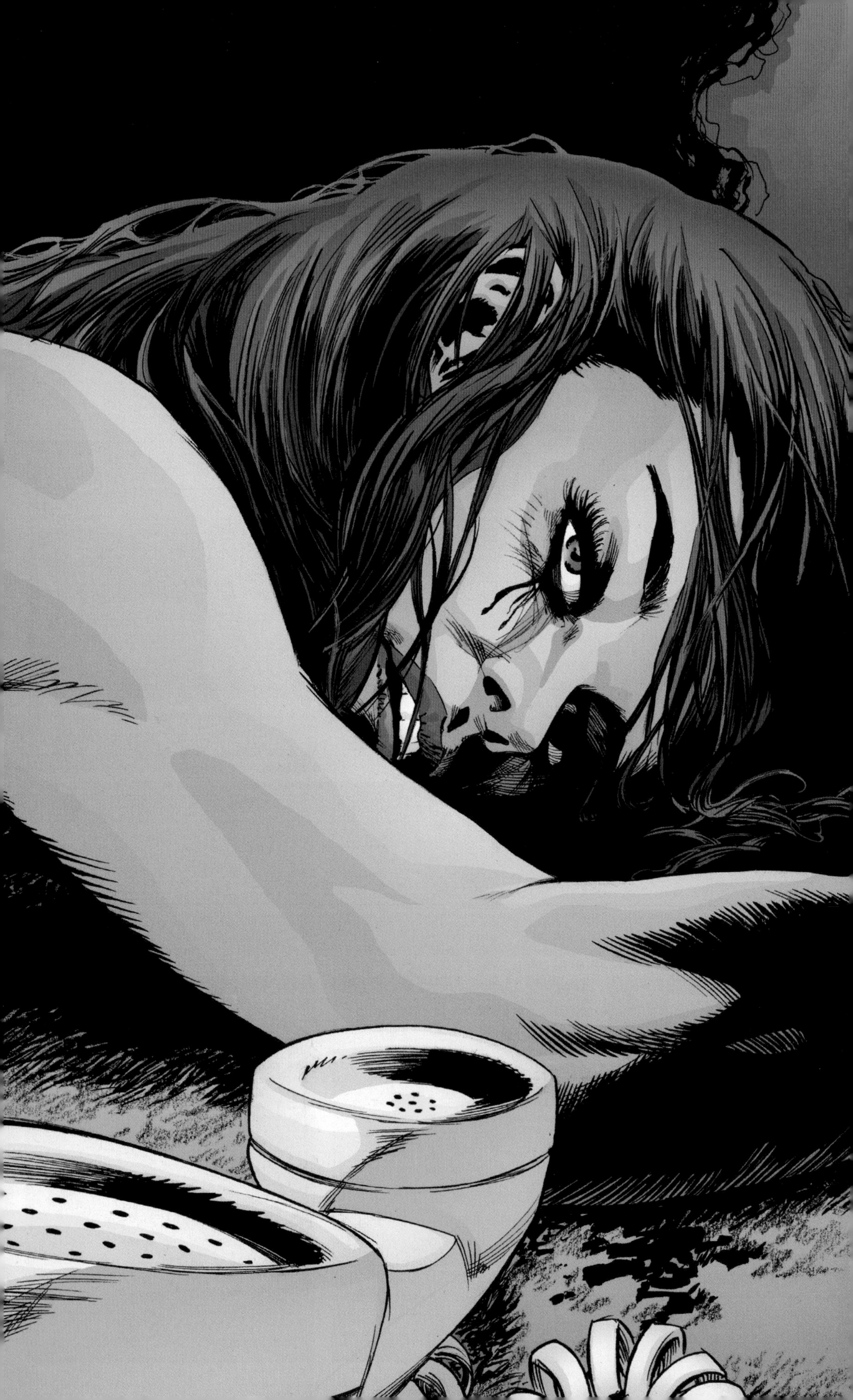

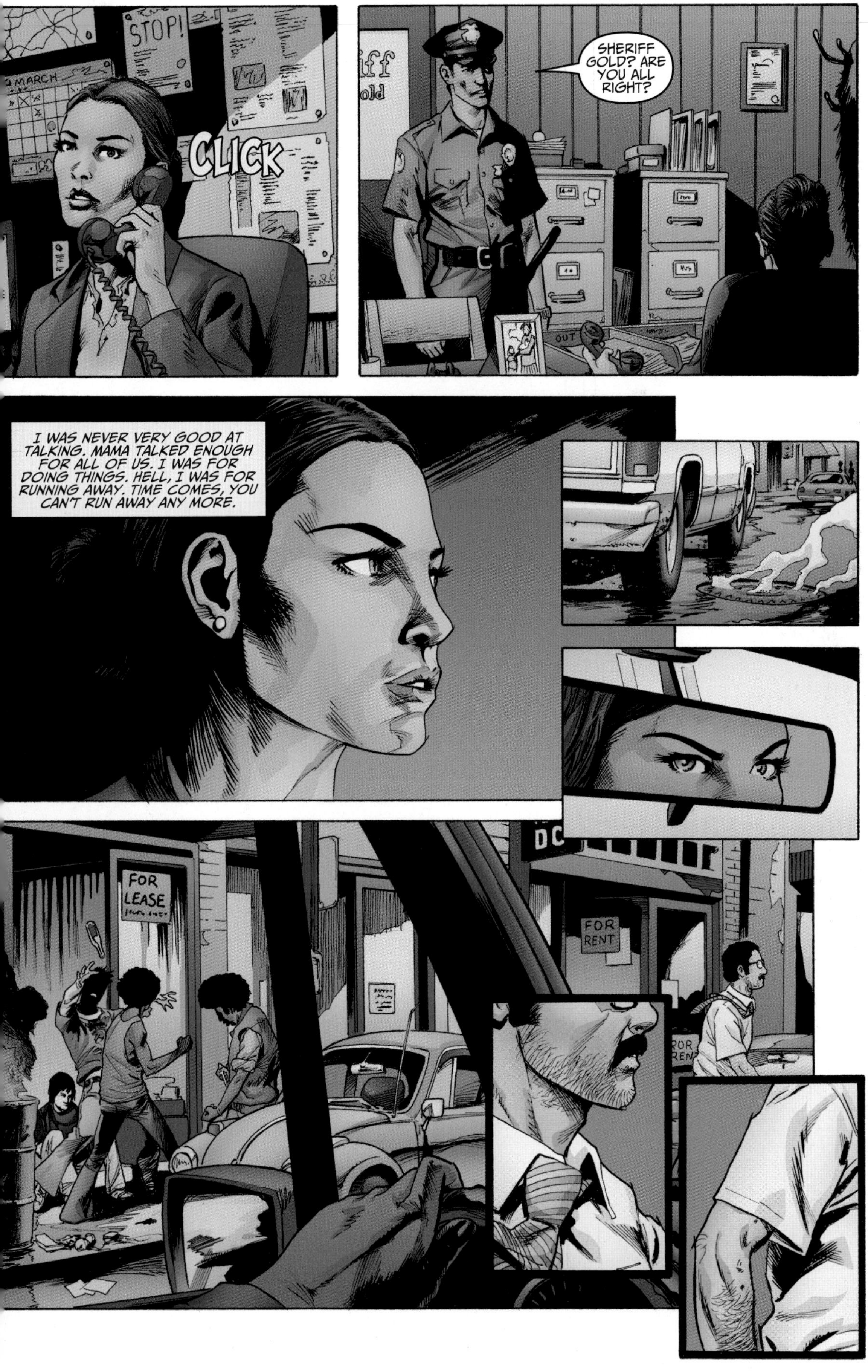
STOP!
MARCH
CLICK
SHERIFF GOLD? ARE YOU ALL RIGHT?
OUT
I WAS NEVER VERY GOOD AT TALKING. MAMA TALKED ENOUGH FOR ALL OF US. I WAS FOR DOING THINGS. HELL, I WAS FOR RUNNING AWAY. TIME COMES, YOU CAN'T RUN AWAY ANY MORE.
FOR LEASE
DC
FOR RENT

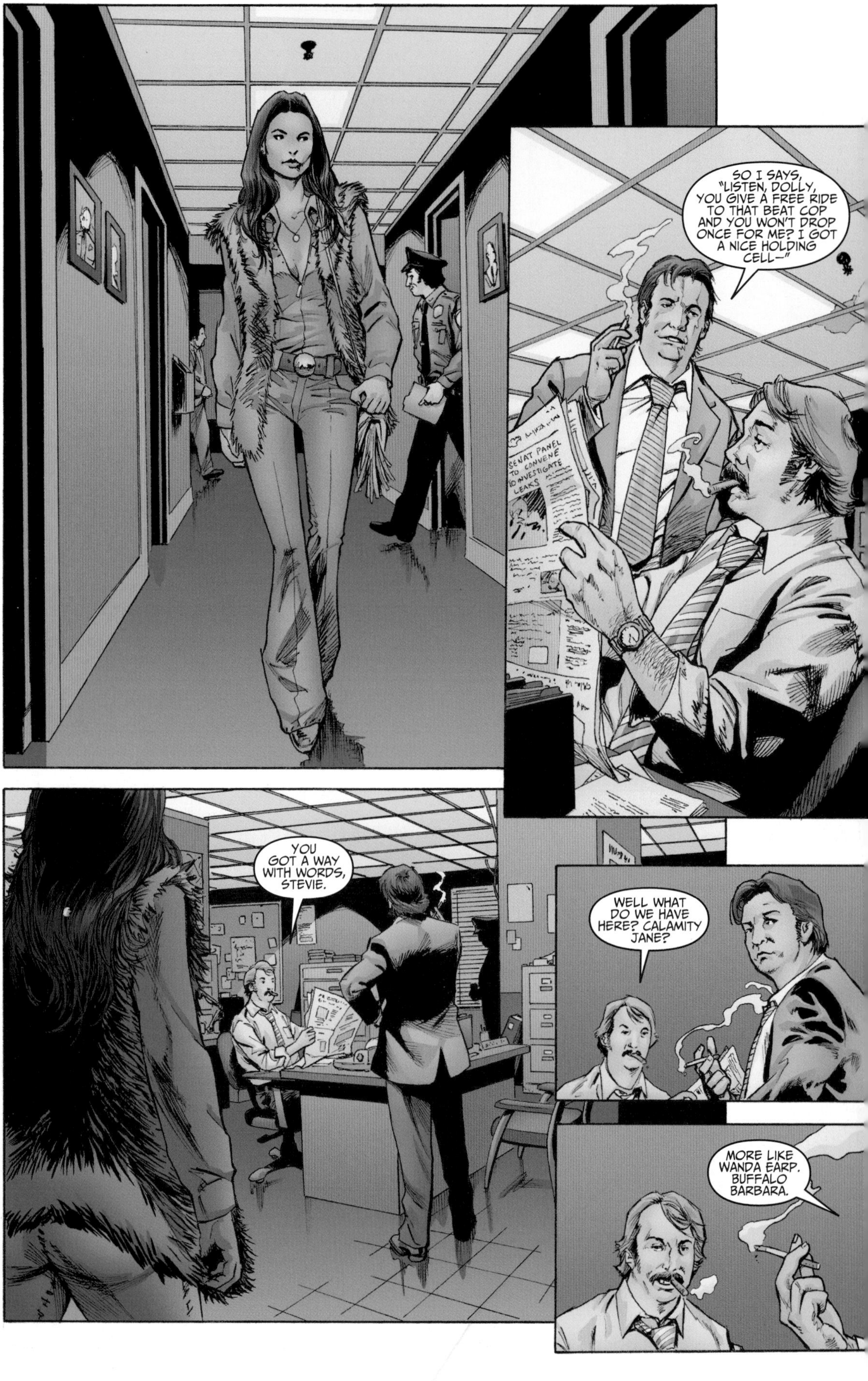

SO I SAYS, "LISTEN, DOLLY, YOU GIVE A FREE RIDE TO THAT BEAT COP AND YOU WON'T DROP ONCE FOR ME? I GOT A NICE HOLDING CELL--"
SENAT PANEL TO CONVENE TO INVESTIGATE LEAKS
YOU GOT A WAY WITH WORDS, STEVIE.
WELL WHAT DO WE HAVE HERE? CALAMITY JANE?
MORE LIKE WANDA EARP. BUFFALO BARBARA.

WHERE'S MY *SISTER*?

THE INDIANS GET HER?

YOU'RE THE ONE WHO CALLED. LOOK, I TOLD YA...

SHE HAD A RAP SHEET LONG AS JOHN HOLMES' BALONEY PONY. A *WHORE*. THEY GO MISSING EVERY DAY.

D.C.

POLICE DEPT. CASE FILE

TE	TIME	OFFICER #
5	17:30	740
	12:25	827

SHE WAS PRACTICALLY SELLING IT ON THE *NATIONAL MALL*. AT A HIGH PRICE, SURE, BUT THAT'S JUST *NUMBERS*.

IS THAT *YOUR GIG TOO*, ANNIE OAKLEY? YOU WANT TO LASSO *THIS*?

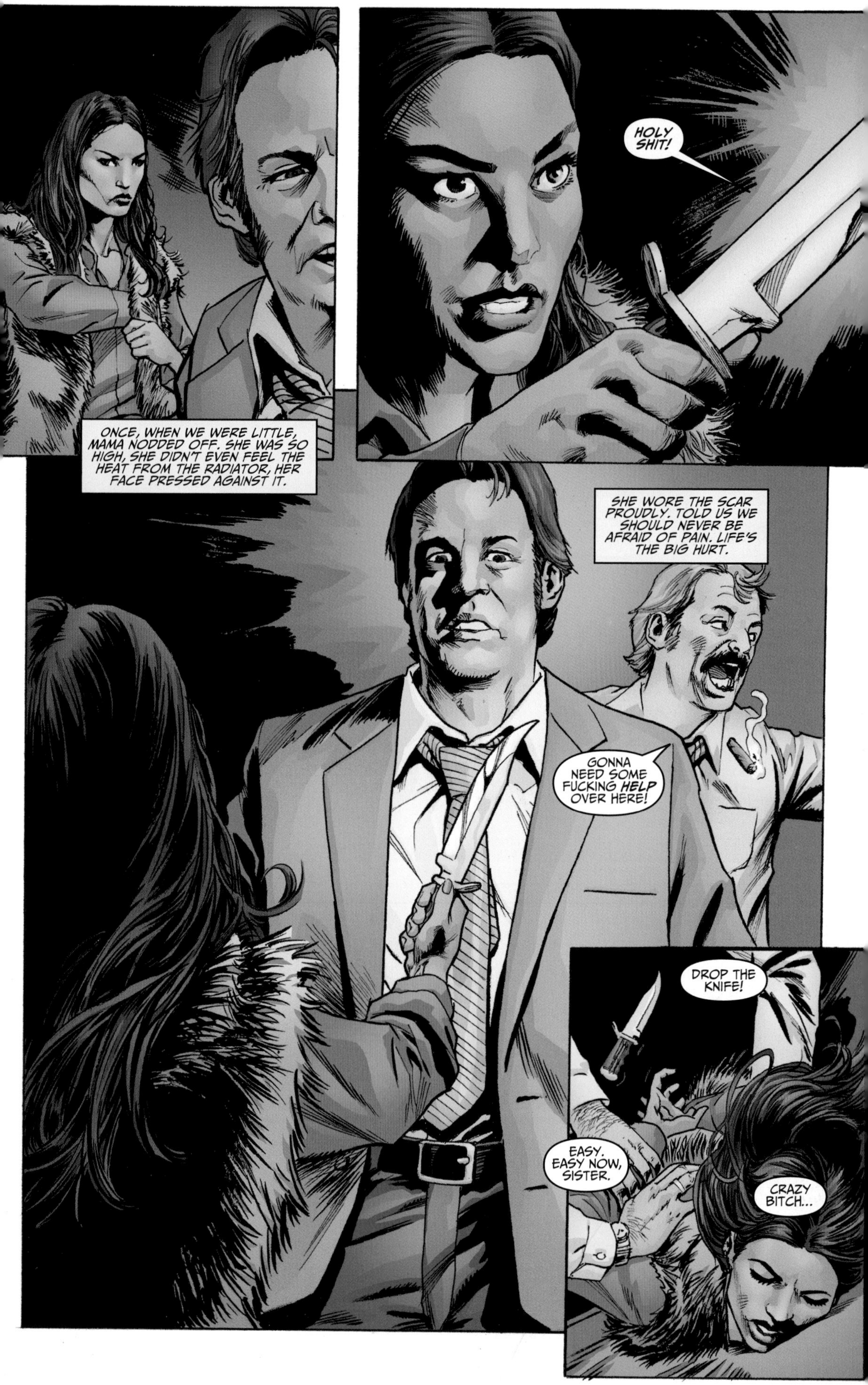
HOLY SHIT!
ONCE, WHEN WE WERE LITTLE, MAMA NODDED OFF. SHE WAS SO HIGH, SHE DIDN'T EVEN FEEL THE HEAT FROM THE RADIATOR, HER FACE PRESSED AGAINST IT.
SHE WORE THE SCAR PROUDLY. TOLD US WE SHOULD NEVER BE AFRAID OF PAIN. LIFE'S THE BIG HURT.
GONNA NEED SOME FUCKING HELP OVER HERE!
DROP THE KNIFE!
EASY. EASY NOW, SISTER.
CRAZY BITCH...

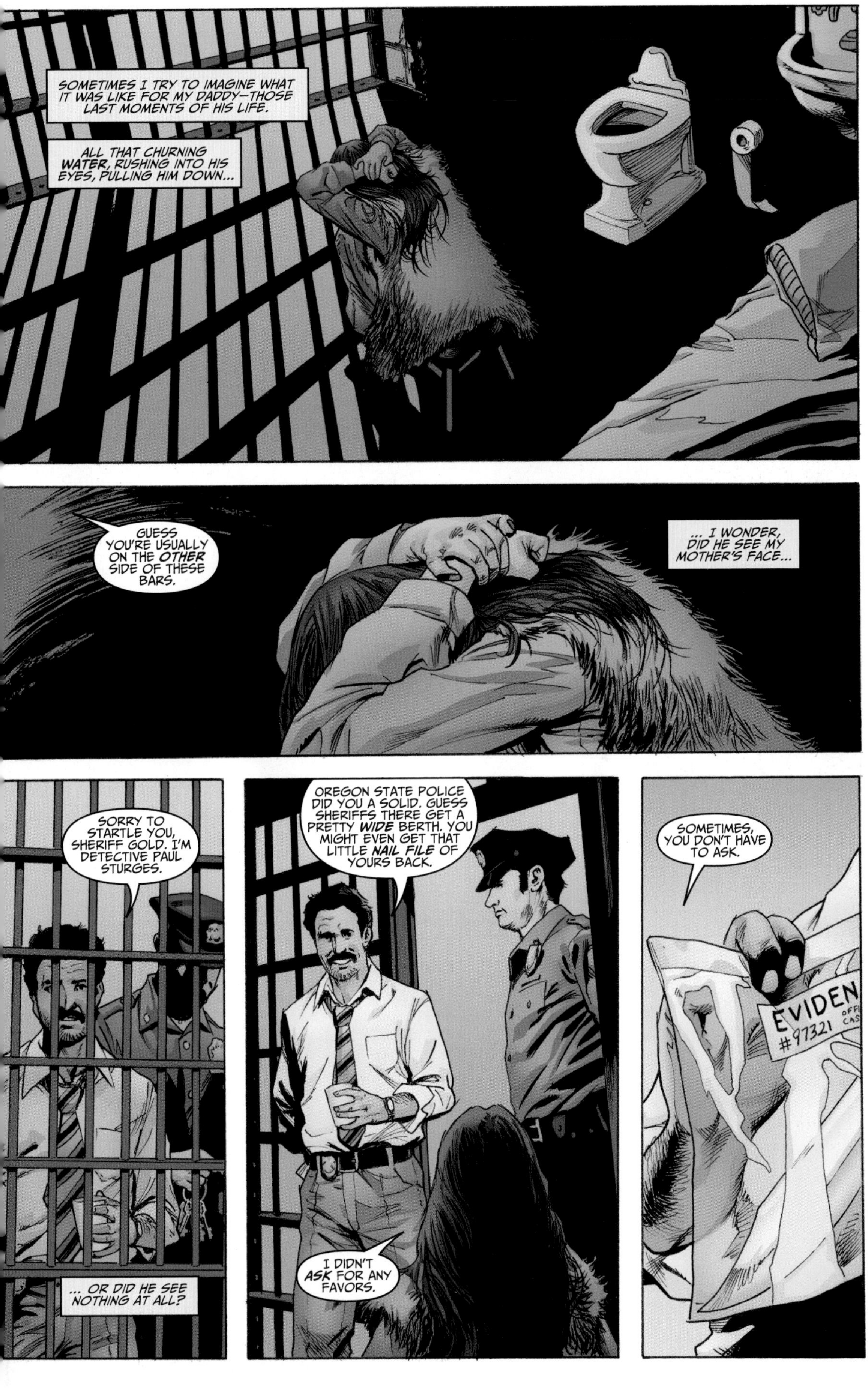
SOMETIMES I TRY TO IMAGINE WHAT IT WAS LIKE FOR MY DADDY—THOSE LAST MOMENTS OF HIS LIFE.
ALL THAT CHURNING WATER, RUSHING INTO HIS EYES, PULLING HIM DOWN...
GUESS YOU'RE USUALLY ON THE OTHER SIDE OF THESE BARS.
... I WONDER, DID HE SEE MY MOTHER'S FACE...
SORRY TO STARTLE YOU, SHERIFF GOLD. I'M DETECTIVE PAUL STURGES.
... OR DID HE SEE NOTHING AT ALL?
OREGON STATE POLICE DID YOU A SOLID. GUESS SHERIFFS THERE GET A PRETTY WIDE BERTH. YOU MIGHT EVEN GET THAT LITTLE NAIL FILE OF YOURS BACK.
I DIDN'T ASK FOR ANY FAVORS.
SOMETIMES, YOU DON'T HAVE TO ASK.
EVIDEN
#97321

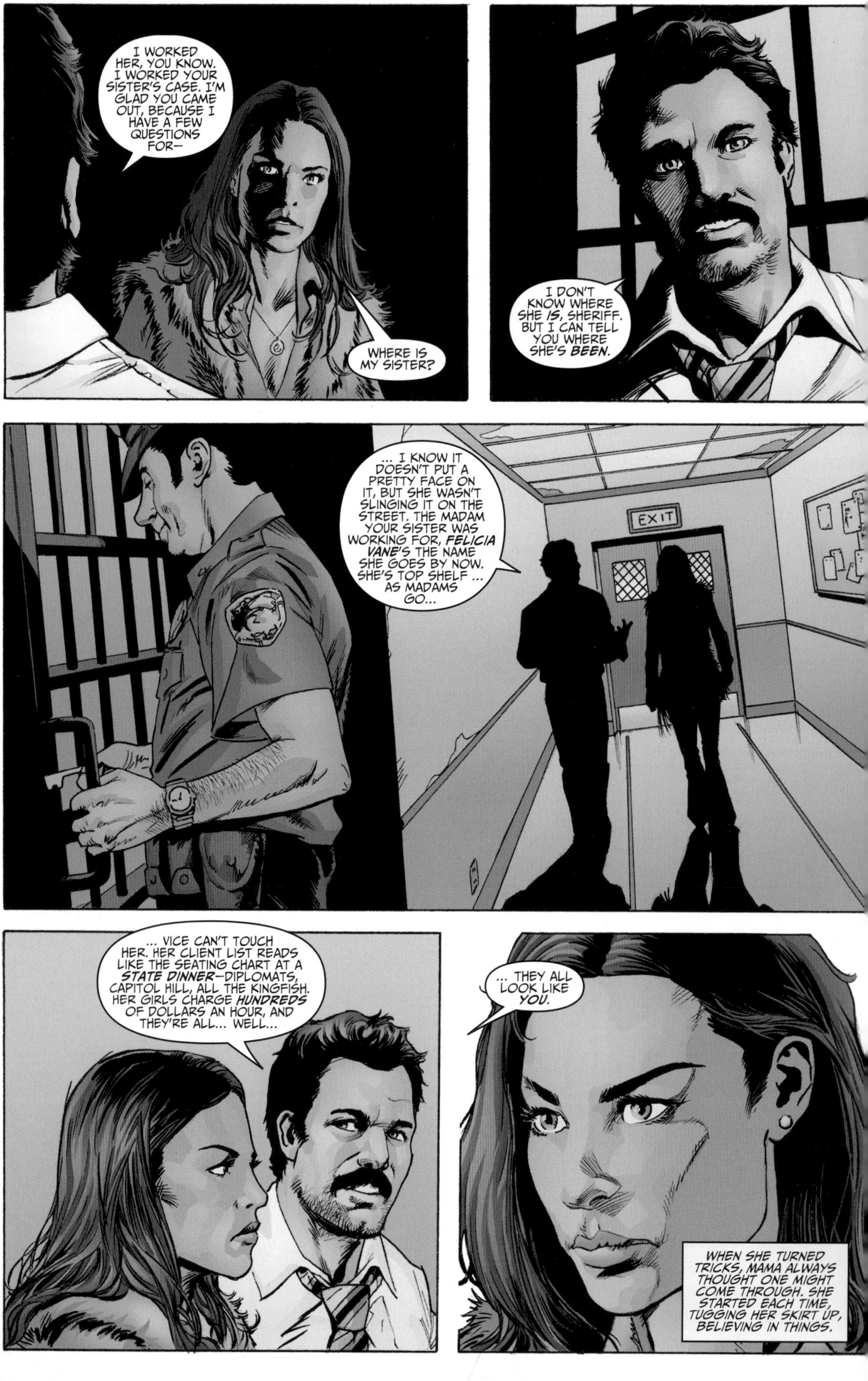
I WORKED HER, YOU KNOW. I WORKED YOUR SISTER'S CASE. I'M GLAD YOU CAME OUT, BECAUSE I HAVE A FEW QUESTIONS FOR–
WHERE IS MY SISTER?
I DON'T KNOW WHERE SHE *IS*, SHERIFF. BUT I CAN TELL YOU WHERE SHE'S ***BEEN***.
... I KNOW IT DOESN'T PUT A PRETTY FACE ON IT, BUT SHE WASN'T SLINGING IT ON THE STREET. THE MADAM YOUR SISTER WAS WORKING FOR, ***FELICIA VANE***'S THE NAME SHE GOES BY NOW. SHE'S TOP SHELF ... AS MADAMS GO...
EXIT
... VICE CAN'T TOUCH HER. HER CLIENT LIST READS LIKE THE SEATING CHART AT A ***STATE DINNER***–DIPLOMATS, CAPITOL HILL, ALL THE KINGFISH. HER GIRLS CHARGE ***HUNDREDS*** OF DOLLARS AN HOUR, AND THEY'RE ALL... WELL...
... THEY ALL LOOK LIKE ***YOU***.
WHEN SHE TURNED TRICKS, MAMA ALWAYS THOUGHT ONE MIGHT COME THROUGH. SHE STARTED EACH TIME, TUGGING HER SKIRT UP, BELIEVING IN THINGS.

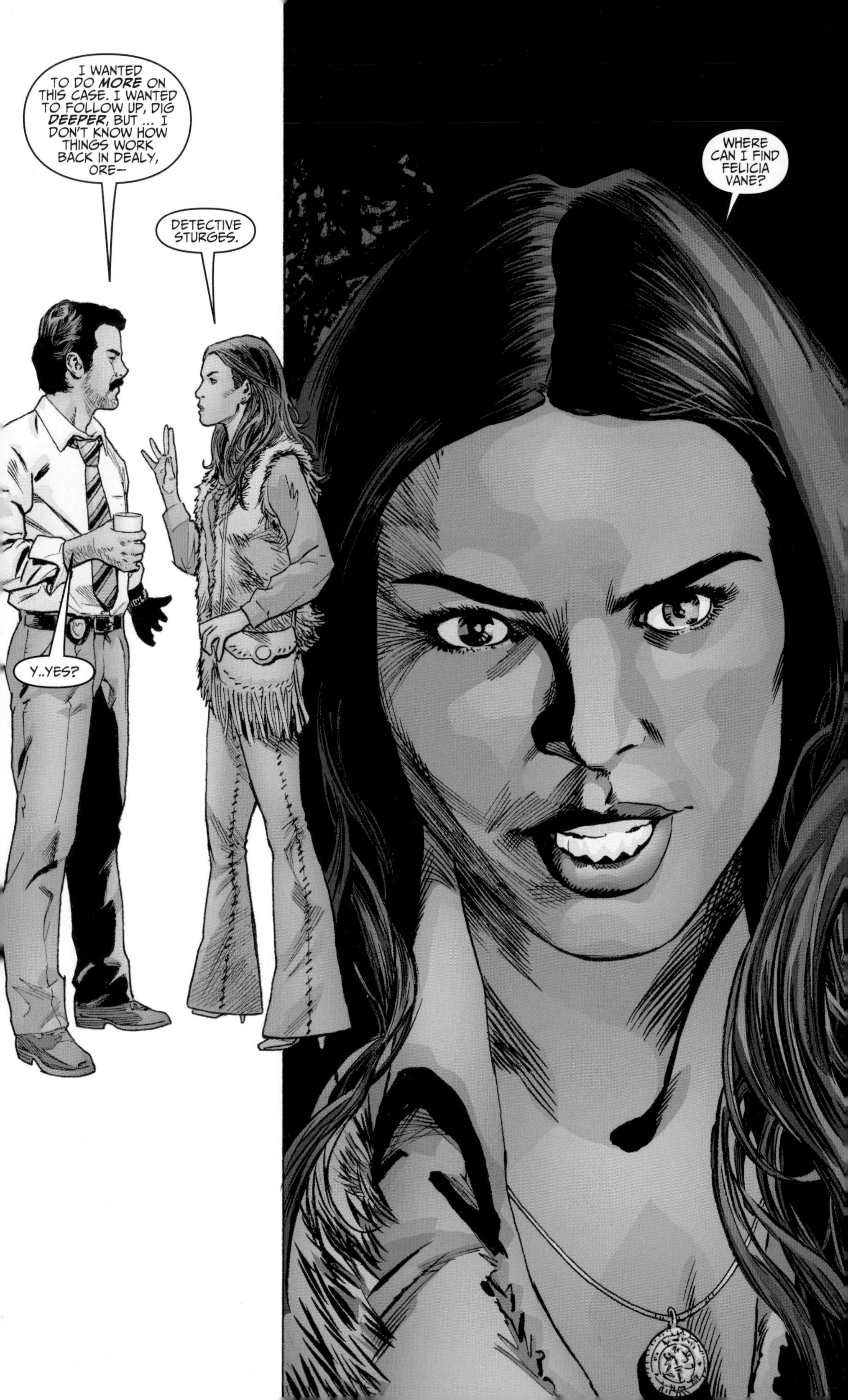
I WANTED TO DO **MORE** ON THIS CASE. I WANTED TO FOLLOW UP, DIG **DEEPER**, BUT ... I DON'T KNOW HOW THINGS WORK BACK IN DEALY, ORE–
DETECTIVE STURGES.
Y..YES?
WHERE CAN I FIND FELICIA VANE?

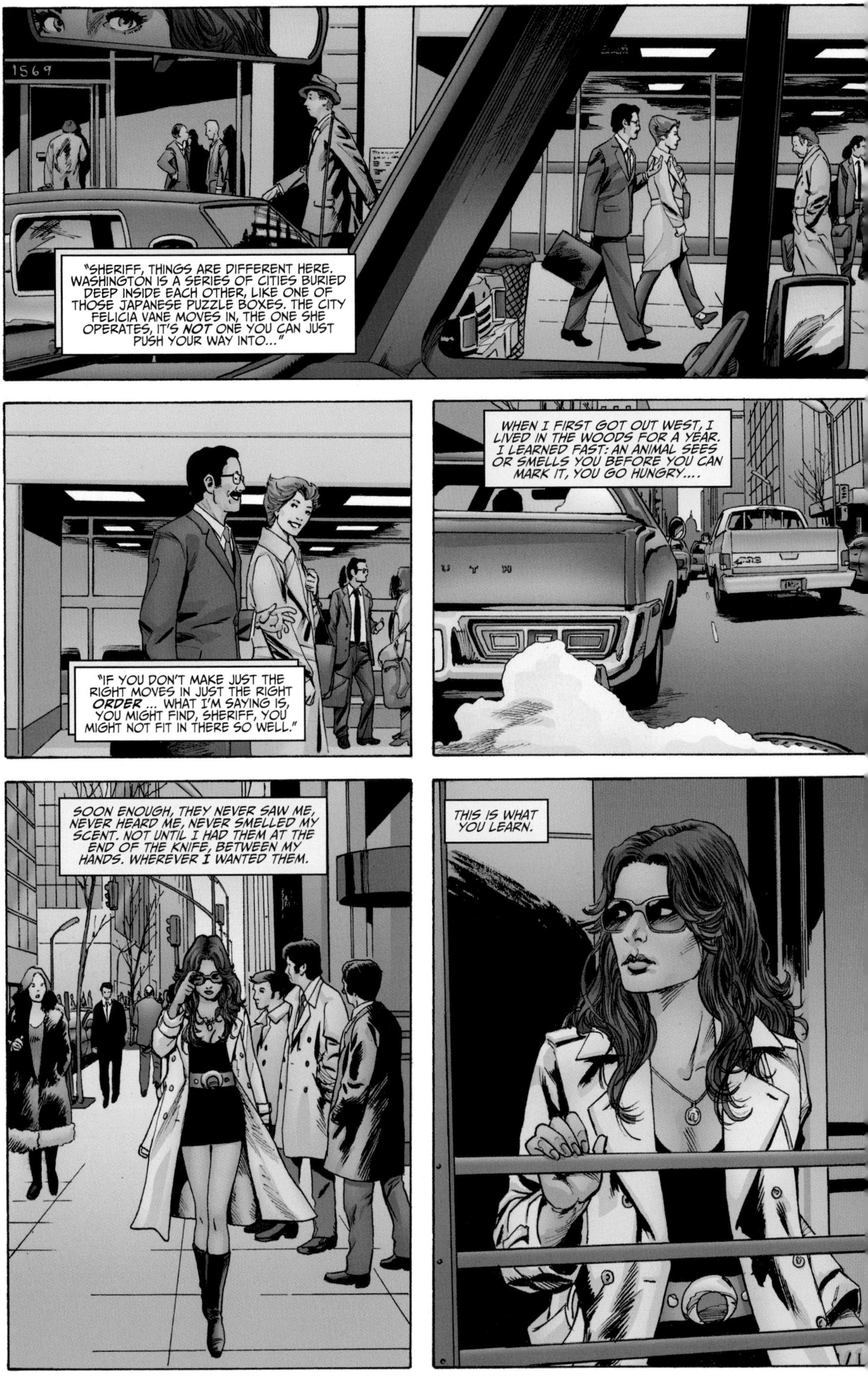
1569
"SHERIFF, THINGS ARE DIFFERENT HERE. WASHINGTON IS A SERIES OF CITIES BURIED DEEP INSIDE EACH OTHER, LIKE ONE OF THOSE JAPANESE PUZZLE BOXES. THE CITY FELICIA VANE MOVES IN, THE ONE SHE OPERATES, IT'S **NOT** ONE YOU CAN JUST PUSH YOUR WAY INTO..."
"IF YOU DON'T MAKE JUST THE RIGHT MOVES IN JUST THE RIGHT **ORDER** ... WHAT I'M SAYING IS, YOU MIGHT FIND, SHERIFF, YOU MIGHT NOT FIT IN THERE SO WELL."
WHEN I FIRST GOT OUT WEST, I LIVED IN THE WOODS FOR A YEAR. I LEARNED FAST: AN ANIMAL SEES OR SMELLS YOU BEFORE YOU CAN MARK IT, YOU GO HUNGRY....
SOON ENOUGH, THEY NEVER SAW ME, NEVER HEARD ME, NEVER SMELLED MY SCENT. NOT UNTIL I HAD THEM AT THE END OF THE KNIFE, BETWEEN MY HANDS. WHEREVER *I* WANTED THEM.
THIS IS WHAT YOU LEARN.

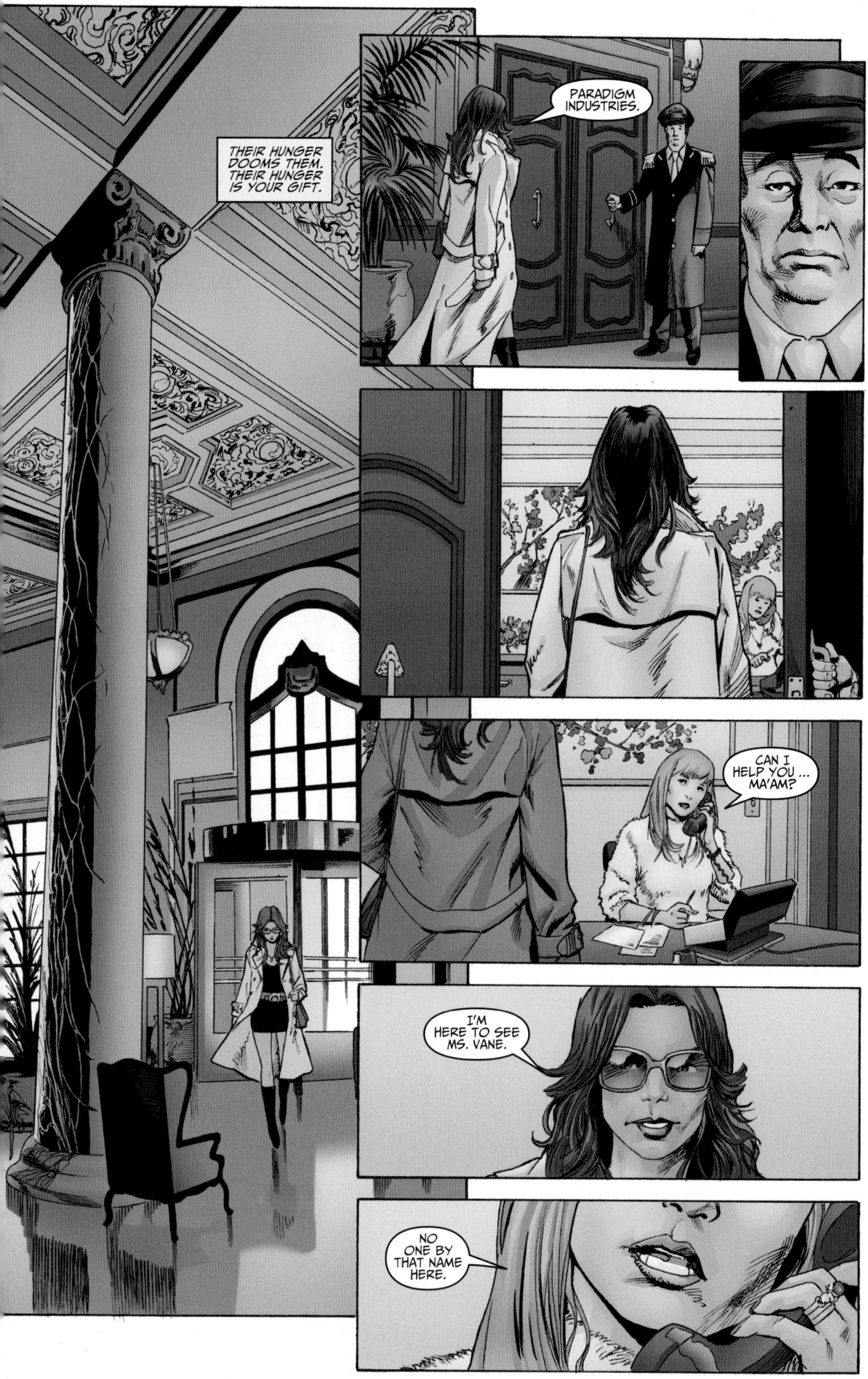
THEIR HUNGER DOOMS THEM. THEIR HUNGER IS YOUR GIFT.
PARADIGM INDUSTRIES.
CAN I HELP YOU ... MA'AM?
I'M HERE TO SEE MS. VANE.
NO ONE BY THAT NAME HERE.

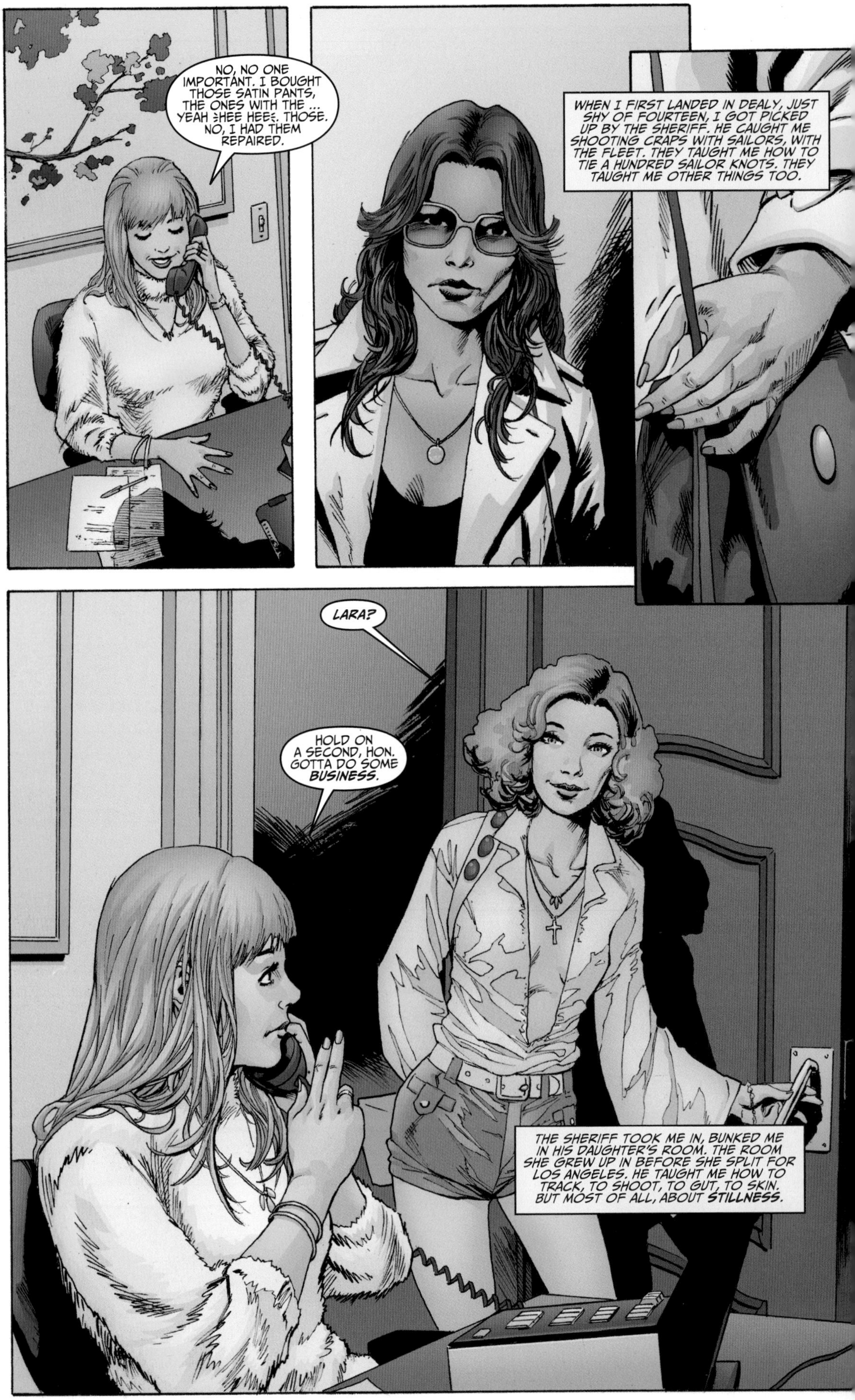
NO, NO ONE IMPORTANT. I BOUGHT THOSE SATIN PANTS, THE ONES WITH THE ... YEAH ≥HEE HEE≤. THOSE. NO, I HAD THEM REPAIRED.
WHEN I FIRST LANDED IN DEALY, JUST SHY OF FOURTEEN, I GOT PICKED UP BY THE SHERIFF. HE CAUGHT ME SHOOTING CRAPS WITH SAILORS, WITH THE FLEET. THEY TAUGHT ME HOW TO TIE A HUNDRED SAILOR KNOTS. THEY TAUGHT ME OTHER THINGS TOO.
LARA?
HOLD ON A SECOND, HON. GOTTA DO SOME BUSINESS.
THE SHERIFF TOOK ME IN, BUNKED ME IN HIS DAUGHTER'S ROOM. THE ROOM SHE GREW UP IN BEFORE SHE SPLIT FOR LOS ANGELES. HE TAUGHT ME HOW TO TRACK, TO SHOOT, TO GUT, TO SKIN. BUT MOST OF ALL, ABOUT STILLNESS.

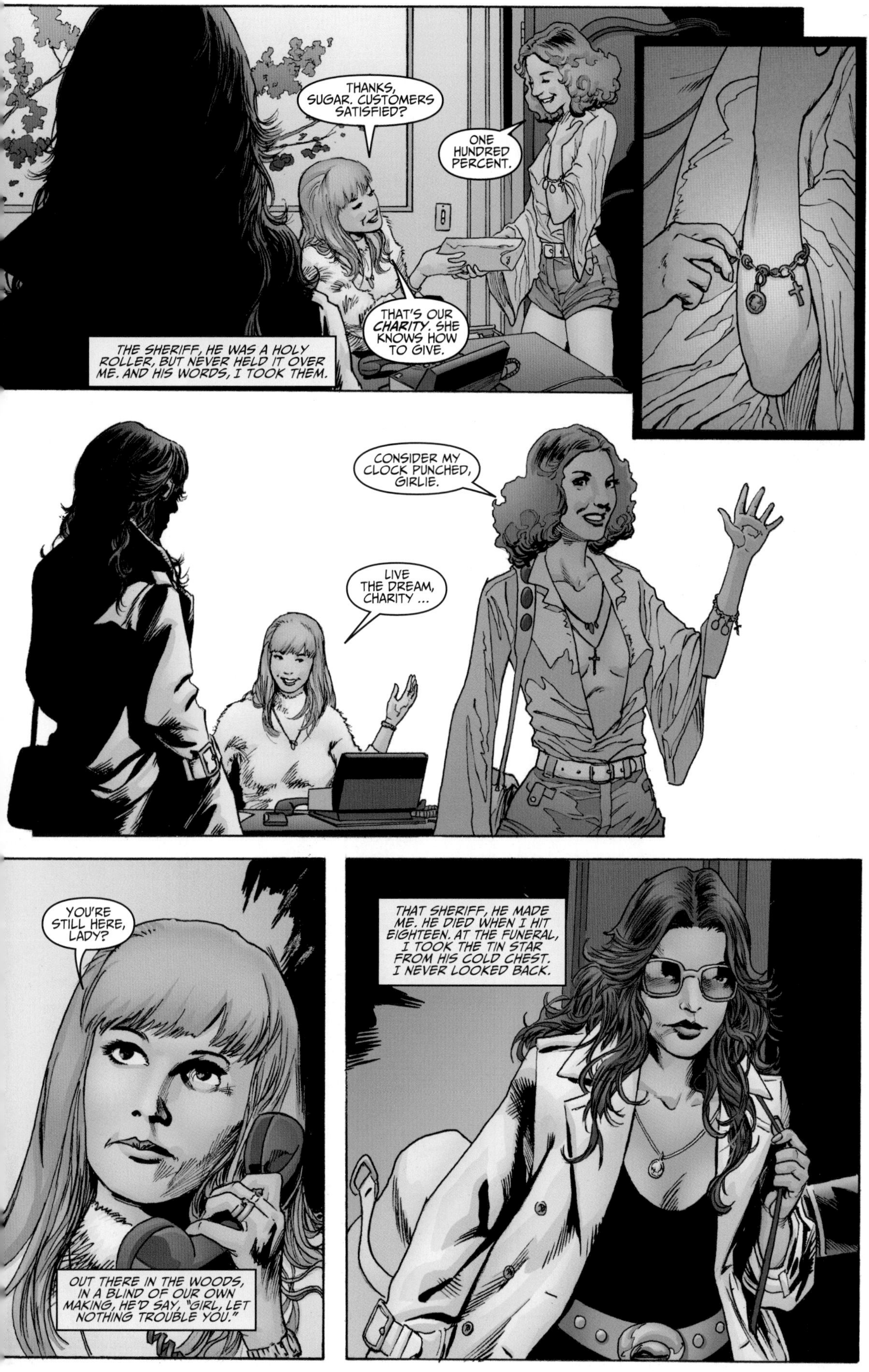
THANKS, SUGAR. CUSTOMERS SATISFIED?
ONE HUNDRED PERCENT.
THAT'S OUR CHARITY. SHE KNOWS HOW TO GIVE.
THE SHERIFF, HE WAS A HOLY ROLLER, BUT NEVER HELD IT OVER ME. AND HIS WORDS, I TOOK THEM.
CONSIDER MY CLOCK PUNCHED, GIRLIE.
LIVE THE DREAM, CHARITY ...
YOU'RE STILL HERE, LADY?
OUT THERE IN THE WOODS, IN A BLIND OF OUR OWN MAKING, HE'D SAY, "GIRL, LET NOTHING TROUBLE YOU."
THAT SHERIFF, HE MADE ME. HE DIED WHEN I HIT EIGHTEEN. AT THE FUNERAL, I TOOK THE TIN STAR FROM HIS COLD CHEST. I NEVER LOOKED BACK.

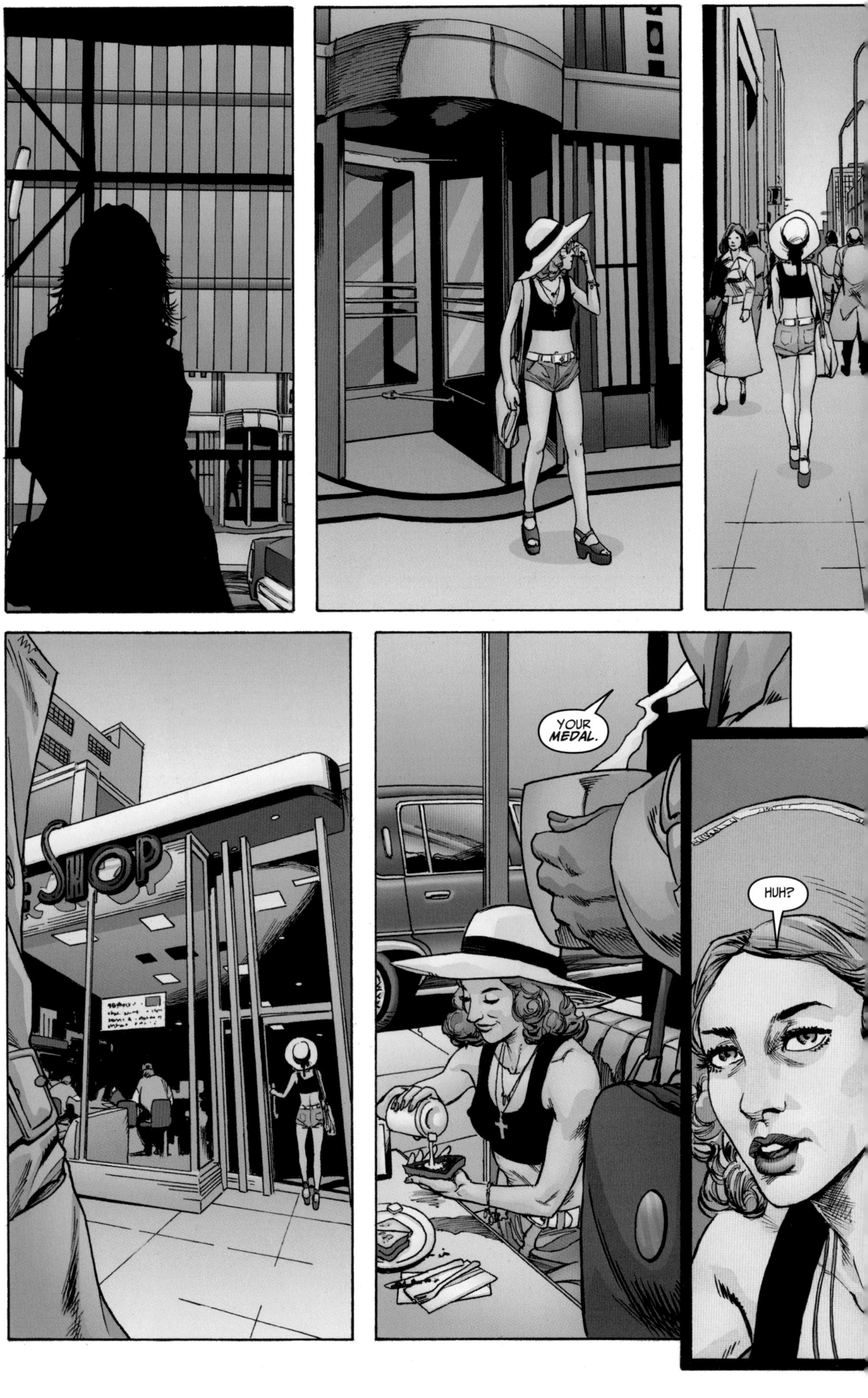
SHOP
YOUR MEDAL.
HUH?

WHOA... MY MOM GAVE ME THIS WHEN I FIRST WENT AWAY TO GIRL SCOUT CAMP. SAFE TRAVELS, AND ALL THAT.

ME TOO. NOT MY MOM, THOUGH. MY DADDY. IT'S ST. IGNATIUS. PATRON SAINT OF SOLDIERS.

MAN, THAT IS SOOOO *FREAKY*. YOU KNOW, WHAT *SIGN* ARE YOU? I BELIEVE IN ALL THAT SHIT. SIT DOWN!

I'M *CHARITY*. WHAT'S YOUR NAME?

VICTORY.

VICTORY, HUH? YOU MUST BE A *WINNER*.

I'M TRYING.

THE THING ABOUT THE SHERIFF, HE MATTERED MORE TO ME THAN ANY *BLOOD* I EVER HAD. EVEN LILA. LILA WAS A KID I REMEMBERED FROM LONG AGO.

MY OLD MAN, HE LEFT. I CAN'T MAKE RENT. MY NEW BOYFRIEND, HE HAS THIS IDEA OF ME DOING LOOPS FOR THE FOXCHASE.

FUCK ME, MOMMA. THAT'S *NO LIFE*.

YOU DON'T HAVE TO TELL ME. I TRIED TO GET IN TO SEE FELICIA VANE.

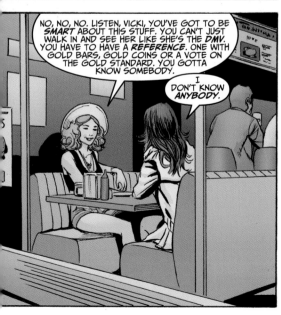

NO, NO, NO. LISTEN, VICKI, YOU'VE GOT TO BE *SMART* ABOUT THIS STUFF. YOU CAN'T JUST WALK IN AND SEE HER LIKE SHE'S THE *DMV*. YOU HAVE TO HAVE A *REFERENCE*. ONE WITH GOLD BARS, GOLD COINS OR A VOTE ON THE GOLD STANDARD. YOU GOTTA KNOW SOMEBODY.

I DON'T KNOW *ANYBODY*.

YOU DO *NOW*.

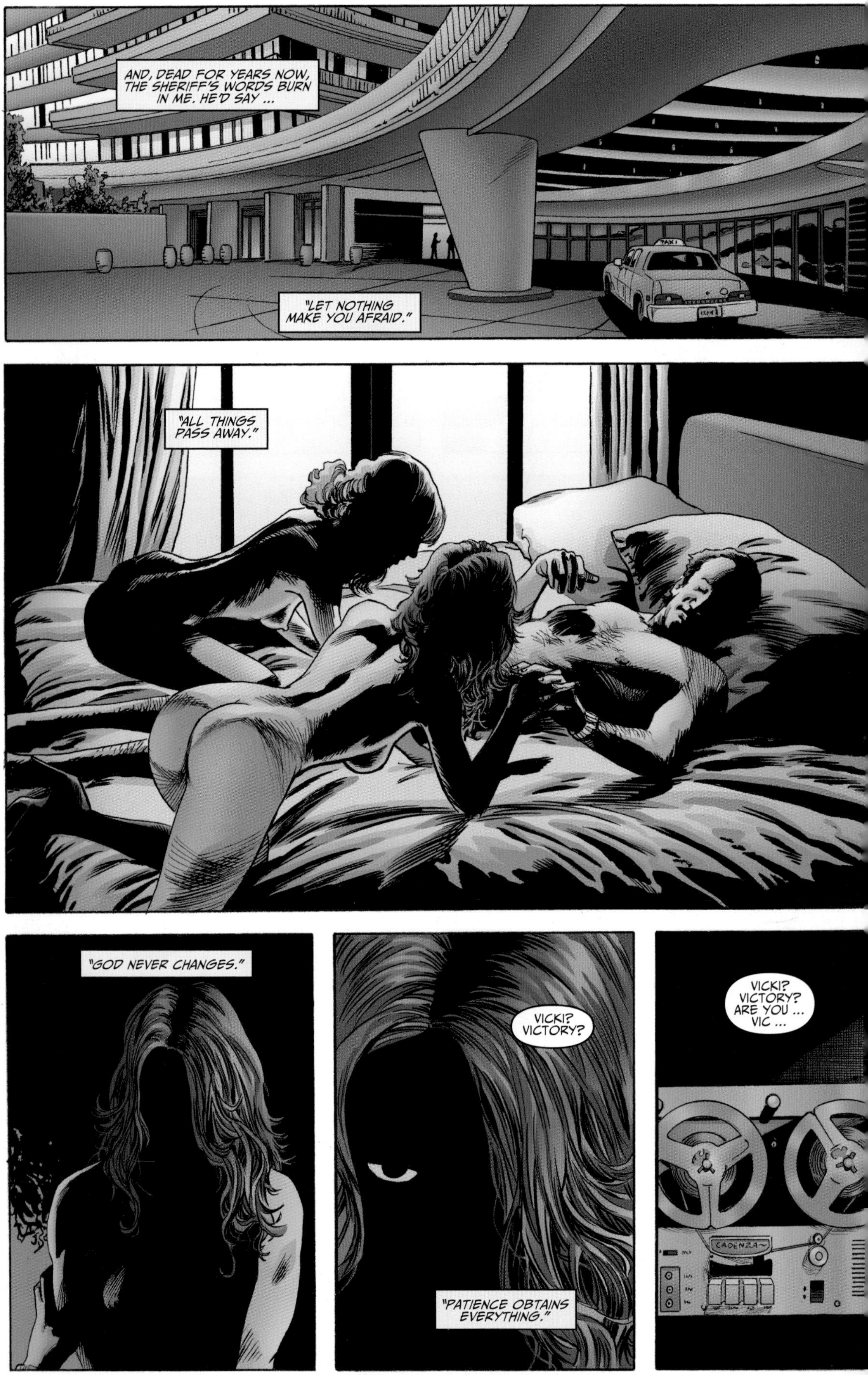
AND, DEAD FOR YEARS NOW, THE SHERIFF'S WORDS BURN IN ME. HE'D SAY ...
"LET NOTHING MAKE YOU AFRAID."
"ALL THINGS PASS AWAY."
"GOD NEVER CHANGES."
VICKI? VICTORY?
"PATIENCE OBTAINS EVERYTHING."
VICKI? VICTORY? ARE YOU ... VIC ...
CADENZA

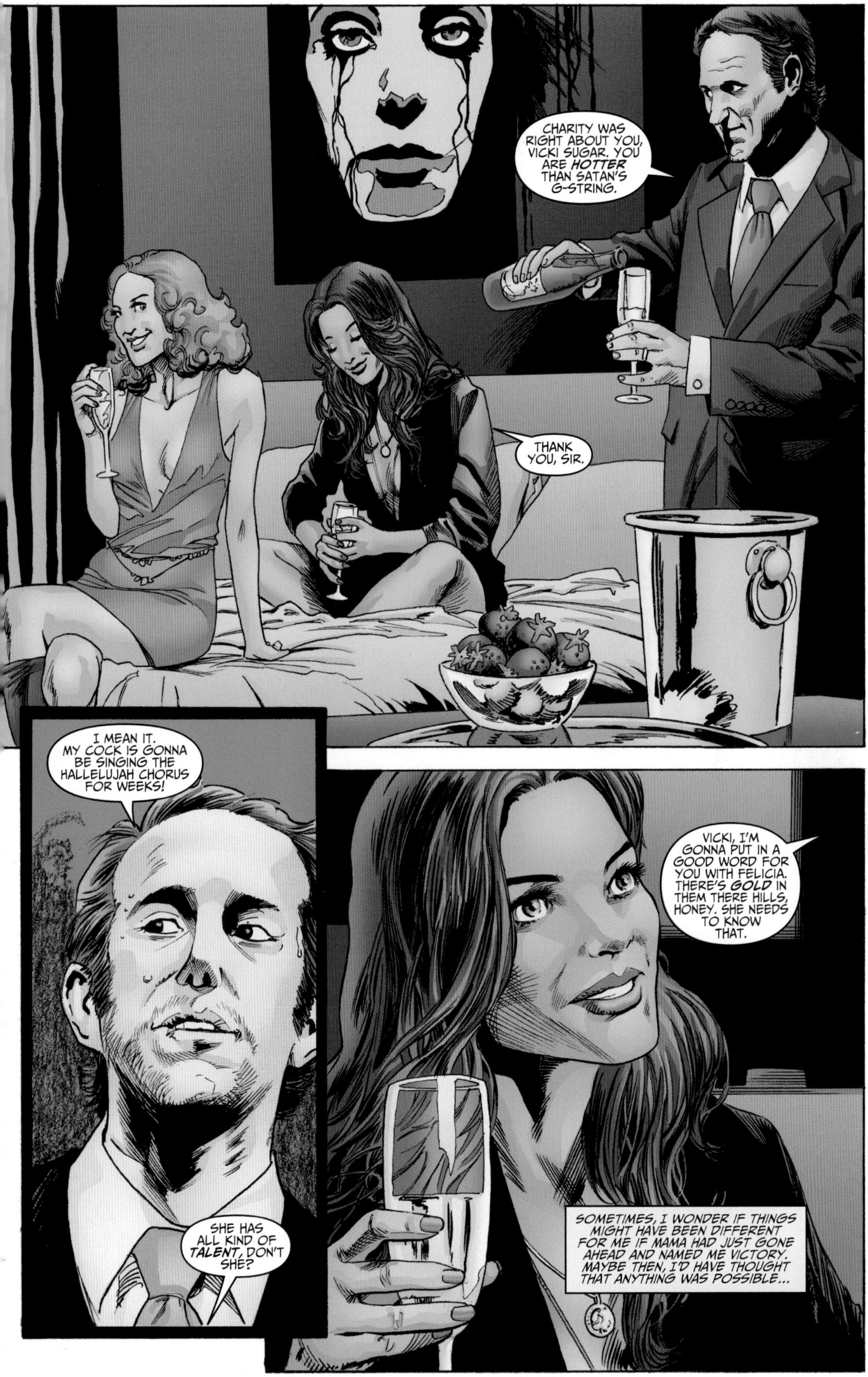
CHARITY WAS RIGHT ABOUT YOU, VICKI SUGAR. YOU ARE *HOTTER* THAN SATAN'S G-STRING.
THANK YOU, SIR.
I MEAN IT. MY COCK IS GONNA BE SINGING THE HALLELUJAH CHORUS FOR WEEKS!
VICKI, I'M GONNA PUT IN A GOOD WORD FOR YOU WITH FELICIA. THERE'S *GOLD* IN THEM THERE HILLS, HONEY. SHE NEEDS TO KNOW THAT.
SHE HAS ALL KIND OF *TALENT*, DON'T SHE?
SOMETIMES, I WONDER IF THINGS MIGHT HAVE BEEN DIFFERENT FOR ME IF MAMA HAD JUST GONE AHEAD AND NAMED ME VICTORY. MAYBE THEN, I'D HAVE THOUGHT THAT ANYTHING WAS POSSIBLE...

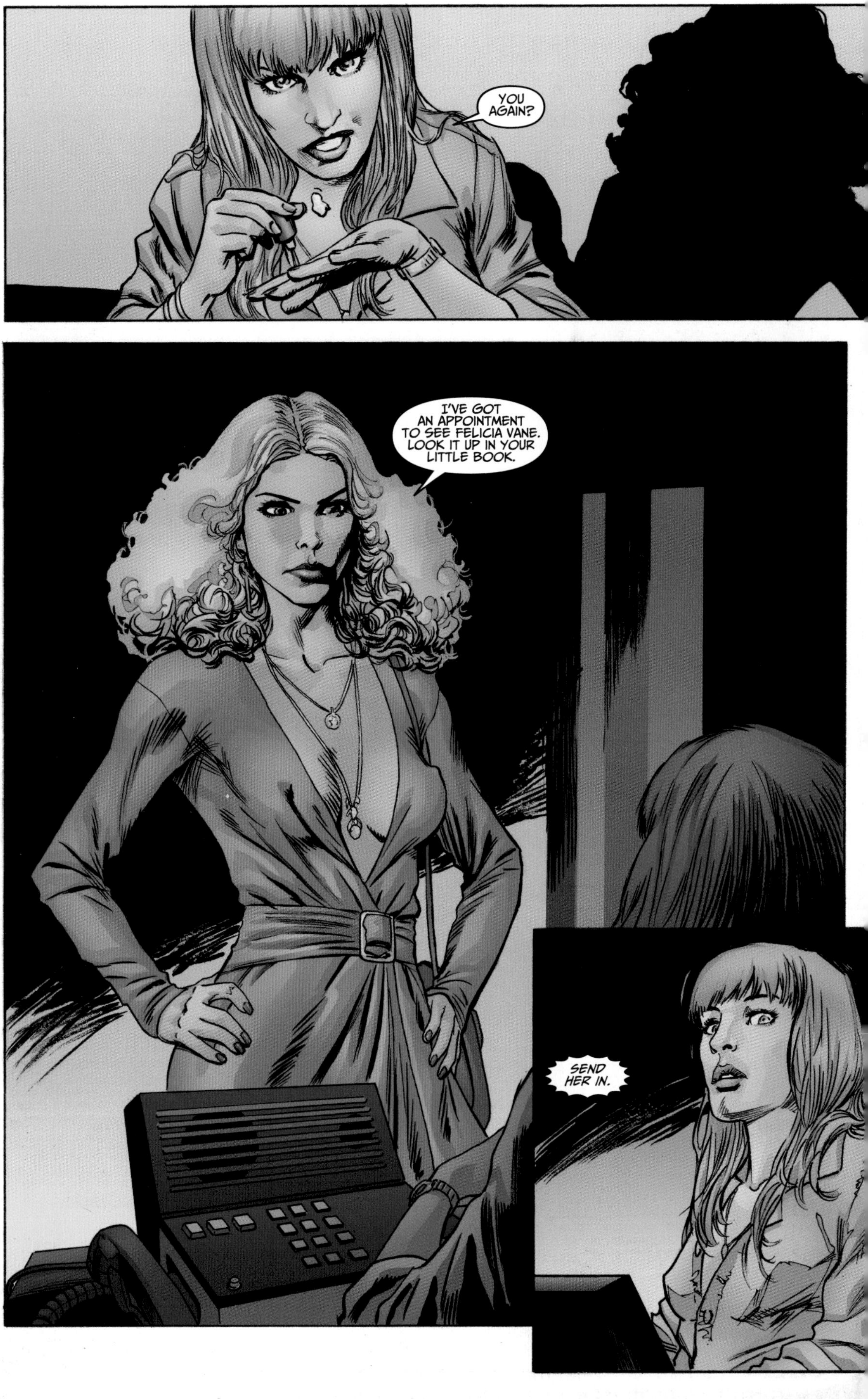
YOU AGAIN?
I'VE GOT AN APPOINTMENT TO SEE FELICIA VANE. LOOK IT UP IN YOUR LITTLE BOOK.
SEND HER IN.

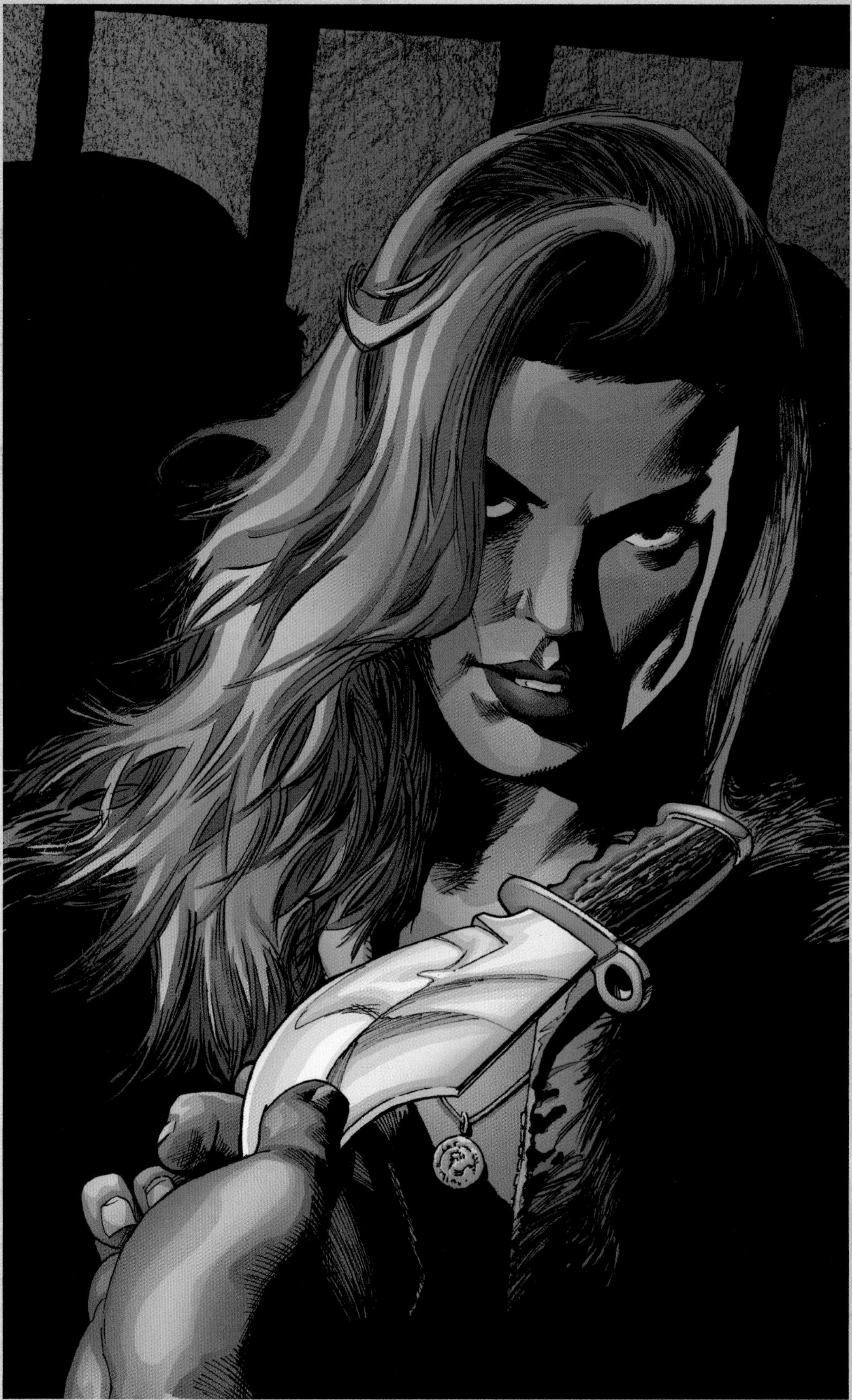

ILLUSTRATED BY **STEVE SCOTT**

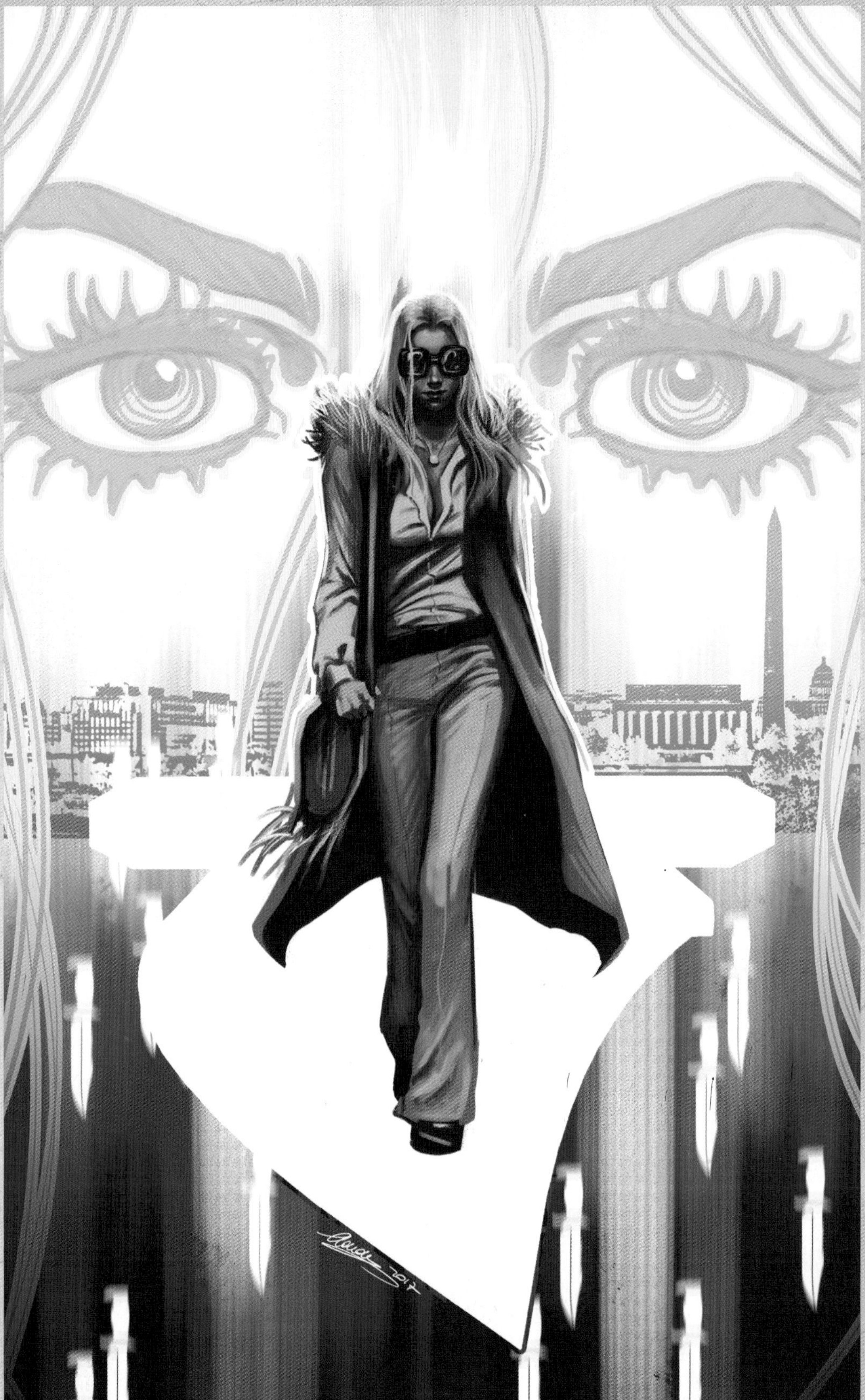

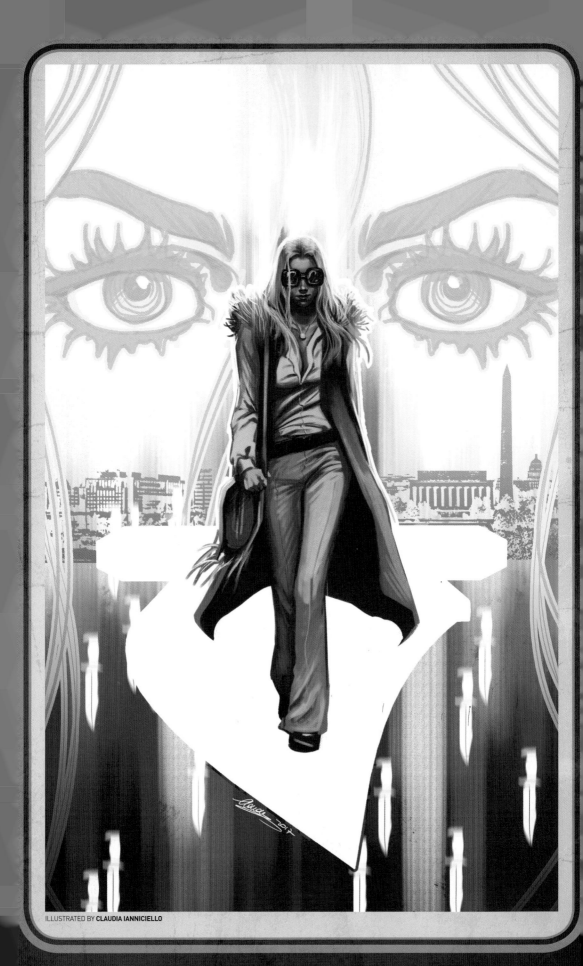

ILLUSTRATED BY **CLAUDIA IANNICIELLO**

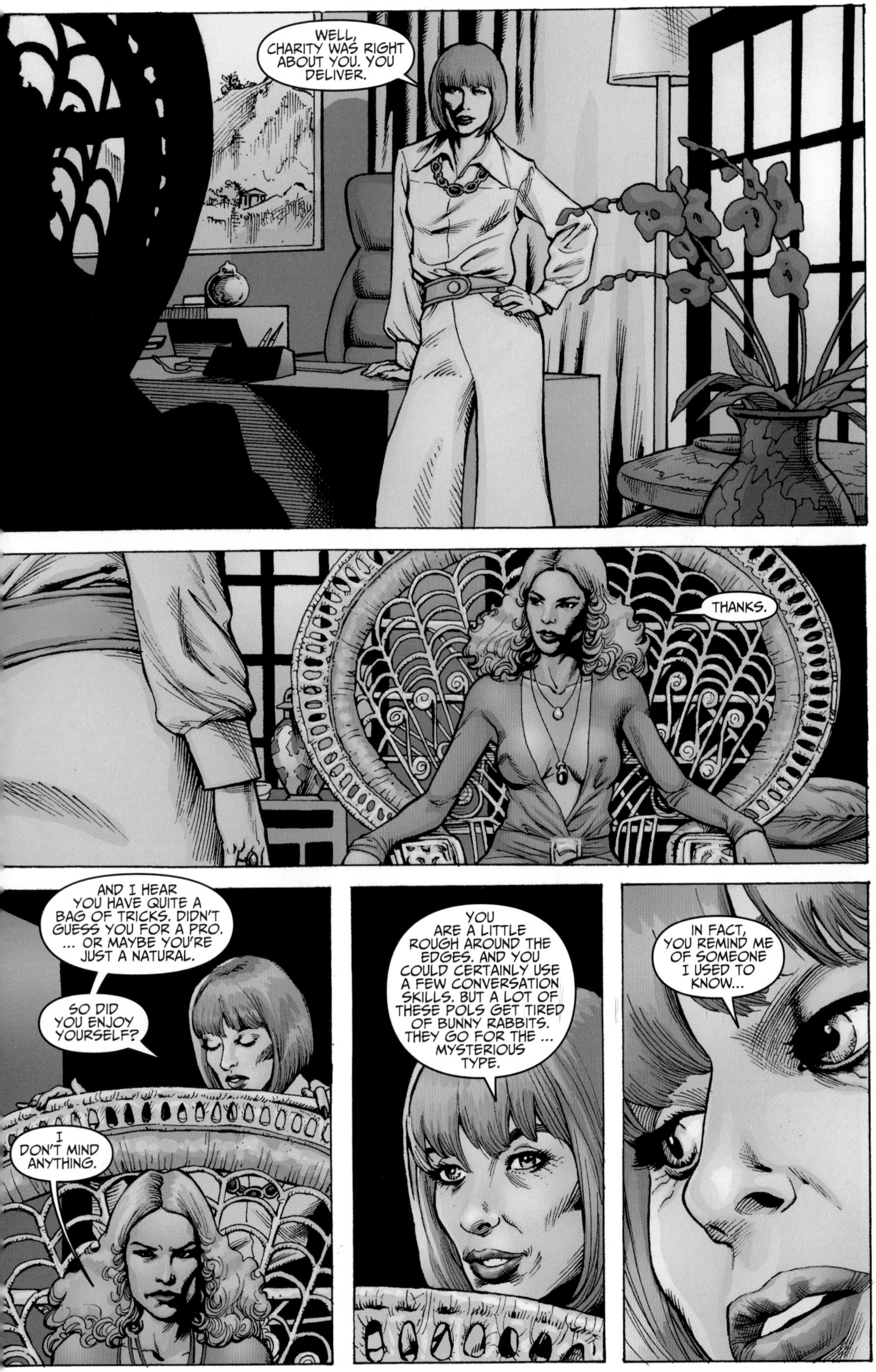
WELL, CHARITY WAS RIGHT ABOUT YOU. YOU DELIVER.
THANKS.
AND I HEAR YOU HAVE QUITE A BAG OF TRICKS. DIDN'T GUESS YOU FOR A PRO. ... OR MAYBE YOU'RE JUST A NATURAL.
SO DID YOU ENJOY YOURSELF?
I DON'T MIND ANYTHING.
YOU ARE A LITTLE ROUGH AROUND THE EDGES. AND YOU COULD CERTAINLY USE A FEW CONVERSATION SKILLS. BUT A LOT OF THESE POLS GET TIRED OF BUNNY RABBITS. THEY GO FOR THE ... MYSTERIOUS TYPE.
IN FACT, YOU REMIND ME OF SOMEONE I USED TO KNOW...

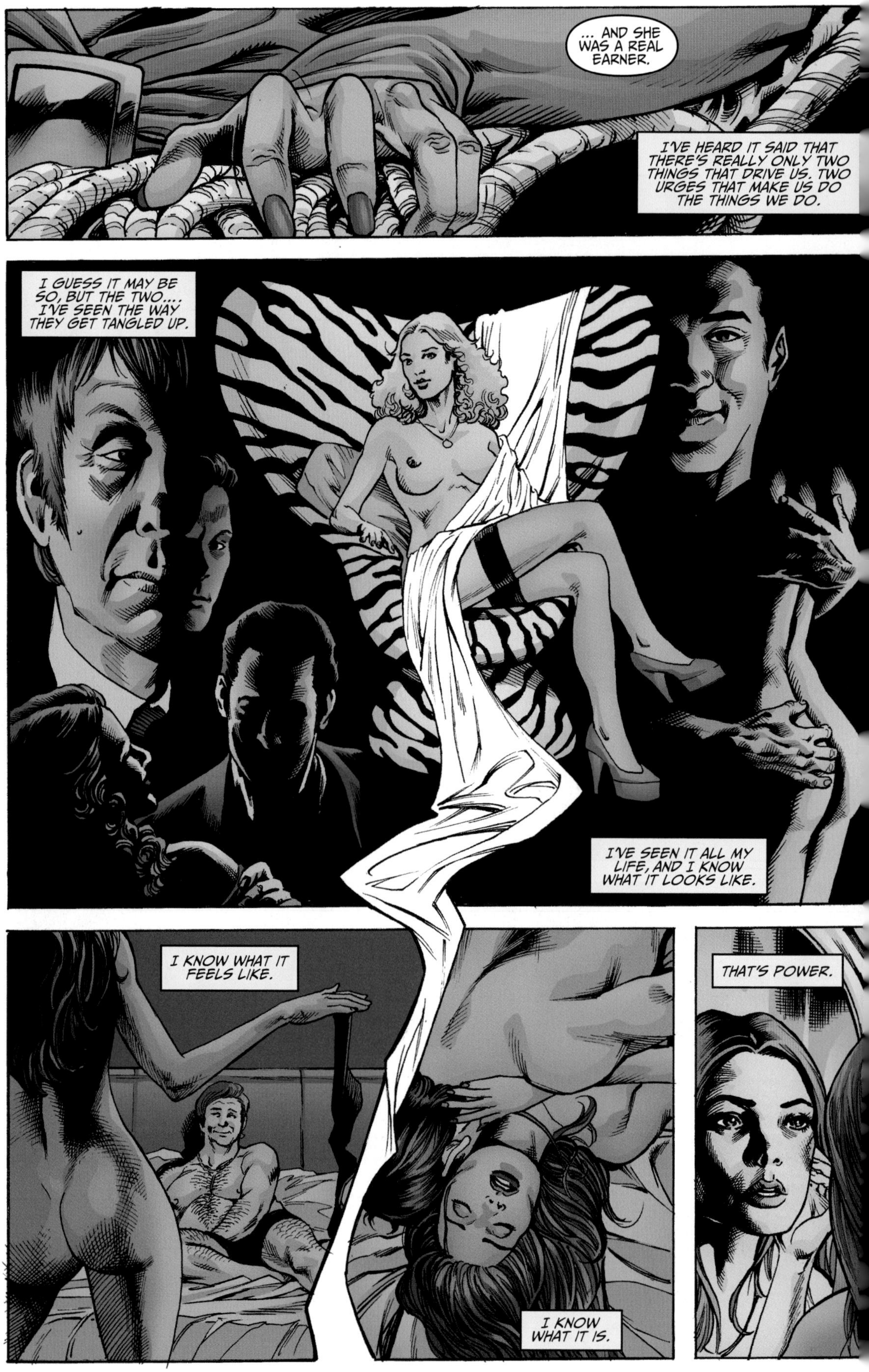
... AND SHE WAS A REAL EARNER.
I'VE HEARD IT SAID THAT THERE'S REALLY ONLY TWO THINGS THAT DRIVE US. TWO URGES THAT MAKE US DO THE THINGS WE DO.
I GUESS IT MAY BE SO, BUT THE TWO.... I'VE SEEN THE WAY THEY GET TANGLED UP.
I'VE SEEN IT ALL MY LIFE, AND I KNOW WHAT IT LOOKS LIKE.
I KNOW WHAT IT FEELS LIKE.
I KNOW WHAT IT IS.
THAT'S POWER.

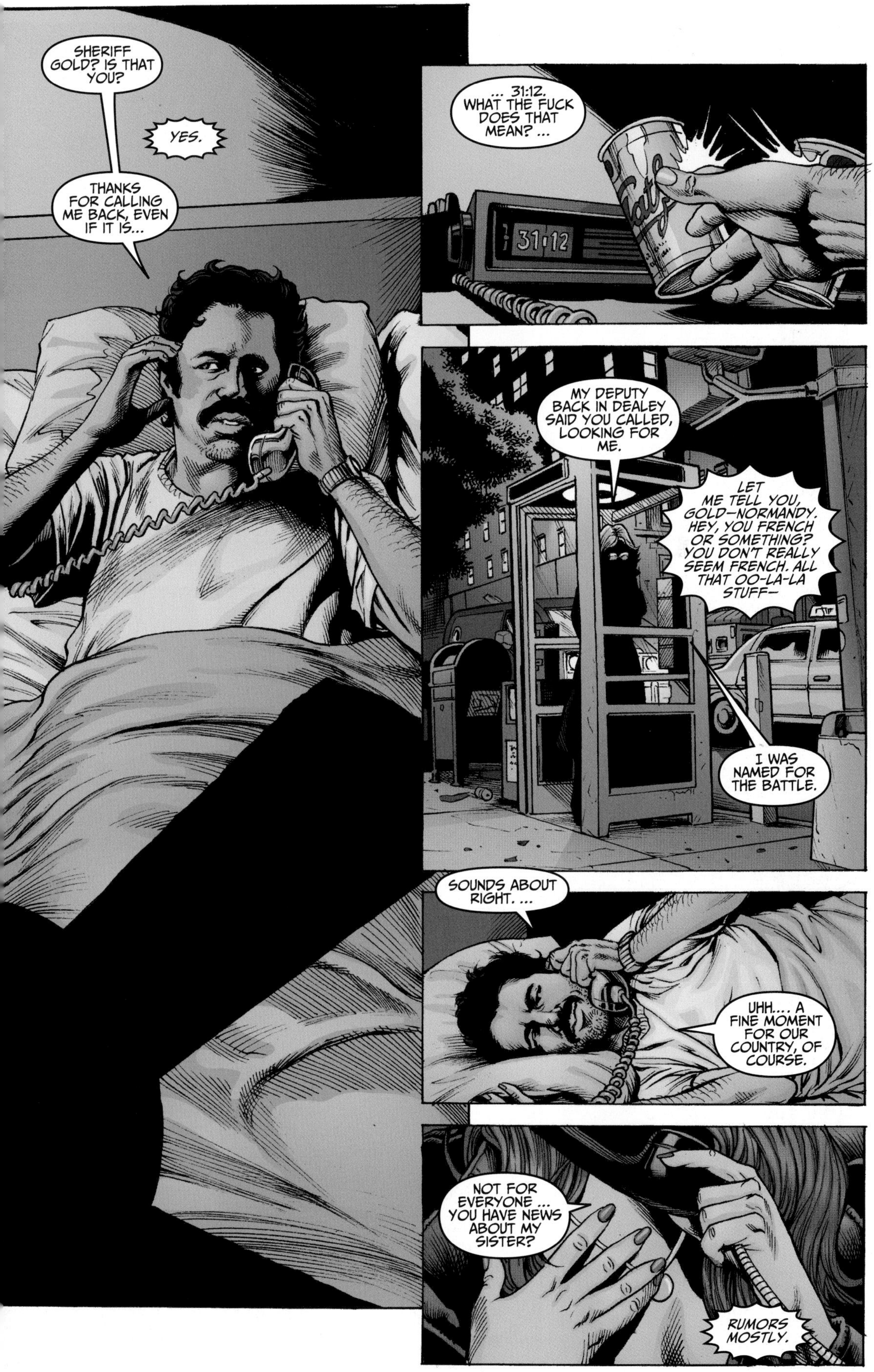
SHERIFF GOLD? IS THAT YOU?
YES.
THANKS FOR CALLING ME BACK, EVEN IF IT IS...
... 31:12. WHAT THE FUCK DOES THAT MEAN? ...
31:12
MY DEPUTY BACK IN DEALEY SAID YOU CALLED, LOOKING FOR ME.
LET ME TELL YOU, GOLD—NORMANDY. HEY, YOU FRENCH OR SOMETHING? YOU DON'T REALLY SEEM FRENCH. ALL THAT OO-LA-LA STUFF—
I WAS NAMED FOR THE BATTLE.
SOUNDS ABOUT RIGHT. ...
UHH.... A FINE MOMENT FOR OUR COUNTRY, OF COURSE.
NOT FOR EVERYONE ... YOU HAVE NEWS ABOUT MY SISTER?
RUMORS MOSTLY.

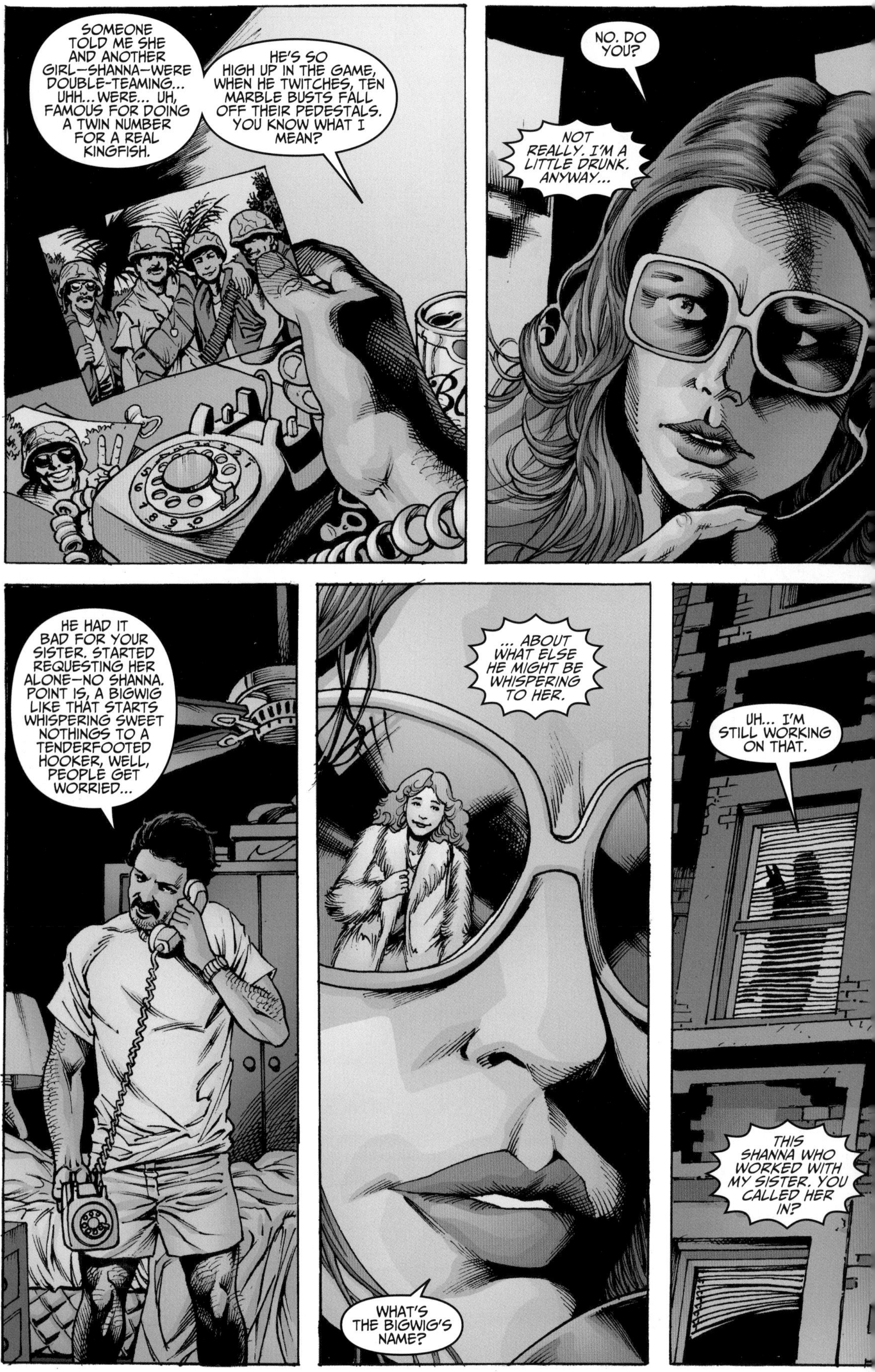
SOMEONE TOLD ME SHE AND ANOTHER GIRL—SHANNA—WERE DOUBLE-TEAMING... UHH... WERE... UH, FAMOUS FOR DOING A TWIN NUMBER FOR A REAL KINGFISH.
HE'S SO HIGH UP IN THE GAME, WHEN HE TWITCHES, TEN MARBLE BUSTS FALL OFF THEIR PEDESTALS. YOU KNOW WHAT I MEAN?
NO. DO YOU?
NOT REALLY. I'M A LITTLE DRUNK. ANYWAY...
HE HAD IT BAD FOR YOUR SISTER. STARTED REQUESTING HER ALONE—NO SHANNA. POINT IS, A BIGWIG LIKE THAT STARTS WHISPERING SWEET NOTHINGS TO A TENDERFOOTED HOOKER, WELL, PEOPLE GET WORRIED...
... ABOUT WHAT ELSE HE MIGHT BE WHISPERING TO HER.
WHAT'S THE BIGWIG'S NAME?
UH... I'M STILL WORKING ON THAT.
THIS SHANNA WHO WORKED WITH MY SISTER. YOU CALLED HER IN?

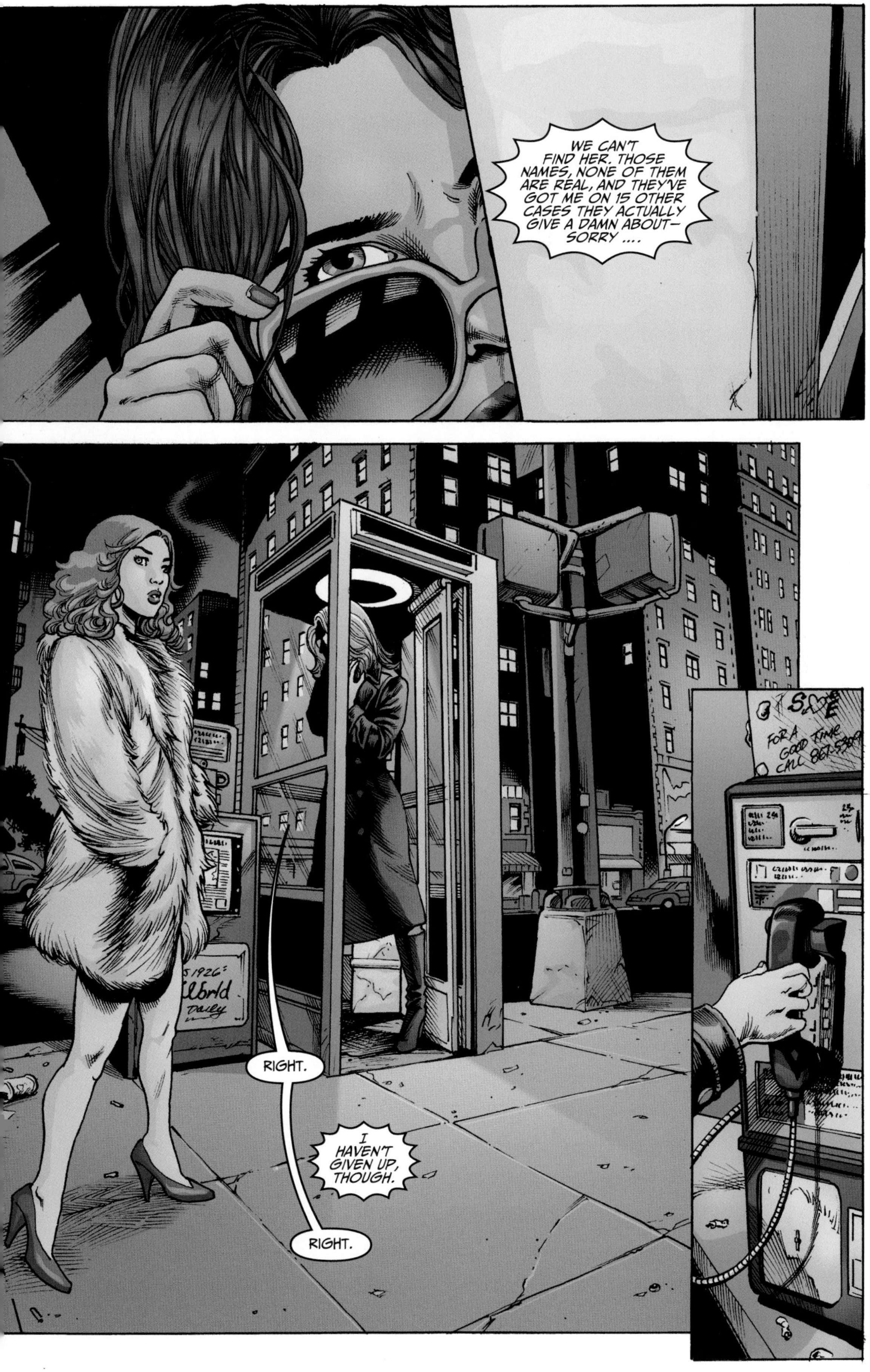
WE CAN'T FIND HER. THOSE NAMES, NONE OF THEM ARE REAL, AND THEY'VE GOT ME ON 15 OTHER CASES THEY ACTUALLY GIVE A DAMN ABOUT— SORRY ....
RIGHT.
I HAVEN'T GIVEN UP, THOUGH.
RIGHT.
FOR A GOOD TIME CALL

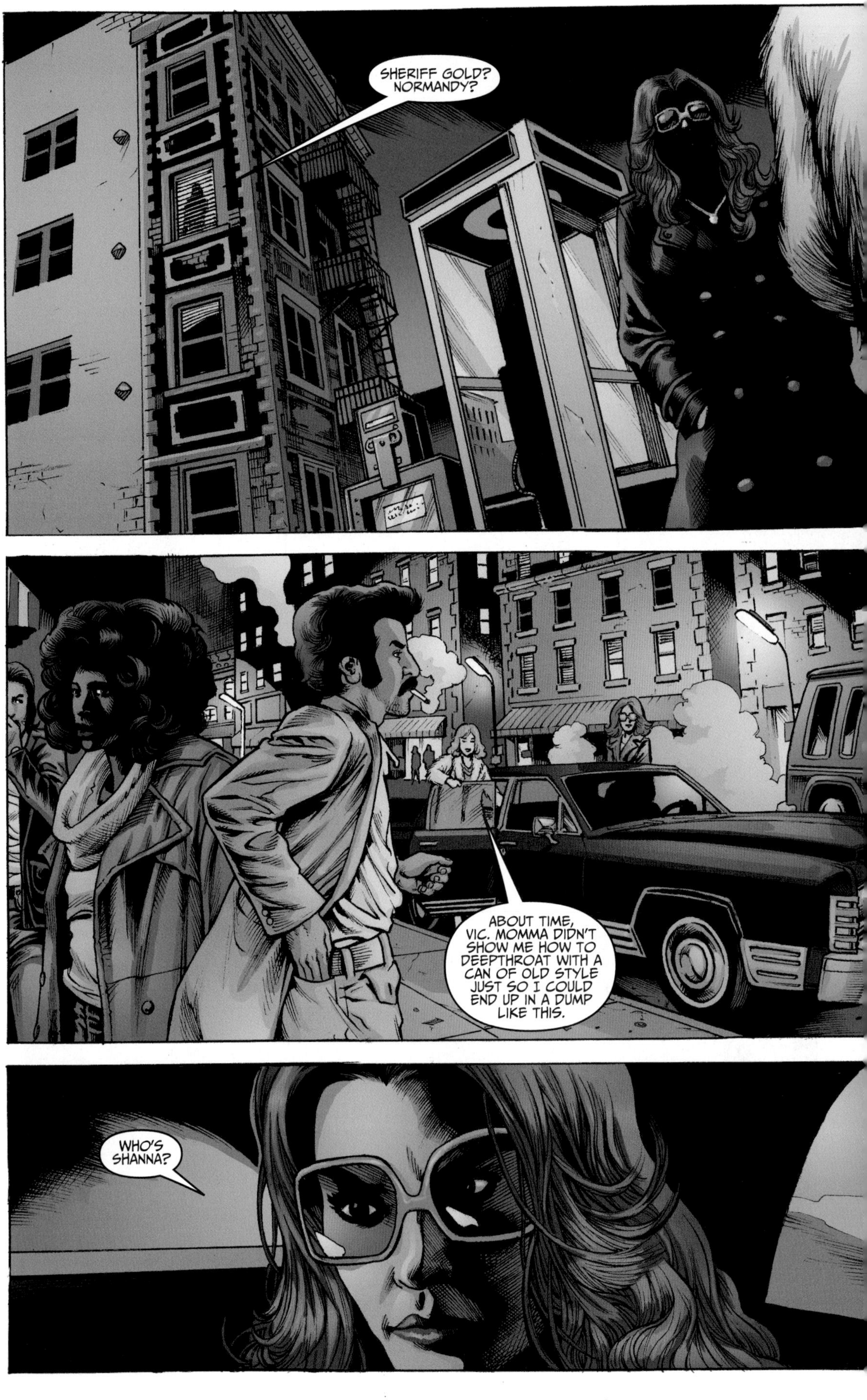
SHERIFF GOLD? NORMANDY?
ABOUT TIME, VIC. MOMMA DIDN'T SHOW ME HOW TO DEEPTHROAT WITH A CAN OF OLD STYLE JUST SO I COULD END UP IN A DUMP LIKE THIS.
WHO'S SHANNA?

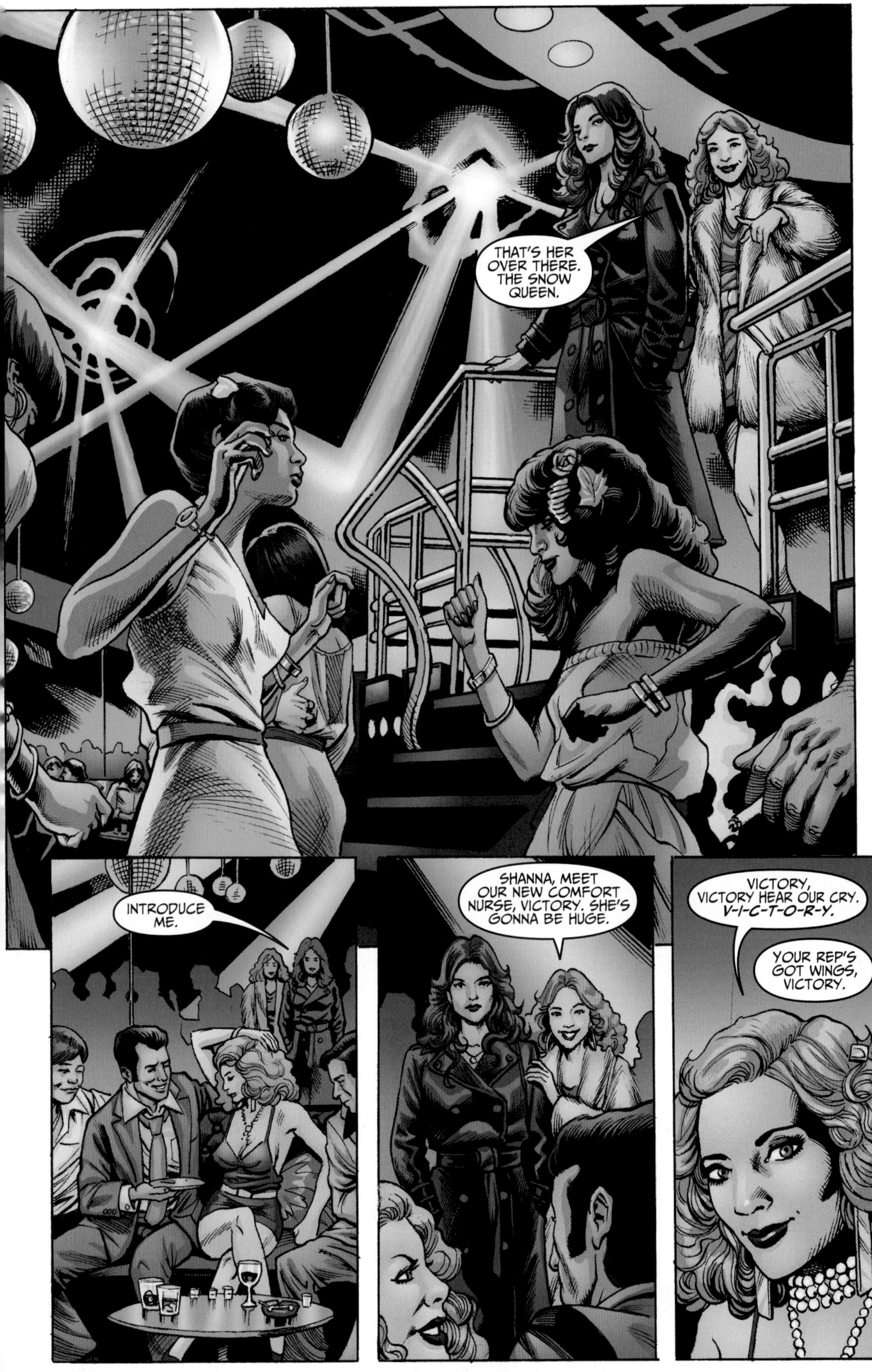
THAT'S HER OVER THERE. THE SNOW QUEEN.
INTRODUCE ME.
SHANNA, MEET OUR NEW COMFORT NURSE, VICTORY. SHE'S GONNA BE HUGE.
VICTORY, VICTORY HEAR OUR CRY. V-I-C-T-O-R-Y.
YOUR REP'S GOT WINGS, VICTORY.

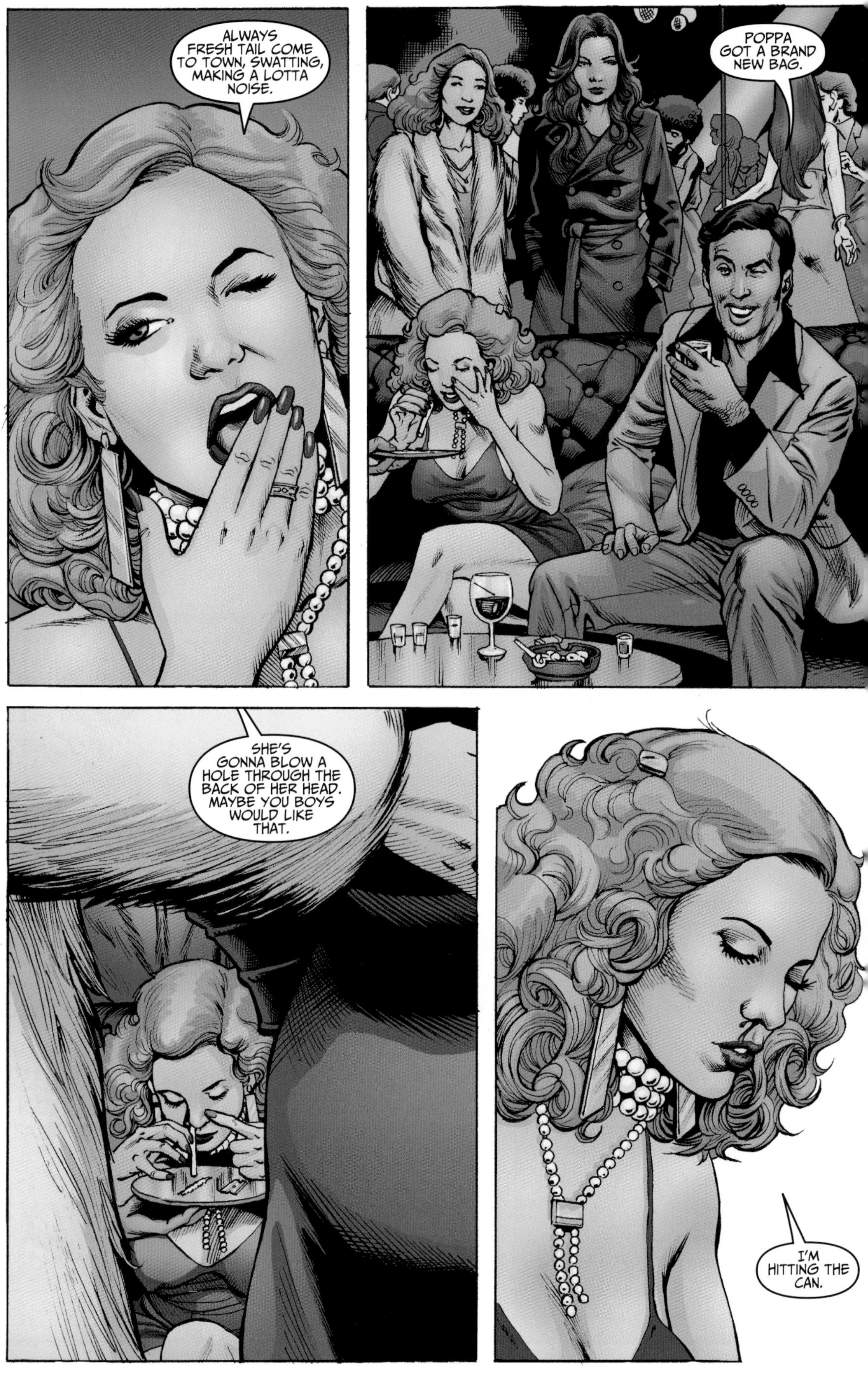
ALWAYS FRESH TAIL COME TO TOWN, SWATTING, MAKING A LOTTA NOISE.
POPPA GOT A BRAND NEW BAG.
SHE'S GONNA BLOW A HOLE THROUGH THE BACK OF HER HEAD. MAYBE YOU BOYS WOULD LIKE THAT.
I'M HITTING THE CAN.

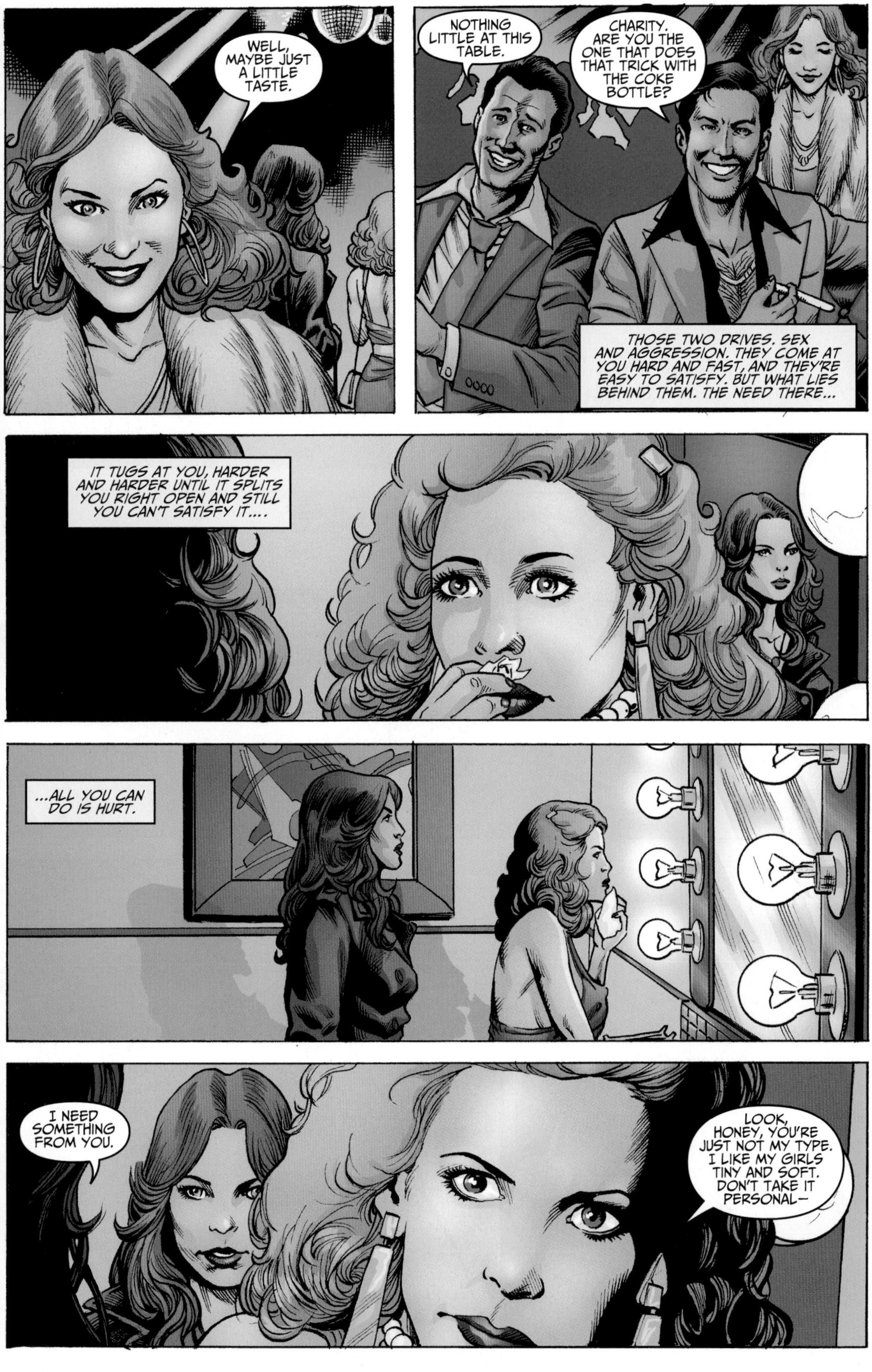

WELL, MAYBE JUST A LITTLE TASTE.
NOTHING LITTLE AT THIS TABLE.
CHARITY. ARE YOU THE ONE THAT DOES THAT TRICK WITH THE COKE BOTTLE?
THOSE TWO DRIVES. SEX AND AGGRESSION. THEY COME AT YOU HARD AND FAST, AND THEY'RE EASY TO SATISFY. BUT WHAT LIES BEHIND THEM. THE NEED THERE...
IT TUGS AT YOU, HARDER AND HARDER UNTIL IT SPLITS YOU RIGHT OPEN AND STILL YOU CAN'T SATISFY IT....
...ALL YOU CAN DO IS HURT.
I NEED SOMETHING FROM YOU.
LOOK, HONEY, YOU'RE JUST NOT MY TYPE. I LIKE MY GIRLS TINY AND SOFT. DON'T TAKE IT PERSONAL—

AHHH!

SMASHHH

YOU'RE TAKING TOO MUCH TIME. I DON'T HAVE TIME.

W-WHAT DO YOU WANT?

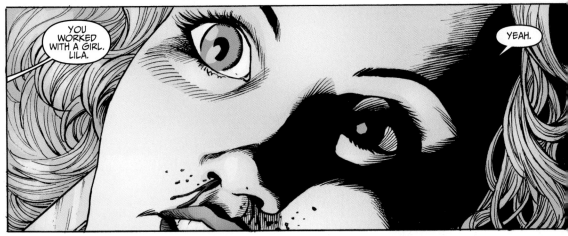

YOU WORKED WITH A GIRL. LILA.

YEAH.

WHERE IS SHE? WHAT HAPPENED TO HER?

NO IDEA.

I MEAN IT. SWEAR ON A STACK. LILA AND ME, WE PLAYED PASS-THE-BATON RELAYS WITH A BUNCH OF SLICK SUITS, AND THEN ONE DAY SHE JUST STOPS SHOWING UP.

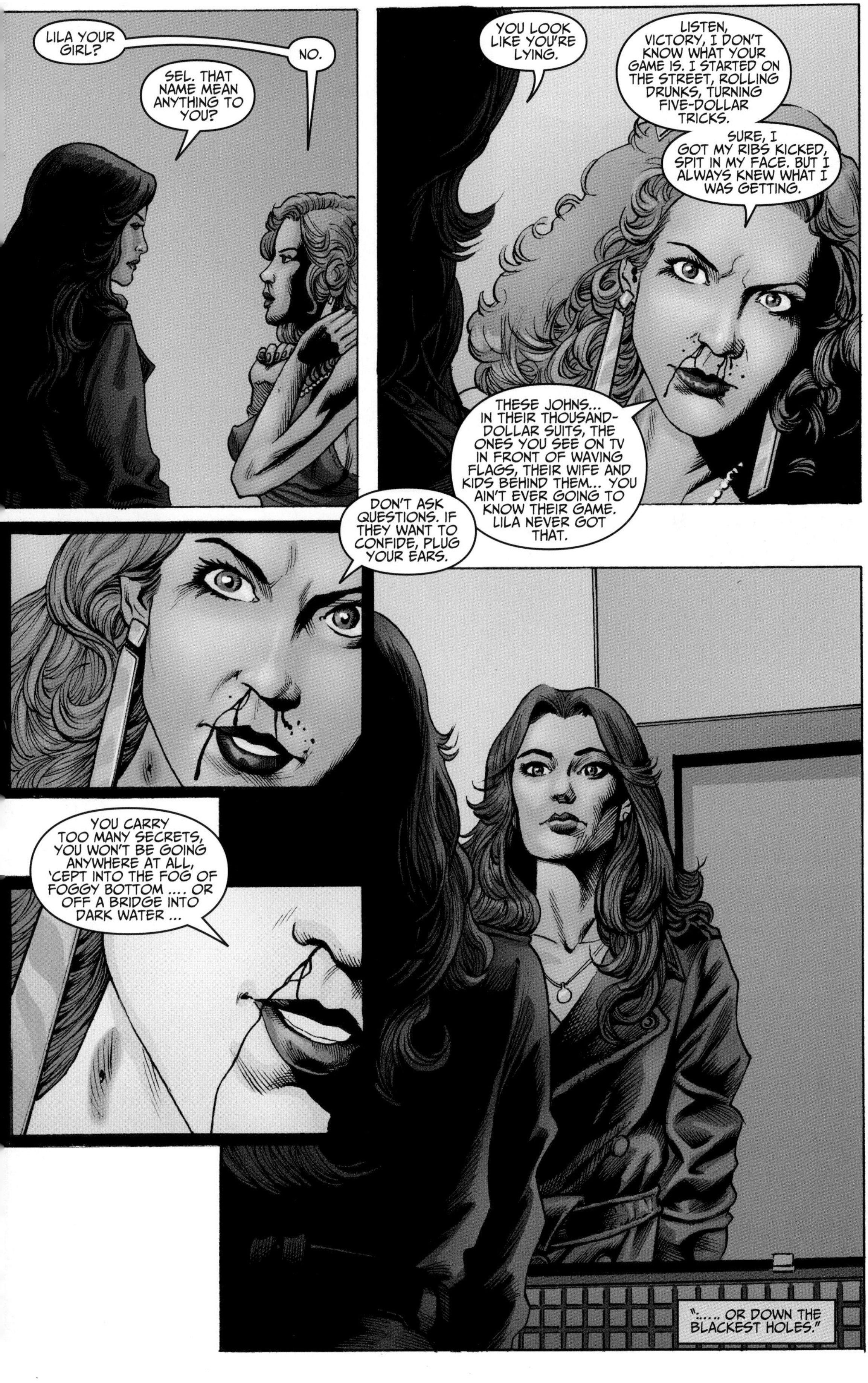
LILA YOUR GIRL?
NO.
SEL. THAT NAME MEAN ANYTHING TO YOU?
YOU LOOK LIKE YOU'RE LYING.
LISTEN, VICTORY, I DON'T KNOW WHAT YOUR GAME IS. I STARTED ON THE STREET, ROLLING DRUNKS, TURNING FIVE-DOLLAR TRICKS.
SURE, I GOT MY RIBS KICKED, SPIT IN MY FACE. BUT I ALWAYS KNEW WHAT I WAS GETTING.
THESE JOHNS... IN THEIR THOUSAND-DOLLAR SUITS, THE ONES YOU SEE ON TV IN FRONT OF WAVING FLAGS, THEIR WIFE AND KIDS BEHIND THEM... YOU AIN'T EVER GOING TO KNOW THEIR GAME. LILA NEVER GOT THAT.
DON'T ASK QUESTIONS. IF THEY WANT TO CONFIDE, PLUG YOUR EARS.
YOU CARRY TOO MANY SECRETS, YOU WON'T BE GOING ANYWHERE AT ALL, 'CEPT INTO THE FOG OF FOGGY BOTTOM .... OR OFF A BRIDGE INTO DARK WATER ...
"..... OR DOWN THE BLACKEST HOLES."

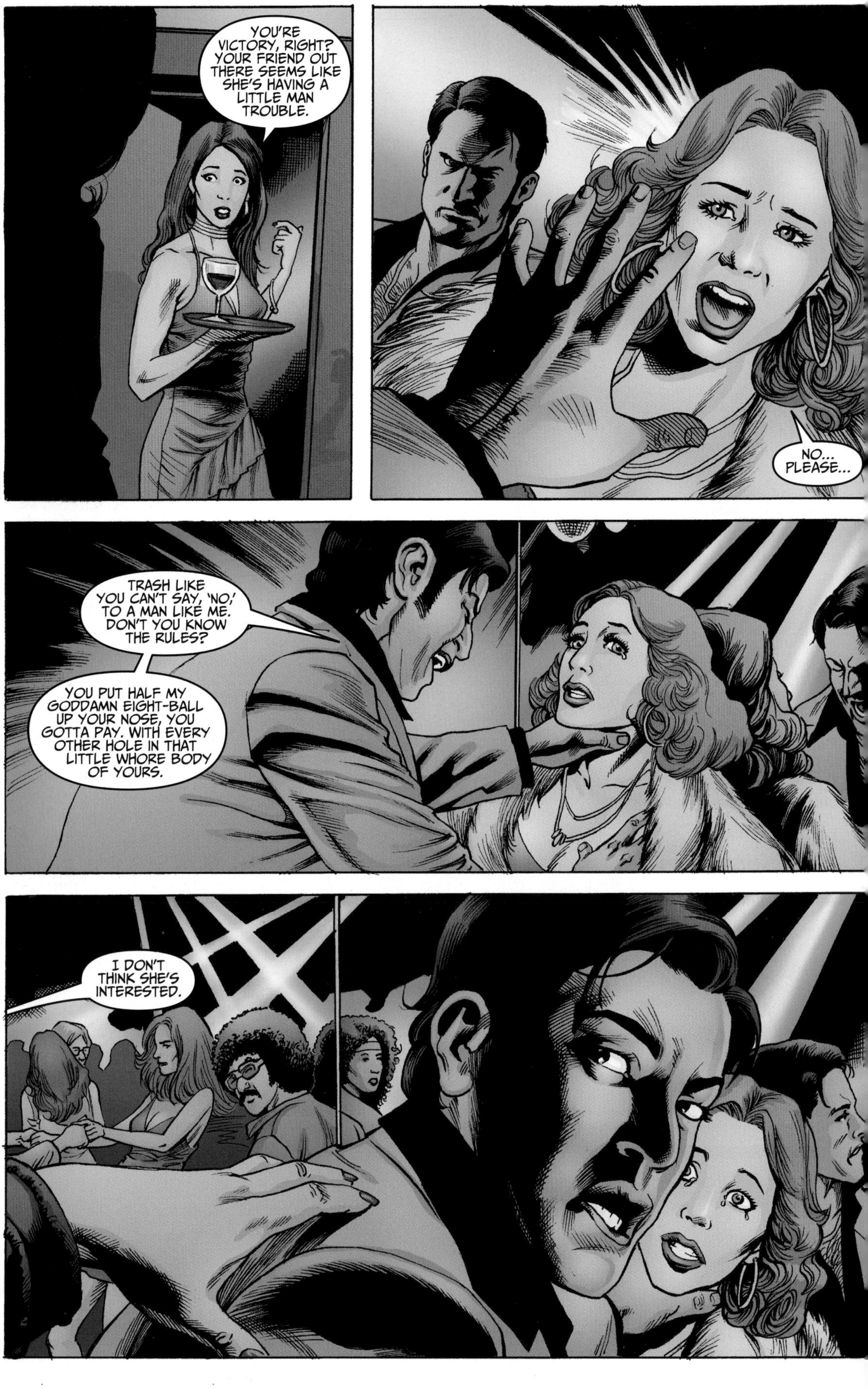
YOU'RE VICTORY, RIGHT? YOUR FRIEND OUT THERE SEEMS LIKE SHE'S HAVING A LITTLE MAN TROUBLE.
NO... PLEASE...
TRASH LIKE YOU CAN'T SAY, 'NO,' TO A MAN LIKE ME. DON'T YOU KNOW THE RULES?
YOU PUT HALF MY GODDAMN EIGHT-BALL UP YOUR NOSE, YOU GOTTA PAY. WITH EVERY OTHER HOLE IN THAT LITTLE WHORE BODY OF YOURS.
I DON'T THINK SHE'S INTERESTED.

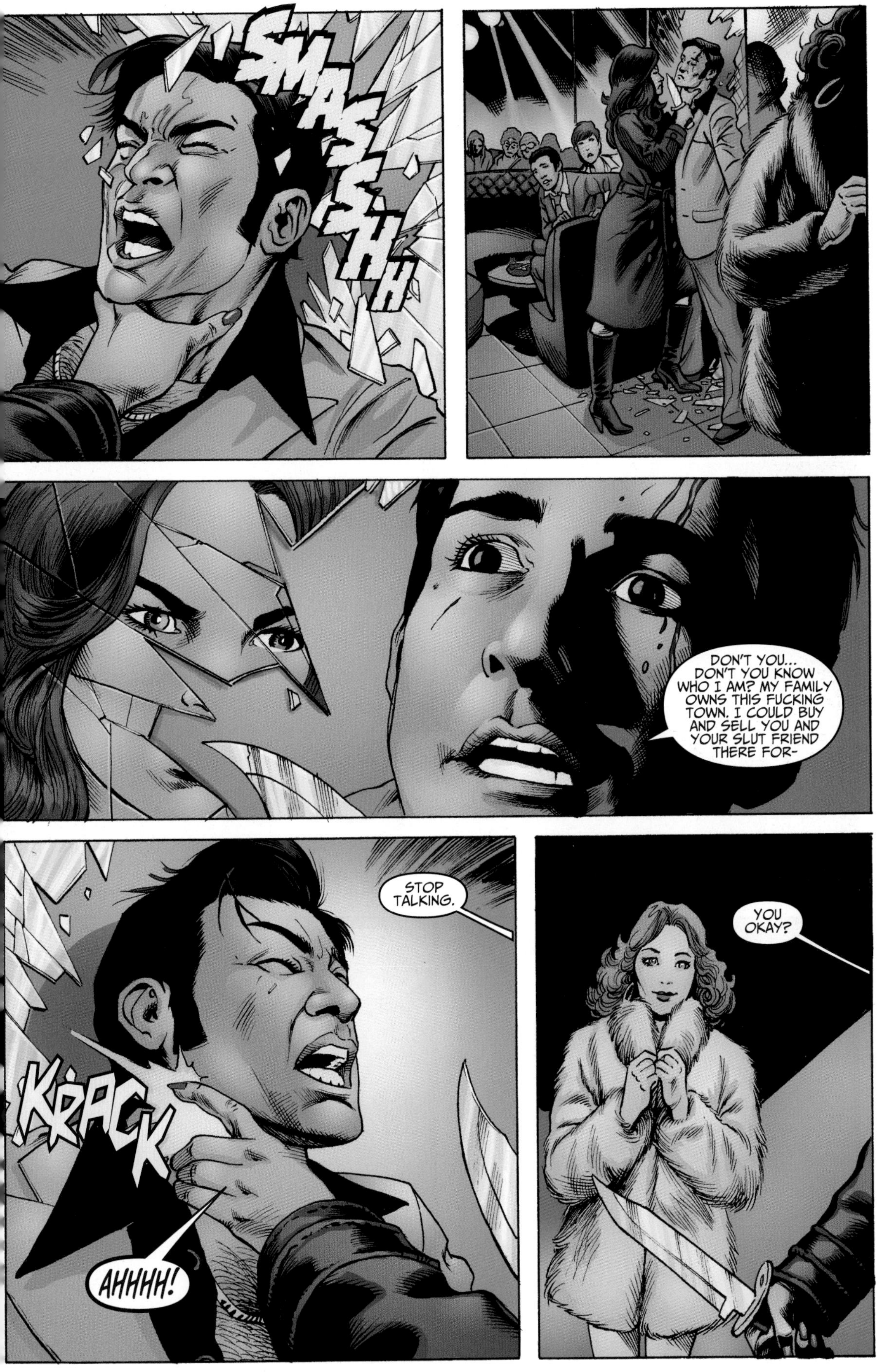
SMASSHH
DON'T YOU... DON'T YOU KNOW WHO I AM? MY FAMILY OWNS THIS FUCKING TOWN. I COULD BUY AND SELL YOU AND YOUR SLUT FRIEND THERE FOR-
STOP TALKING.
KRACK
AHHHH!
YOU OKAY?

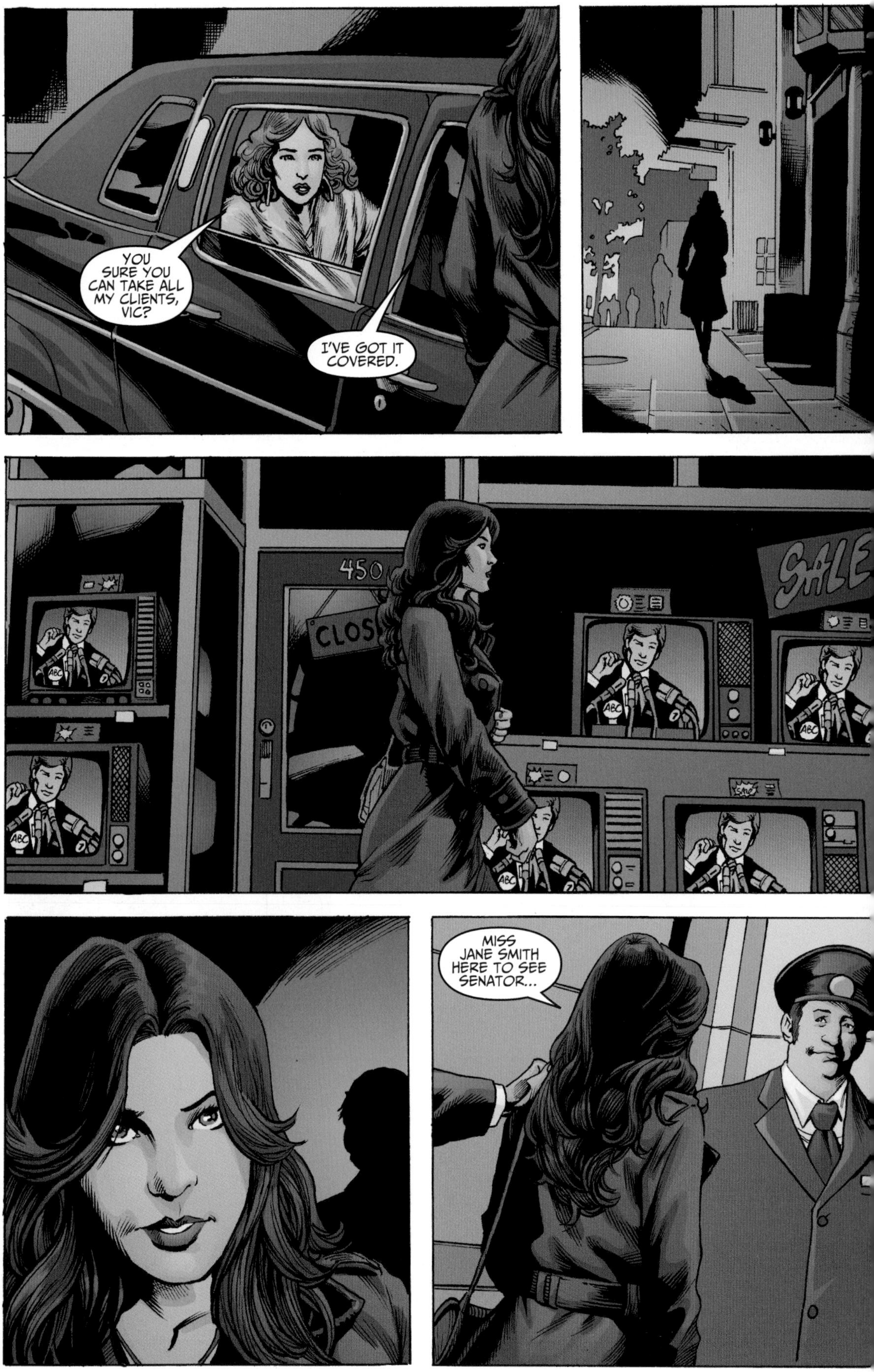
YOU SURE YOU CAN TAKE ALL MY CLIENTS, VIC?
I'VE GOT IT COVERED.
450
CLOS
ABC
SALE
MISS JANE SMITH HERE TO SEE SENATOR...

.... STURGES?

I NEED YOU TO COME WITH ME, SHERIFF GOLD.

IS THIS ABOUT WHAT HAPPENED IN THE CLUB?

NO ....

HELL, GOLD, I'M SO SORRY...

IT'S ABOUT YOUR SISTER.

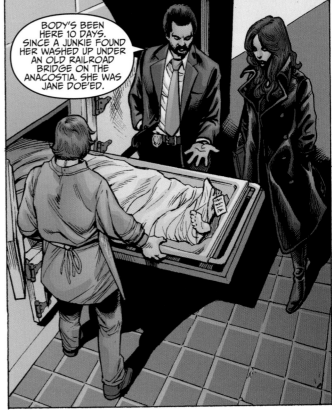

BODY'S BEEN HERE 10 DAYS. SINCE A JUNKIE FOUND HER WASHED UP UNDER AN OLD RAILROAD BRIDGE ON THE ANACOSTIA. SHE WAS JANE DOE'ED.

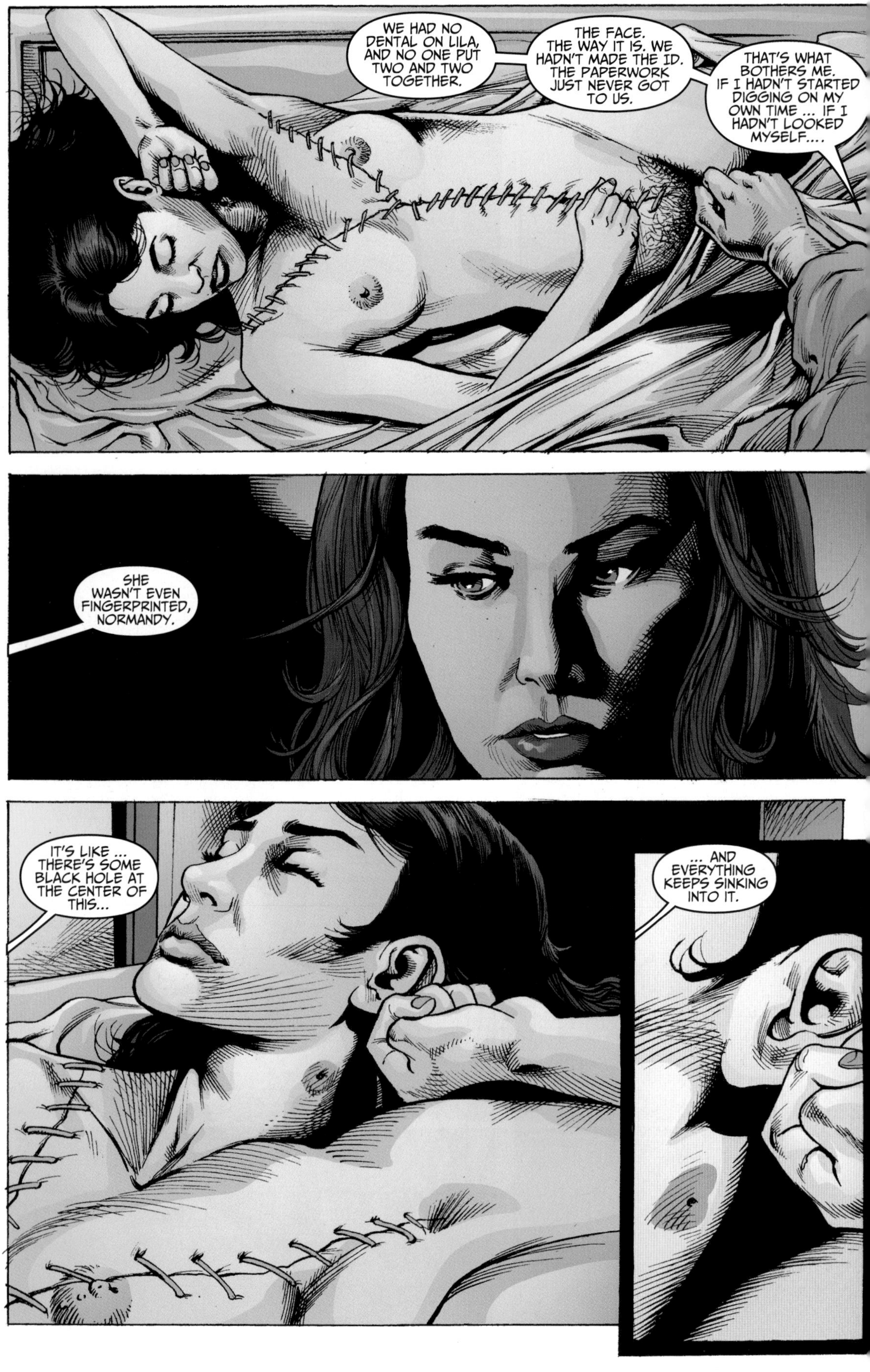

WE HAD NO DENTAL ON LILA, AND NO ONE PUT TWO AND TWO TOGETHER.
THE FACE. THE WAY IT IS. WE HADN'T MADE THE ID. THE PAPERWORK JUST NEVER GOT TO US.
THAT'S WHAT BOTHERS ME. IF I HADN'T STARTED DIGGING ON MY OWN TIME ... IF I HADN'T LOOKED MYSELF....
SHE WASN'T EVEN FINGERPRINTED, NORMANDY.
IT'S LIKE ... THERE'S SOME BLACK HOLE AT THE CENTER OF THIS...
... AND EVERYTHING KEEPS SINKING INTO IT.

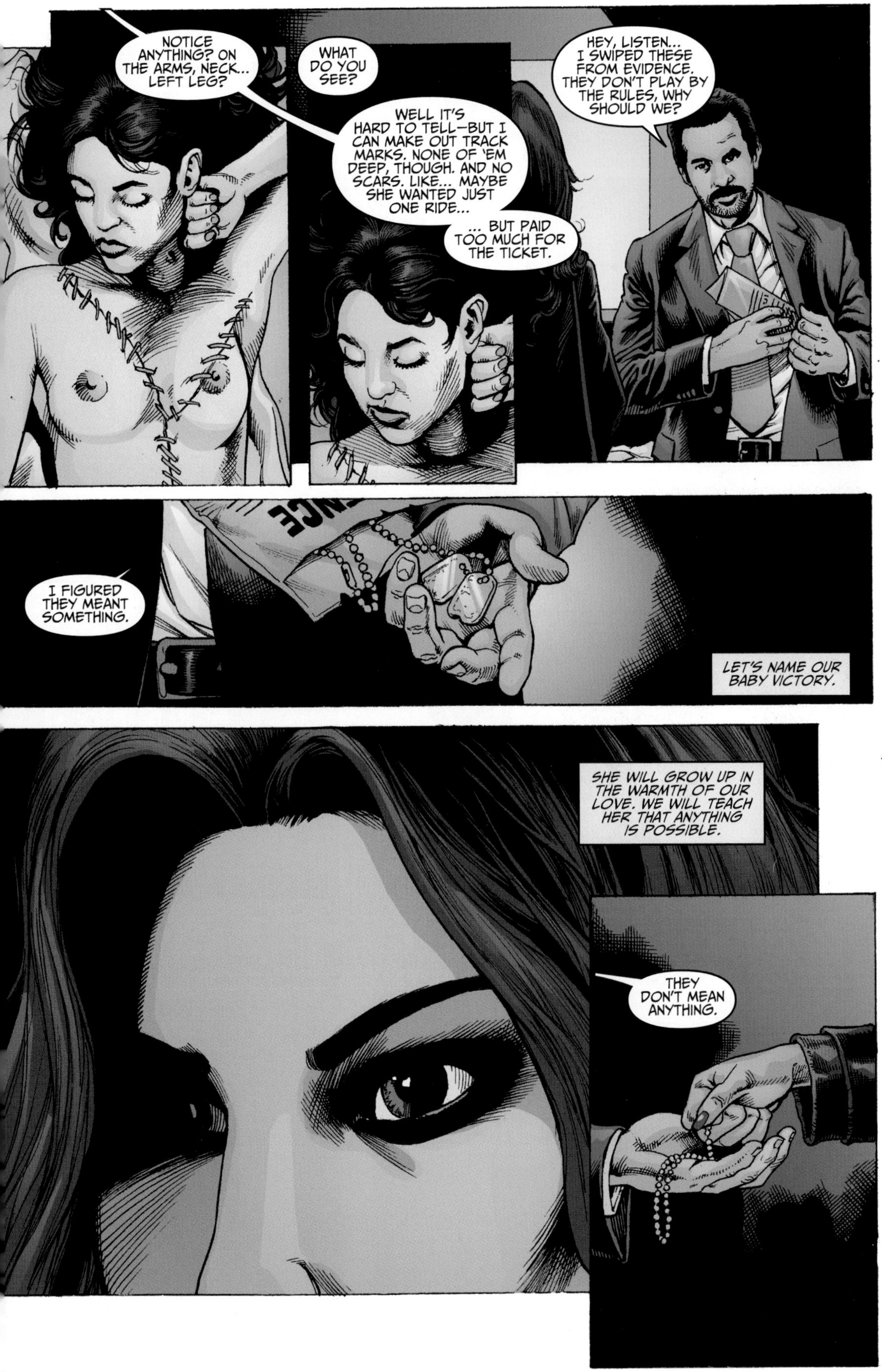
NOTICE ANYTHING? ON THE ARMS, NECK... LEFT LEG?
WHAT DO YOU SEE?
WELL IT'S HARD TO TELL—BUT I CAN MAKE OUT TRACK MARKS. NONE OF 'EM DEEP, THOUGH. AND NO SCARS. LIKE... MAYBE SHE WANTED JUST ONE RIDE...
... BUT PAID TOO MUCH FOR THE TICKET.
HEY, LISTEN... I SWIPED THESE FROM EVIDENCE. THEY DON'T PLAY BY THE RULES, WHY SHOULD WE?
I FIGURED THEY MEANT SOMETHING.
LET'S NAME OUR BABY VICTORY.
SHE WILL GROW UP IN THE WARMTH OF OUR LOVE. WE WILL TEACH HER THAT ANYTHING IS POSSIBLE.
THEY DON'T MEAN ANYTHING.

WHEN I WAS A KID, WE LIVED ACROSS FROM A BUTCHER. MY SISTER -- KNEE HIGH TO A GRASS-HOPPER -- LOVED THE OLD MAN.

EVERY MORNING, HE'D GIVE HER ONE OF THESE ROPES OF RED LICORICE.

SHERIFF GOLD!

SHE'D HANG IT OUT OF HER MOUTH ALL DAY LONG.

ONE DAY, LILA WANTED TO SURPRISE HIM, SHOW HIM SOME NEW DANCE SHE'D LEARNED. SHE SNUCK IN THE BACK OF THE STORE.

THAT'S WHEN SHE SAW IT.

MY SISTER, SHE CRIED ALL DAY AND NIGHT. THERE WAS NO COMFORTING HER.

THE DAY AFTER, WHEN THE BUTCHER WAVED HIS RED VINE, SHE JUST KEPT WALKING. THAT WAS JUST HER WAY. TOO SOFT FOR THIS WORLD.

SOFT LIKE I NEVER WAS.

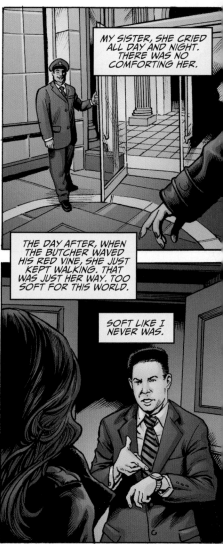

SHE SAW HIM DRAW HIS KNIFE ACROSS THAT CALF'S THROAT, SEVERING THE ARTERY, THE JUGULAR.

LETTING THE BLOOD DRAIN OUT. ALL WHILE CHATTING WITH HIS COUNTER GIRL, LAUGHING AT A SONG ON THE RADIO. THE THING DYING IN HIS ARMS.

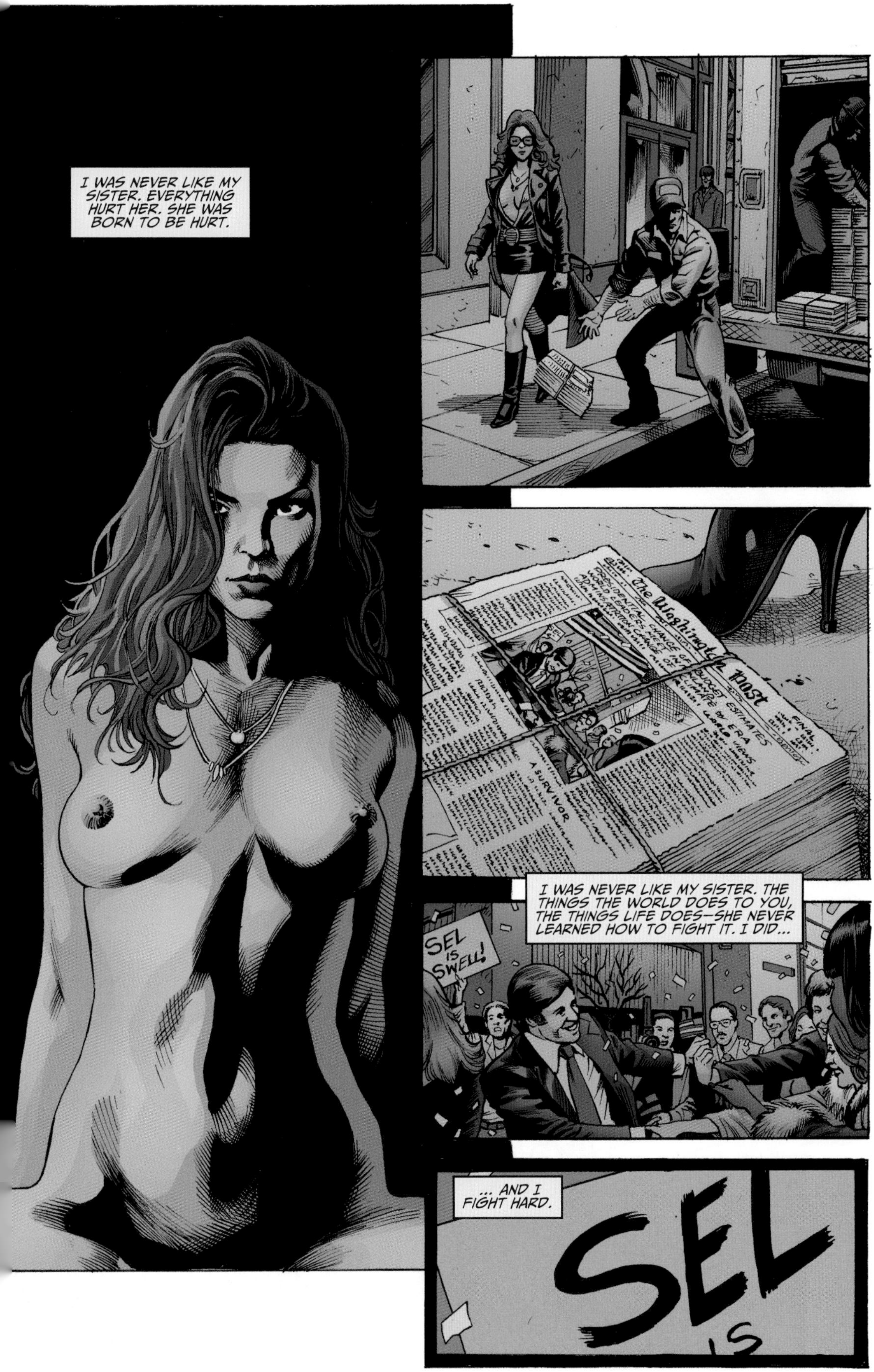
I WAS NEVER LIKE MY SISTER. EVERYTHING HURT HER. SHE WAS BORN TO BE HURT.
The Washington Post
A SURVIVOR
I WAS NEVER LIKE MY SISTER. THE THINGS THE WORLD DOES TO YOU, THE THINGS LIFE DOES—SHE NEVER LEARNED HOW TO FIGHT IT. I DID...
SEL IS SWELL!
... AND I FIGHT HARD.
SEL IS

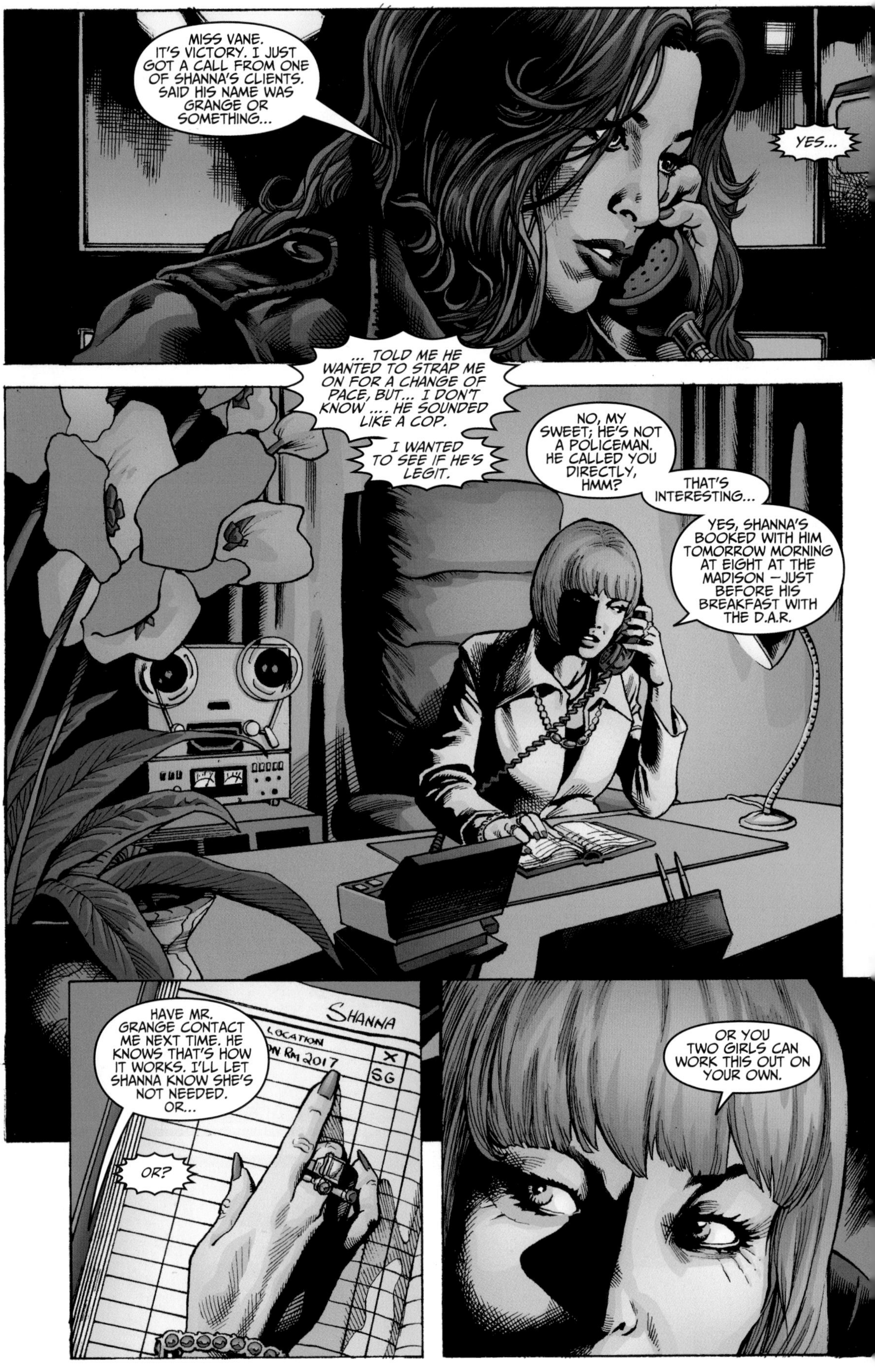
MISS VANE. IT'S VICTORY. I JUST GOT A CALL FROM ONE OF SHANNA'S CLIENTS. SAID HIS NAME WAS GRANGE OR SOMETHING...
YES...
... TOLD ME HE WANTED TO STRAP ME ON FOR A CHANGE OF PACE, BUT... I DON'T KNOW .... HE SOUNDED LIKE A COP.
I WANTED TO SEE IF HE'S LEGIT.
NO, MY SWEET; HE'S NOT A POLICEMAN. HE CALLED YOU DIRECTLY, HMM?
THAT'S INTERESTING...
YES, SHANNA'S BOOKED WITH HIM TOMORROW MORNING AT EIGHT AT THE MADISON —JUST BEFORE HIS BREAKFAST WITH THE D.A.R.
SHANNA
LOCATION
RM 2017
X
SG
HAVE MR. GRANGE CONTACT ME NEXT TIME. HE KNOWS THAT'S HOW IT WORKS. I'LL LET SHANNA KNOW SHE'S NOT NEEDED. OR...
OR?
OR YOU TWO GIRLS CAN WORK THIS OUT ON YOUR OWN.

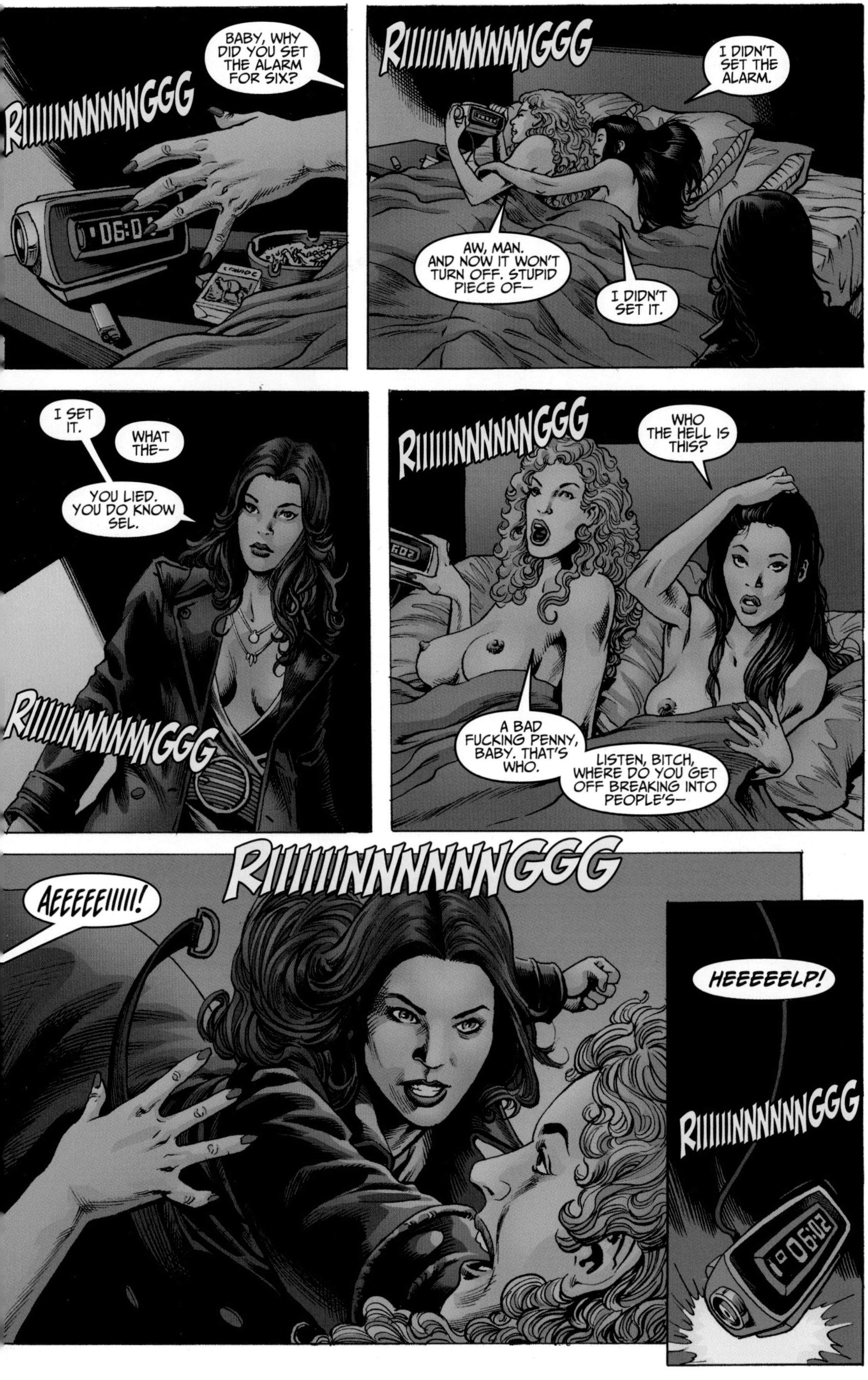
BABY, WHY DID YOU SET THE ALARM FOR SIX?
RIIIIINNNNNNGGG
RIIIIINNNNNNGGG
I DIDN'T SET THE ALARM.
AW, MAN. AND NOW IT WON'T TURN OFF. STUPID PIECE OF—
I DIDN'T SET IT.
I SET IT.
WHAT THE—
YOU LIED. YOU DO KNOW SEL.
RIIIIINNNNNNGGG
RIIIIINNNNNNGGG
WHO THE HELL IS THIS?
A BAD FUCKING PENNY, BABY. THAT'S WHO.
LISTEN, BITCH, WHERE DO YOU GET OFF BREAKING INTO PEOPLE'S—
RIIIIINNNNNNGGG
AEEEEEIIIII!
HEEEEELP!
RIIIIINNNNNNGGG

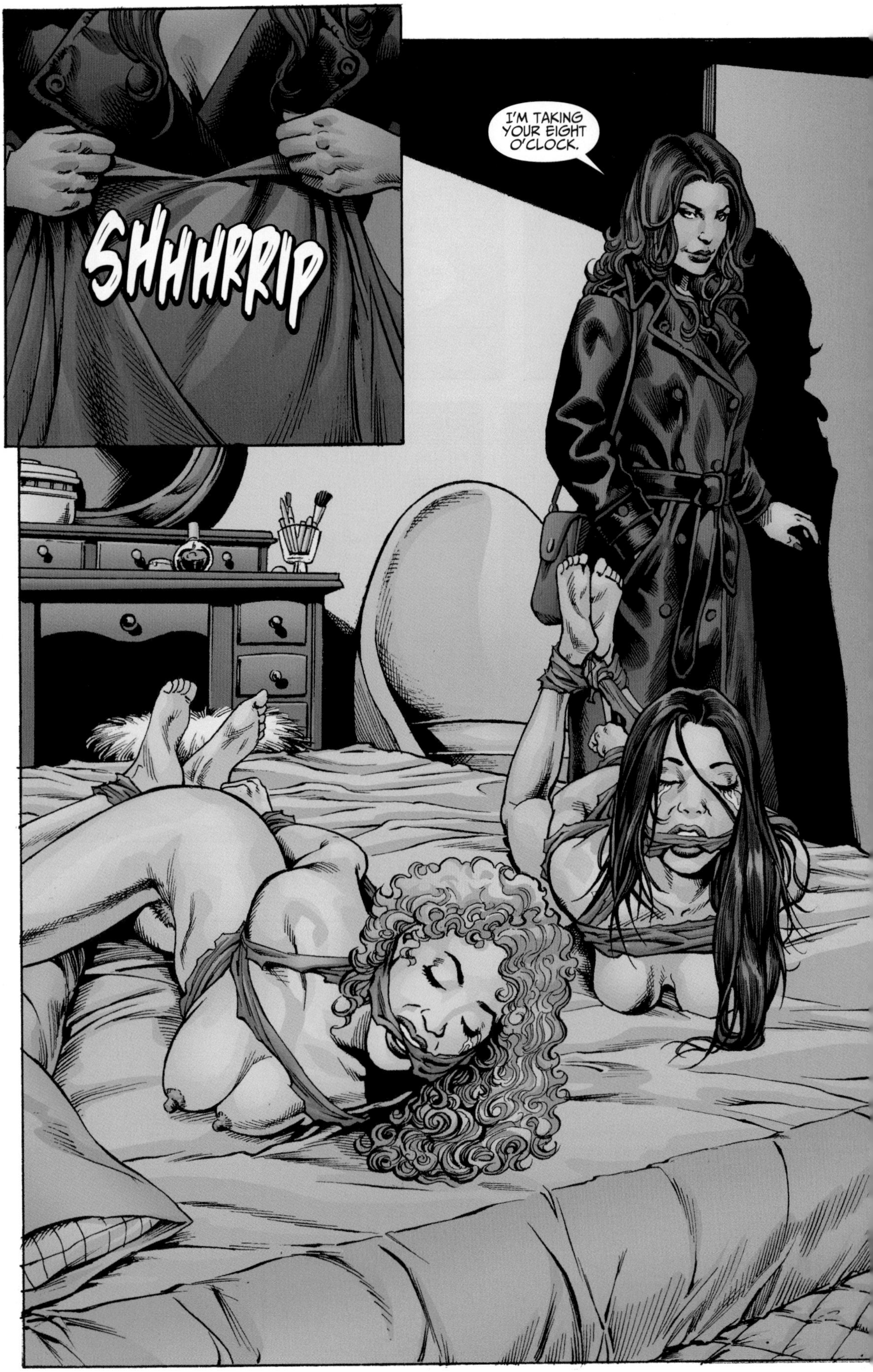
SHHHRRIP
I'M TAKING YOUR EIGHT O'CLOCK.

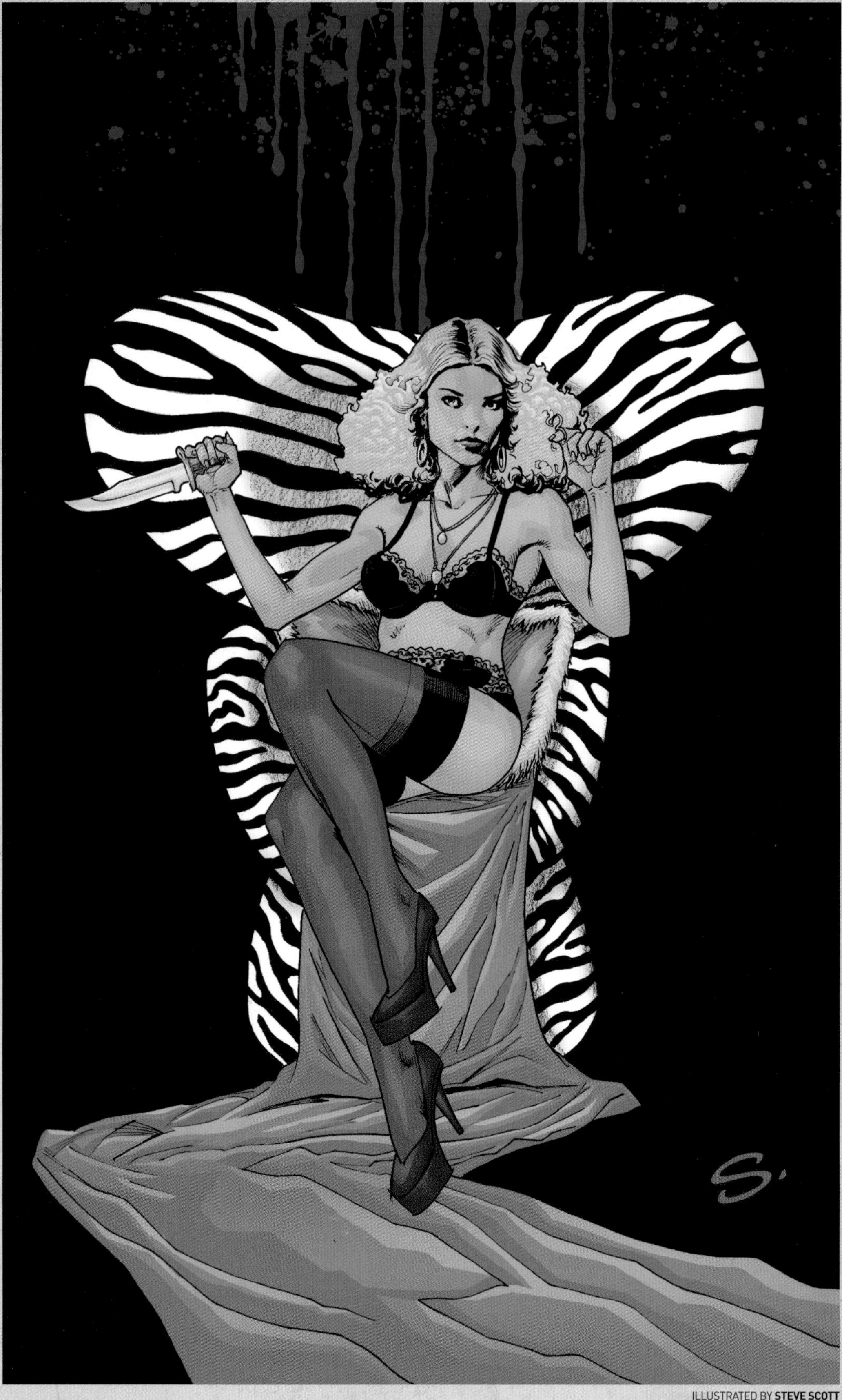

ILLUSTRATED BY **STEVE SCOTT**

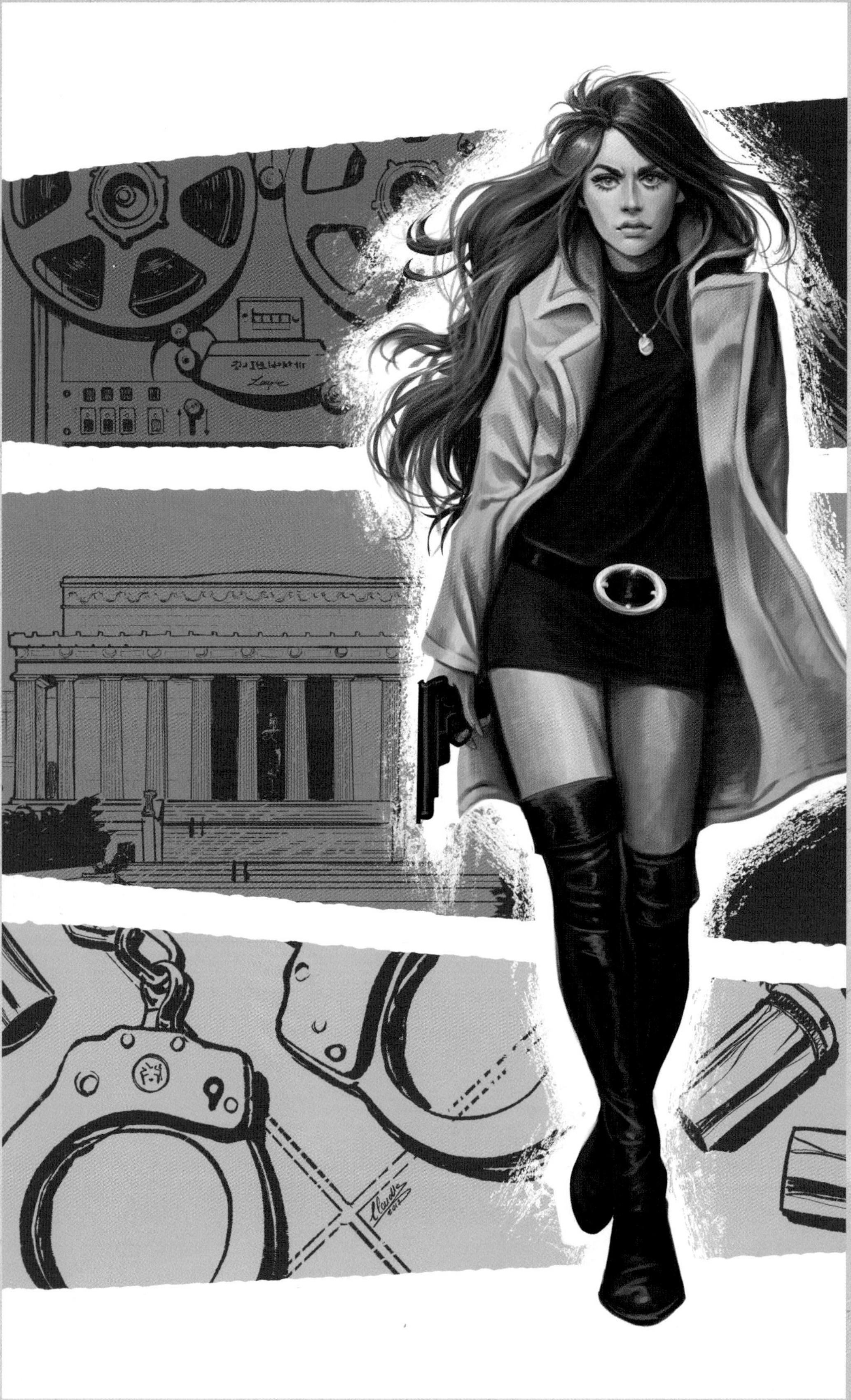

ILLUSTRATED BY **CLAUDIA IANNICIELLO**

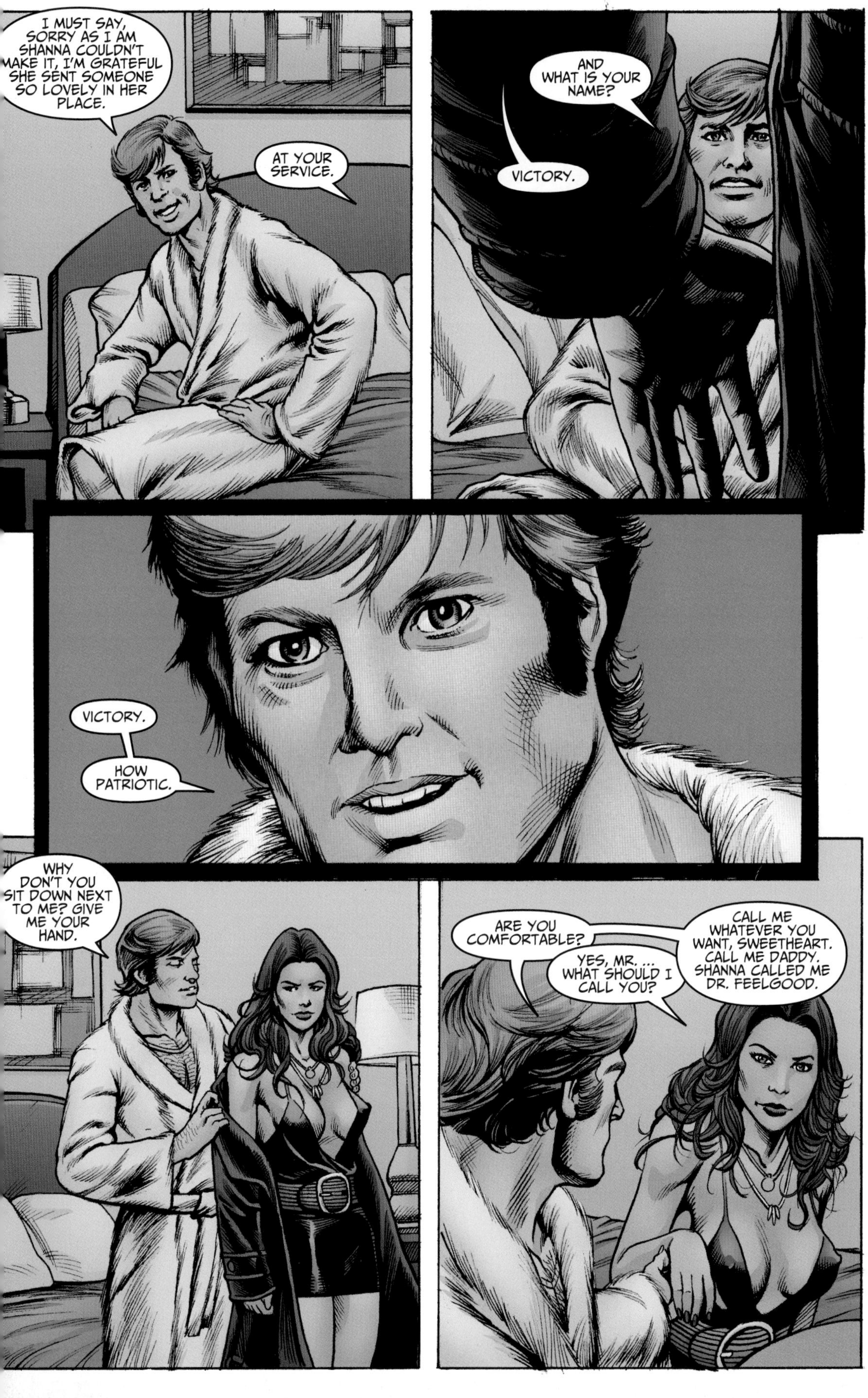
I MUST SAY, SORRY AS I AM SHANNA COULDN'T MAKE IT, I'M GRATEFUL SHE SENT SOMEONE SO LOVELY IN HER PLACE.
AT YOUR SERVICE.
AND WHAT IS YOUR NAME?
VICTORY.
VICTORY.
HOW PATRIOTIC.
WHY DON'T YOU SIT DOWN NEXT TO ME? GIVE ME YOUR HAND.
ARE YOU COMFORTABLE?
YES, MR. ... WHAT SHOULD I CALL YOU?
CALL ME WHATEVER YOU WANT, SWEETHEART. CALL ME DADDY. SHANNA CALLED ME DR. FEELGOOD.

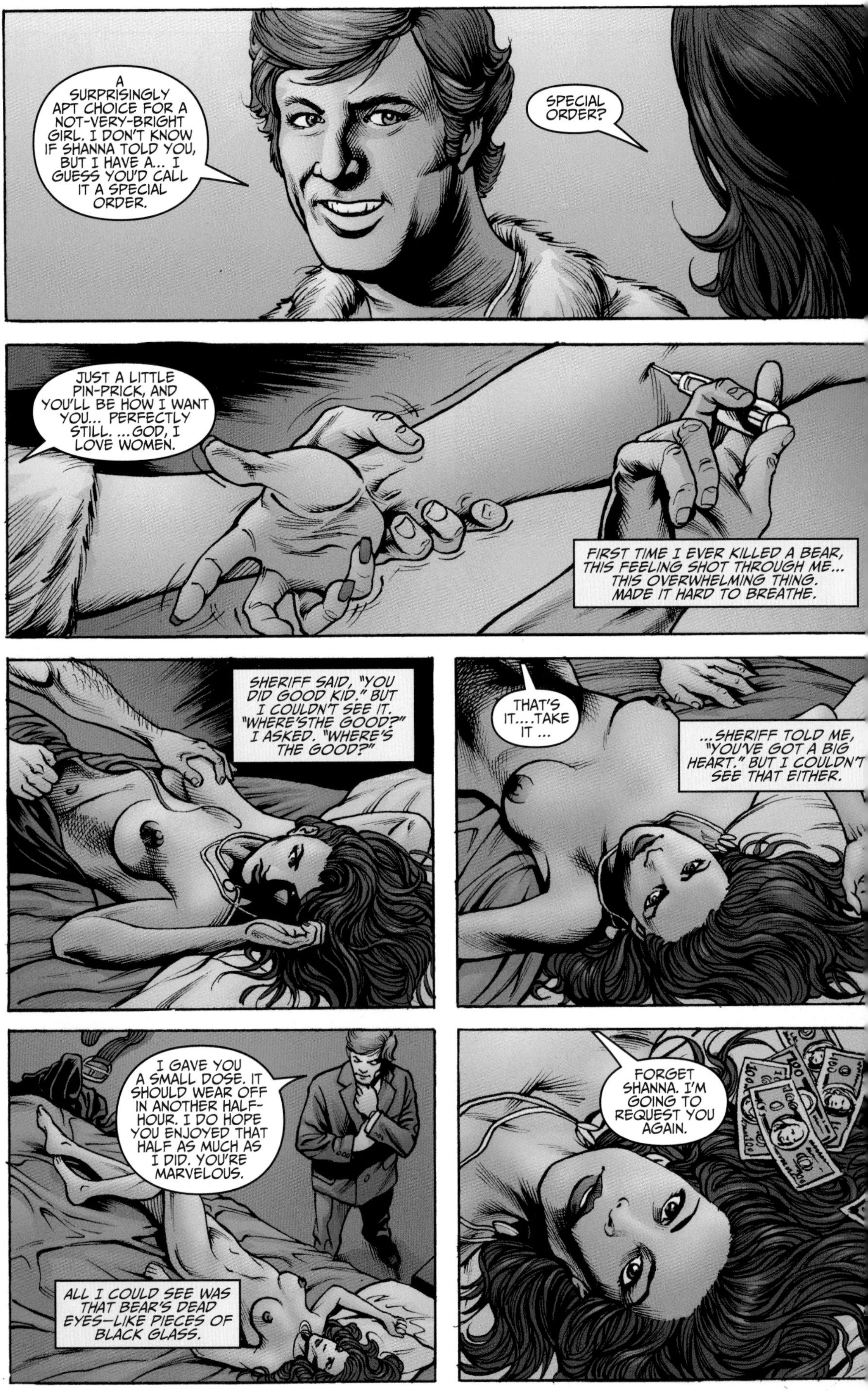
A SURPRISINGLY APT CHOICE FOR A NOT-VERY-BRIGHT GIRL. I DON'T KNOW IF SHANNA TOLD YOU, BUT I HAVE A... I GUESS YOU'D CALL IT A SPECIAL ORDER.
SPECIAL ORDER?
JUST A LITTLE PIN-PRICK, AND YOU'LL BE HOW I WANT YOU... PERFECTLY STILL. ...GOD, I LOVE WOMEN.
FIRST TIME I EVER KILLED A BEAR, THIS FEELING SHOT THROUGH ME... THIS OVERWHELMING THING. MADE IT HARD TO BREATHE.
SHERIFF SAID, "YOU DID GOOD KID." BUT I COULDN'T SEE IT. "WHERE'STHE GOOD?" I ASKED. "WHERE'S THE GOOD?"
THAT'S IT....TAKE IT ...
...SHERIFF TOLD ME, "YOU'VE GOT A BIG HEART." BUT I COULDN'T SEE THAT EITHER.
I GAVE YOU A SMALL DOSE. IT SHOULD WEAR OFF IN ANOTHER HALF-HOUR. I DO HOPE YOU ENJOYED THAT HALF AS MUCH AS I DID. YOU'RE MARVELOUS.
ALL I COULD SEE WAS THAT BEAR'S DEAD EYES—LIKE PIECES OF BLACK GLASS.
FORGET SHANNA. I'M GOING TO REQUEST YOU AGAIN.

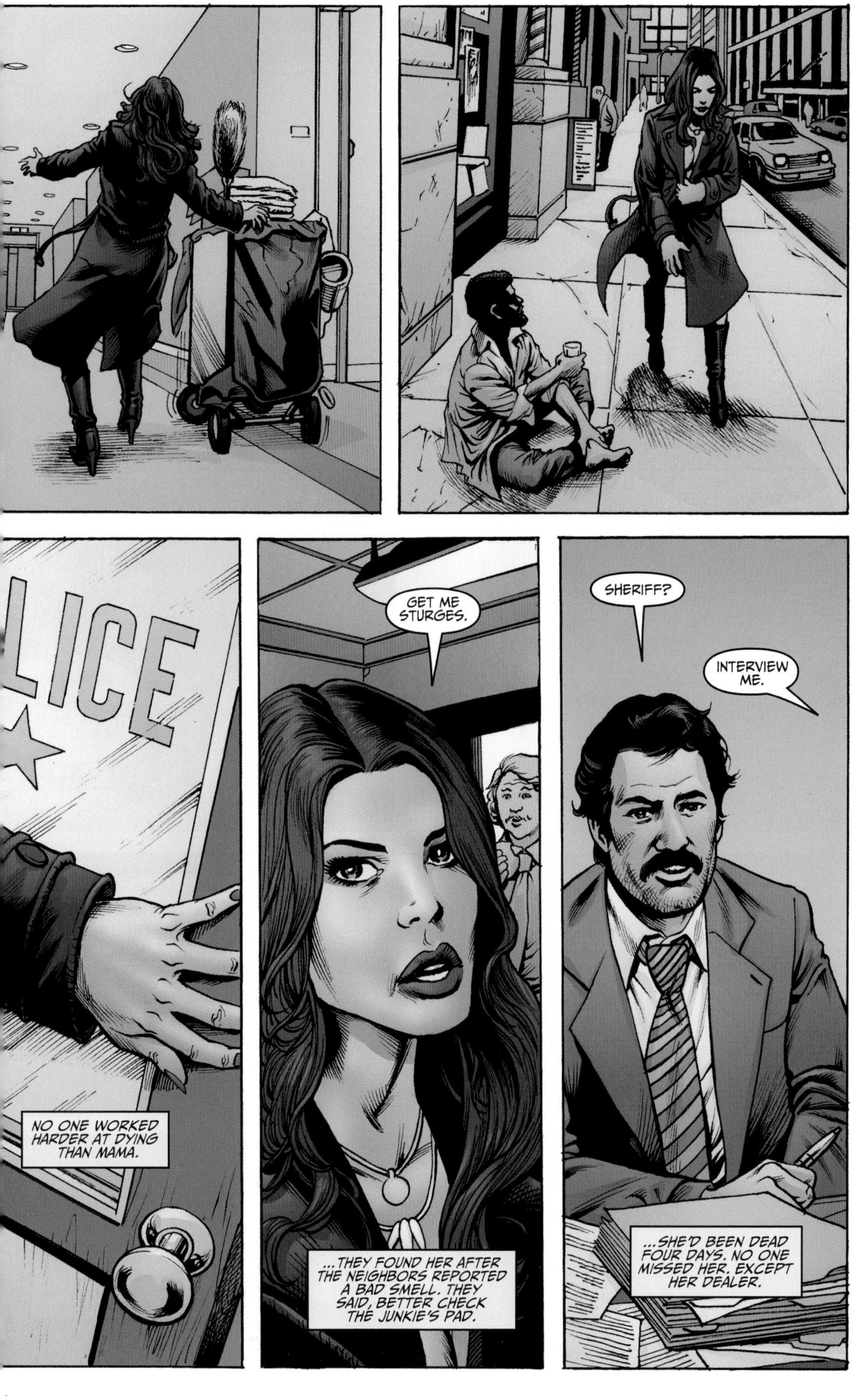
LICE
GET ME STURGES.
NO ONE WORKED HARDER AT DYING THAN MAMA.
...THEY FOUND HER AFTER THE NEIGHBORS REPORTED A BAD SMELL. THEY SAID, BETTER CHECK THE JUNKIE'S PAD.
SHERIFF?
INTERVIEW ME.
...SHE'D BEEN DEAD FOUR DAYS. NO ONE MISSED HER. EXCEPT HER DEALER.

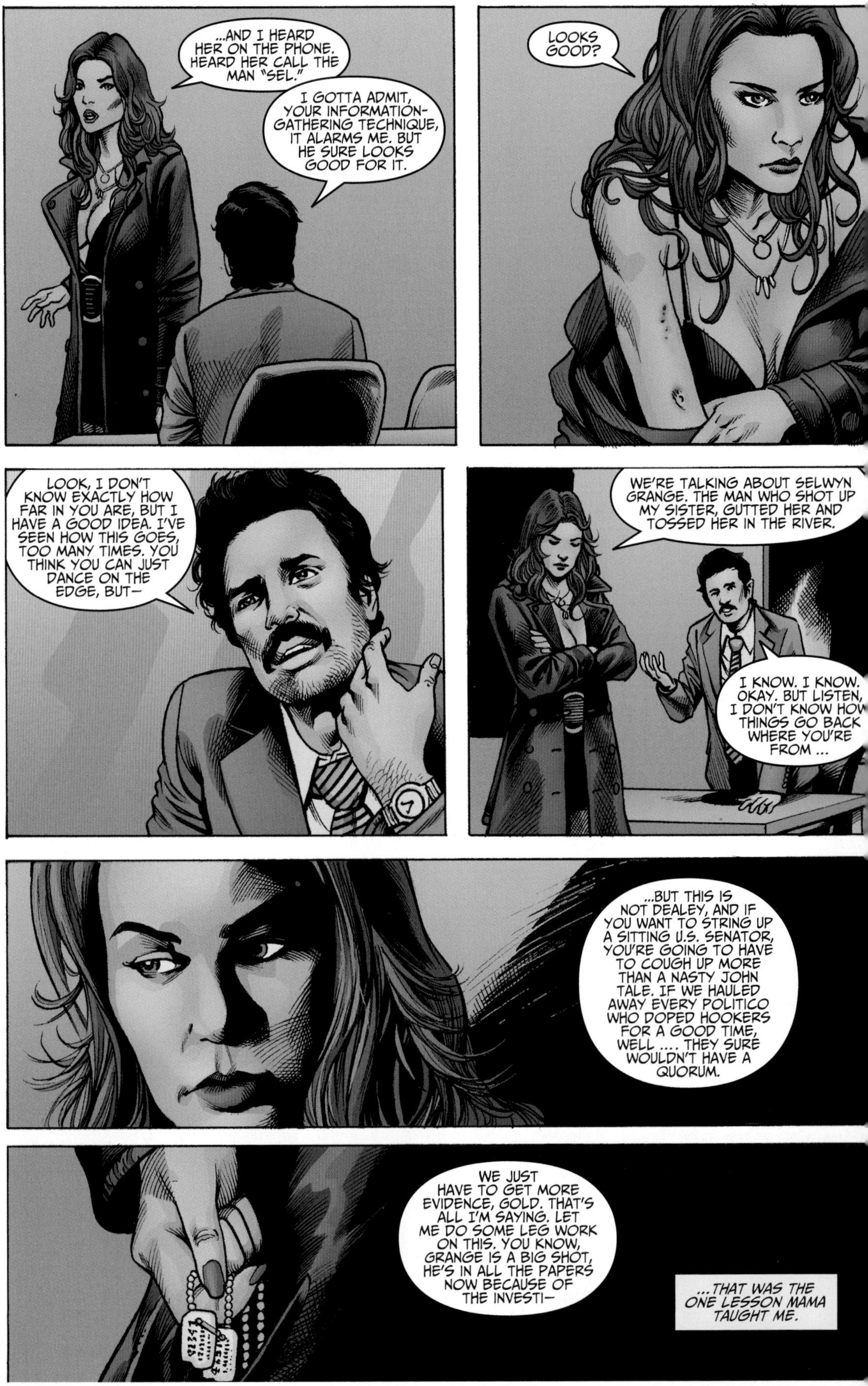
...AND I HEARD HER ON THE PHONE. HEARD HER CALL THE MAN "SEL."
I GOTTA ADMIT, YOUR INFORMATION-GATHERING TECHNIQUE, IT ALARMS ME. BUT HE SURE LOOKS GOOD FOR IT.
LOOKS GOOD?
LOOK, I DON'T KNOW EXACTLY HOW FAR IN YOU ARE, BUT I HAVE A GOOD IDEA. I'VE SEEN HOW THIS GOES, TOO MANY TIMES. YOU THINK YOU CAN JUST DANCE ON THE EDGE, BUT—
WE'RE TALKING ABOUT SELWYN GRANGE. THE MAN WHO SHOT UP MY SISTER, GUTTED HER AND TOSSED HER IN THE RIVER.
I KNOW. I KNOW. OKAY. BUT LISTEN, I DON'T KNOW HOW THINGS GO BACK WHERE YOU'RE FROM ...
...BUT THIS IS NOT DEALEY, AND IF YOU WANT TO STRING UP A SITTING U.S. SENATOR, YOU'RE GOING TO HAVE TO COUGH UP MORE THAN A NASTY JOHN TALE. IF WE HAULED AWAY EVERY POLITICO WHO DOPED HOOKERS FOR A GOOD TIME, WELL .... THEY SURE WOULDN'T HAVE A QUORUM.
WE JUST HAVE TO GET MORE EVIDENCE, GOLD. THAT'S ALL I'M SAYING. LET ME DO SOME LEG WORK ON THIS. YOU KNOW, GRANGE IS A BIG SHOT, HE'S IN ALL THE PAPERS NOW BECAUSE OF THE INVESTI—
...THAT WAS THE ONE LESSON MAMA TAUGHT ME.

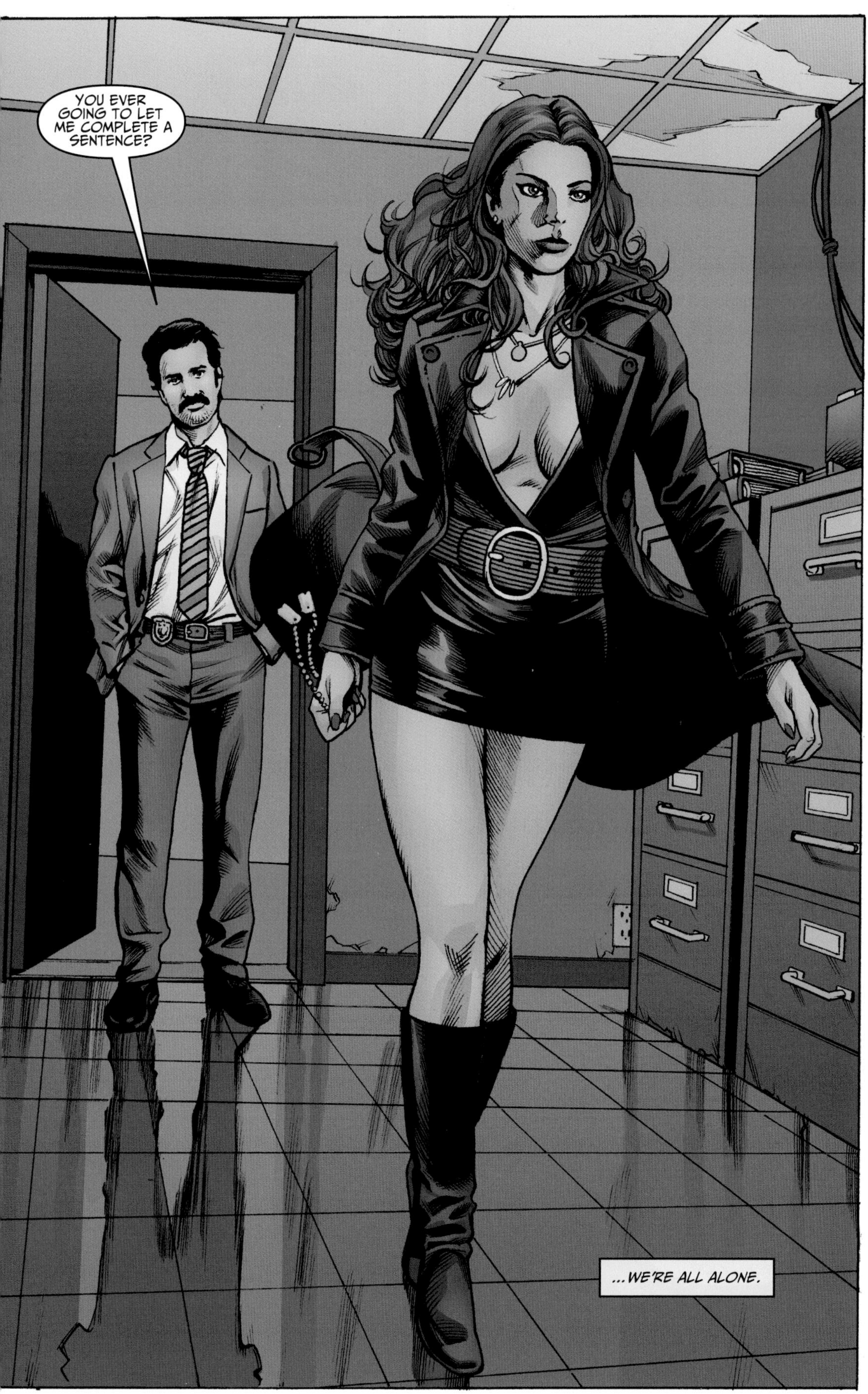
YOU EVER GOING TO LET ME COMPLETE A SENTENCE?
...WE'RE ALL ALONE.

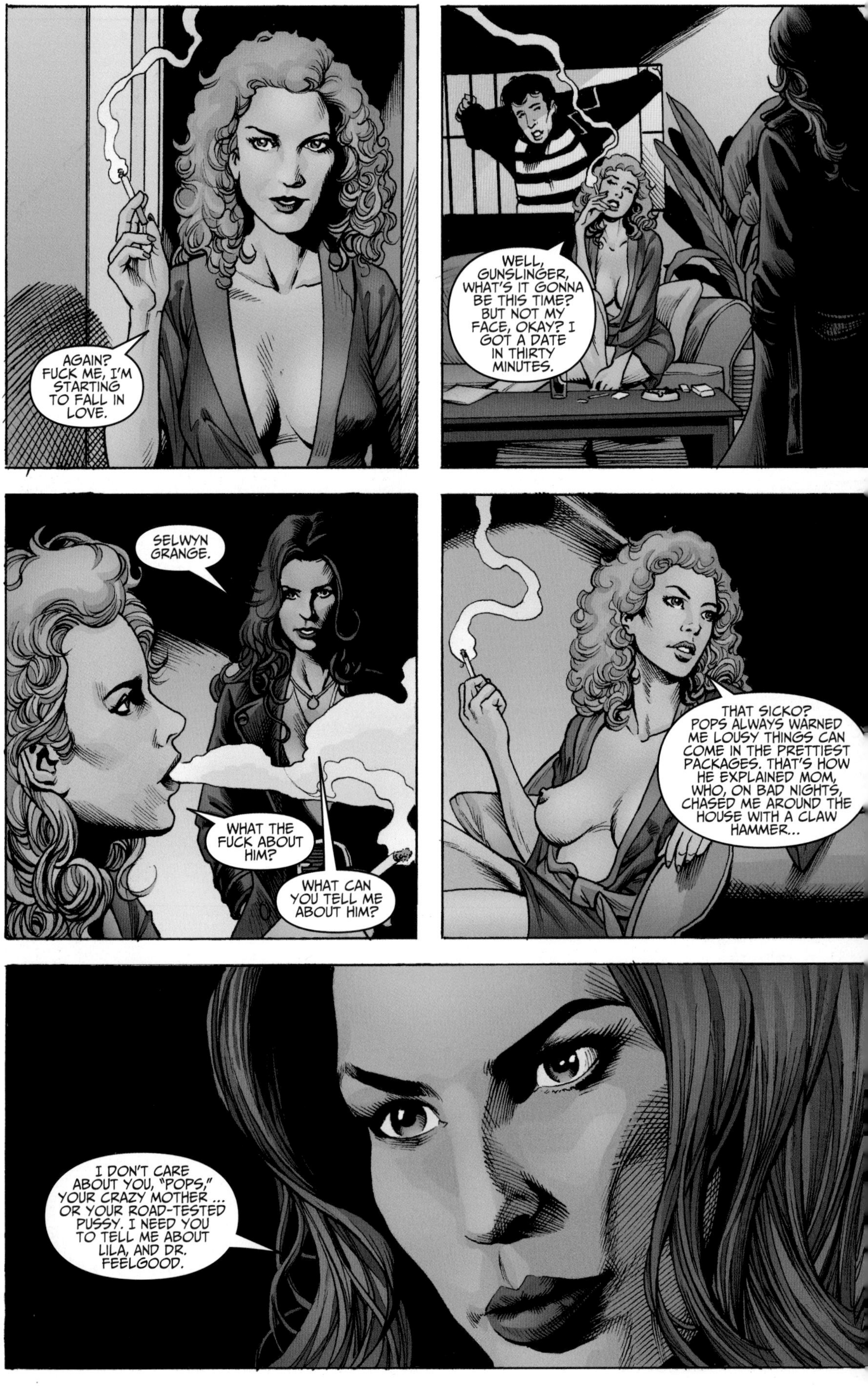
AGAIN? FUCK ME, I'M STARTING TO FALL IN LOVE.
WELL, GUNSLINGER, WHAT'S IT GONNA BE THIS TIME? BUT NOT MY FACE, OKAY? I GOT A DATE IN THIRTY MINUTES.
SELWYN GRANGE.
WHAT THE FUCK ABOUT HIM?
WHAT CAN YOU TELL ME ABOUT HIM?
THAT SICKO? POPS ALWAYS WARNED ME LOUSY THINGS CAN COME IN THE PRETTIEST PACKAGES. THAT'S HOW HE EXPLAINED MOM, WHO, ON BAD NIGHTS, CHASED ME AROUND THE HOUSE WITH A CLAW HAMMER...
I DON'T CARE ABOUT YOU, "POPS," YOUR CRAZY MOTHER ... OR YOUR ROAD-TESTED PUSSY. I NEED YOU TO TELL ME ABOUT LILA, AND DR. FEELGOOD.

WHAT'S THERE TO SAY, ANOTHER JOHN, JUST A LITTLE MORE INTO THE FREAKY DEAKY. HE LIKES LILA. THEY ALL DO. HE ESPECIALLY LIKES IT WHEN I DO THIS ONE TRICK WITH HER. I—

DID SHE LIKE HIM?

SURE, LILA LIKES EVERYBODY. HEY, YOU KEEP TALKING ABOUT HER LIKE SHE'S GONE. WHY?

NEVER YOU. TH CAME A

NO... I FIGURED SHE'D JUST SKIPPED TOWN.

YOU FIGURED SHE HAD A REASON TO BE SCARED. THE SAME REASON YOU HAVE.

I SAW HIM ON TV. ALL THOSE HEARINGS. I KNEW WHO HE WAS. BIG-SHOT SENATOR. I KNEW ABOUT LILA AND HIM ... AND I KNEW WHAT HE WAS. DR. FEELGOOD.

I DON'T WANT TROUBLE. I DON'T WANT TROUBLE.

TROUBLE HAS YOU. ALL YOU CAN DO NOW IS TRY TO CLIMB YOUR WAY OUT.

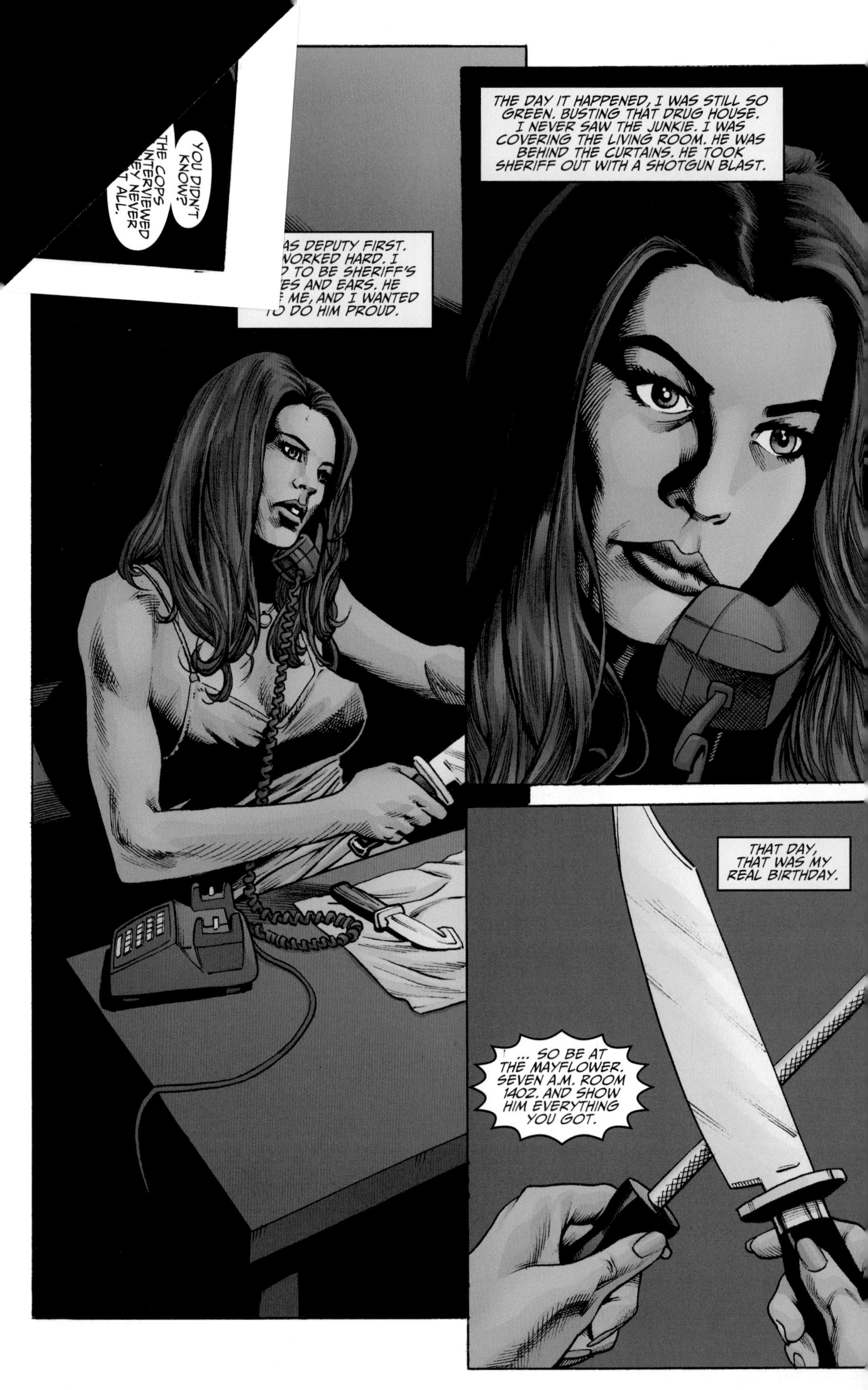
YOU DIDN'T KNOW?
THE COPS INTERVIEWED
AS DEPUTY FIRST. WORKED HARD. I D TO BE SHERIFF'S ES AND EARS. HE E ME, AND I WANTED TO DO HIM PROUD.
THE DAY IT HAPPENED, I WAS STILL SO GREEN. BUSTING THAT DRUG HOUSE. I NEVER SAW THE JUNKIE. I WAS COVERING THE LIVING ROOM. HE WAS BEHIND THE CURTAINS. HE TOOK SHERIFF OUT WITH A SHOTGUN BLAST.
THAT DAY, THAT WAS MY REAL BIRTHDAY.
... SO BE AT THE MAYFLOWER. SEVEN A.M. ROOM 1402. AND SHOW HIM EVERYTHING YOU GOT.

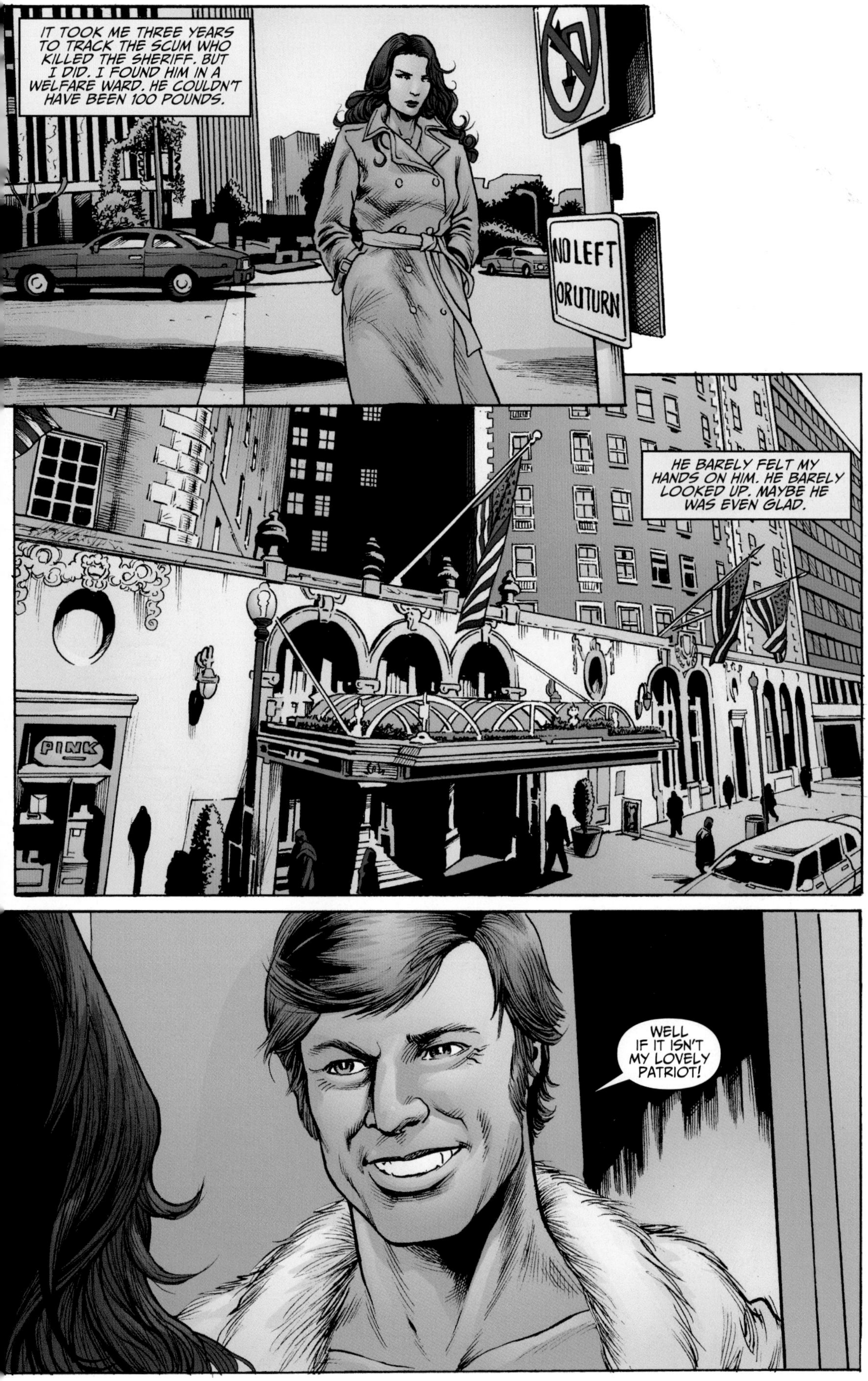
IT TOOK ME THREE YEARS TO TRACK THE SCUM WHO KILLED THE SHERIFF. BUT I DID. I FOUND HIM IN A WELFARE WARD. HE COULDN'T HAVE BEEN 100 POUNDS.
NO LEFT OR U TURN
HE BARELY FELT MY HANDS ON HIM. HE BARELY LOOKED UP. MAYBE HE WAS EVEN GLAD.
PINK
WELL IF IT ISN'T MY LOVELY PATRIOT!

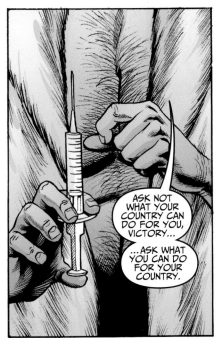

ASK NOT WHAT YOUR COUNTRY CAN DO FOR YOU, VICTORY...

...ASK WHAT YOU CAN DO FOR YOUR COUNTRY.

YOU REALLY DO HAVE THE MOST EXQUISITE, MALLEABLE THIGHS, VEE. I CAN'T WAIT TO GET MY FIST UP BETWEEN THEM AND—

SEL.

WERE YOU JUST... WHAT DID YOU CALL ME?

SEL.

THAT'S SO STRANGE. NO ONE EVER CALLS ME THAT EXCEPT—

LILA?

—MY WIFE.

WHO THE FUCK IS LILA?

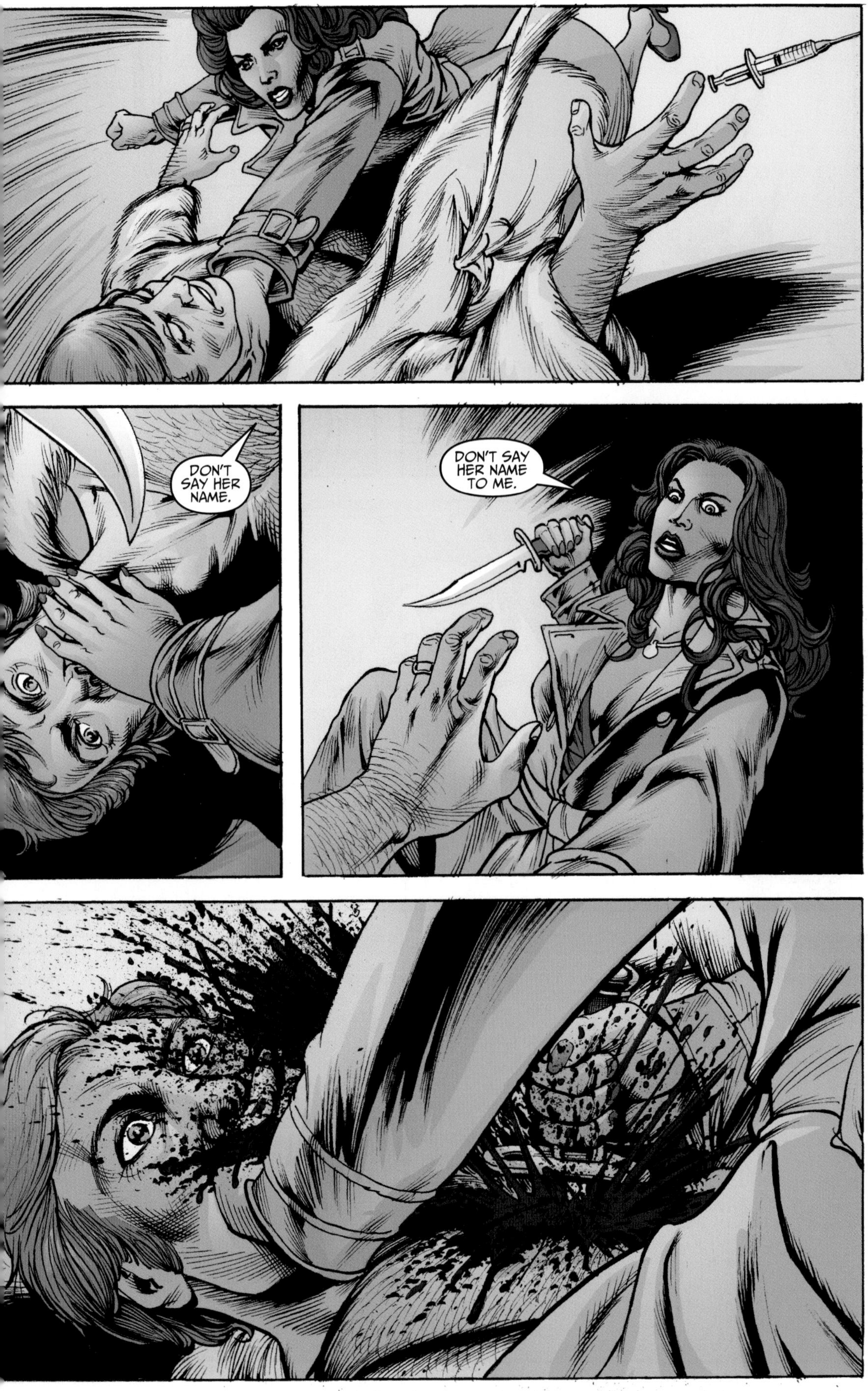
DON'T SAY HER NAME.
DON'T SAY HER NAME TO ME.

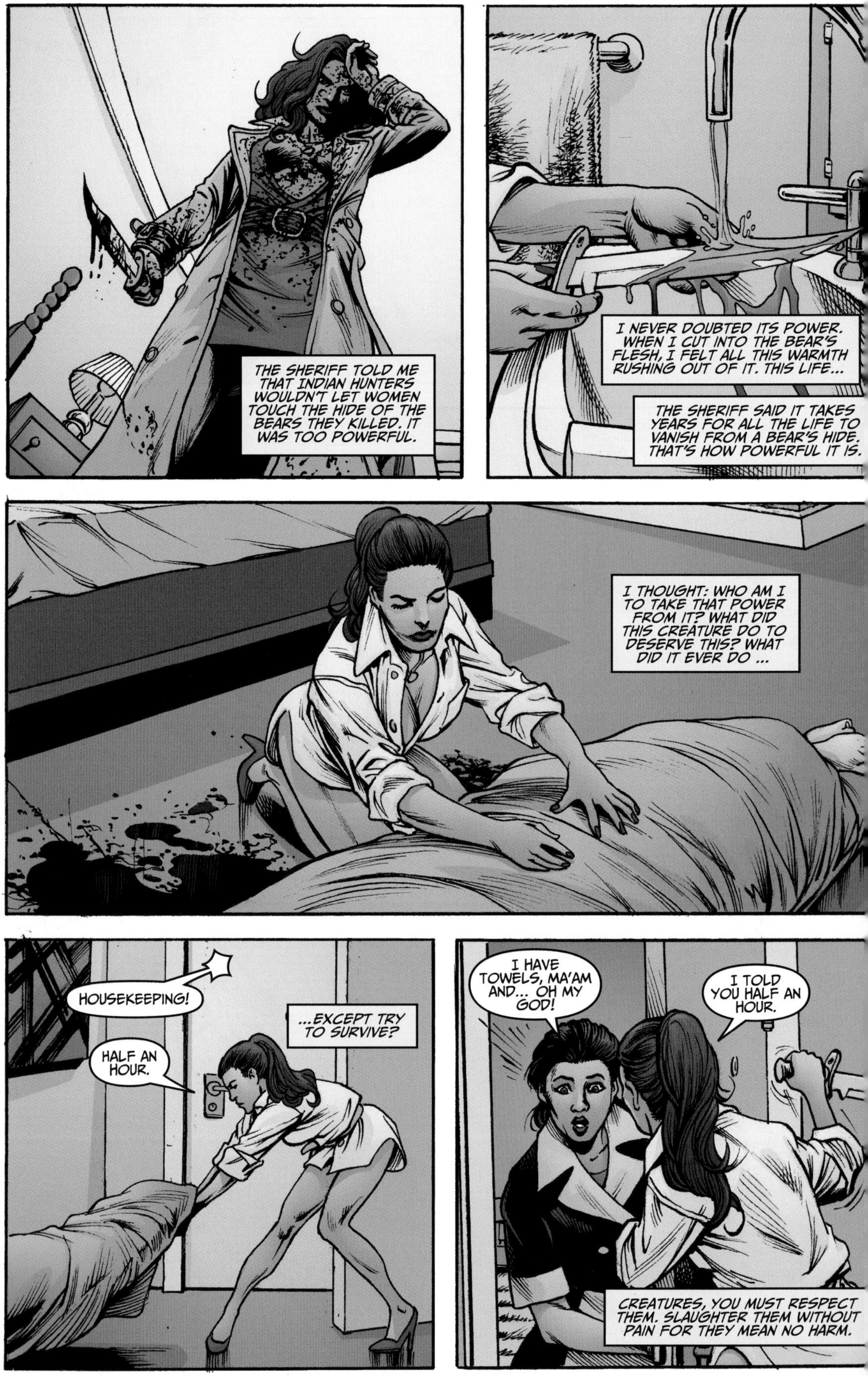
THE SHERIFF TOLD ME THAT INDIAN HUNTERS WOULDN'T LET WOMEN TOUCH THE HIDE OF THE BEARS THEY KILLED. IT WAS TOO POWERFUL.
I NEVER DOUBTED ITS POWER. WHEN I CUT INTO THE BEAR'S FLESH, I FELT ALL THIS WARMTH RUSHING OUT OF IT. THIS LIFE...
THE SHERIFF SAID IT TAKES YEARS FOR ALL THE LIFE TO VANISH FROM A BEAR'S HIDE. THAT'S HOW POWERFUL IT IS.
I THOUGHT: WHO AM I TO TAKE THAT POWER FROM IT? WHAT DID THIS CREATURE DO TO DESERVE THIS? WHAT DID IT EVER DO ...
HOUSEKEEPING!
HALF AN HOUR.
...EXCEPT TRY TO SURVIVE?
I HAVE TOWELS, MA'AM AND... OH MY GOD!
I TOLD YOU HALF AN HOUR.
CREATURES, YOU MUST RESPECT THEM. SLAUGHTER THEM WITHOUT PAIN FOR THEY MEAN NO HARM.

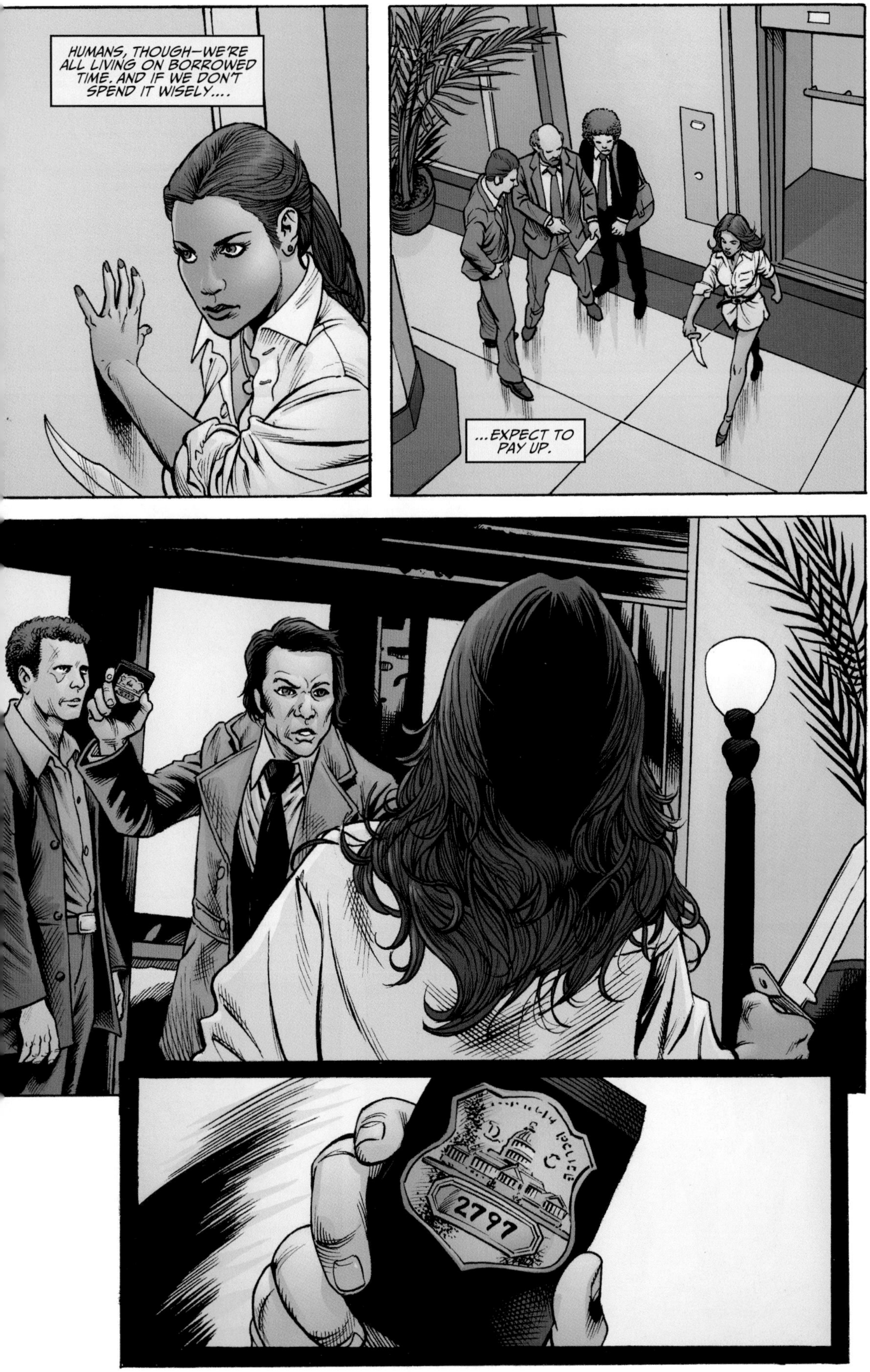
HUMANS, THOUGH—WE'RE ALL LIVING ON BORROWED TIME. AND IF WE DON'T SPEND IT WISELY....
...EXPECT TO PAY UP.
2797

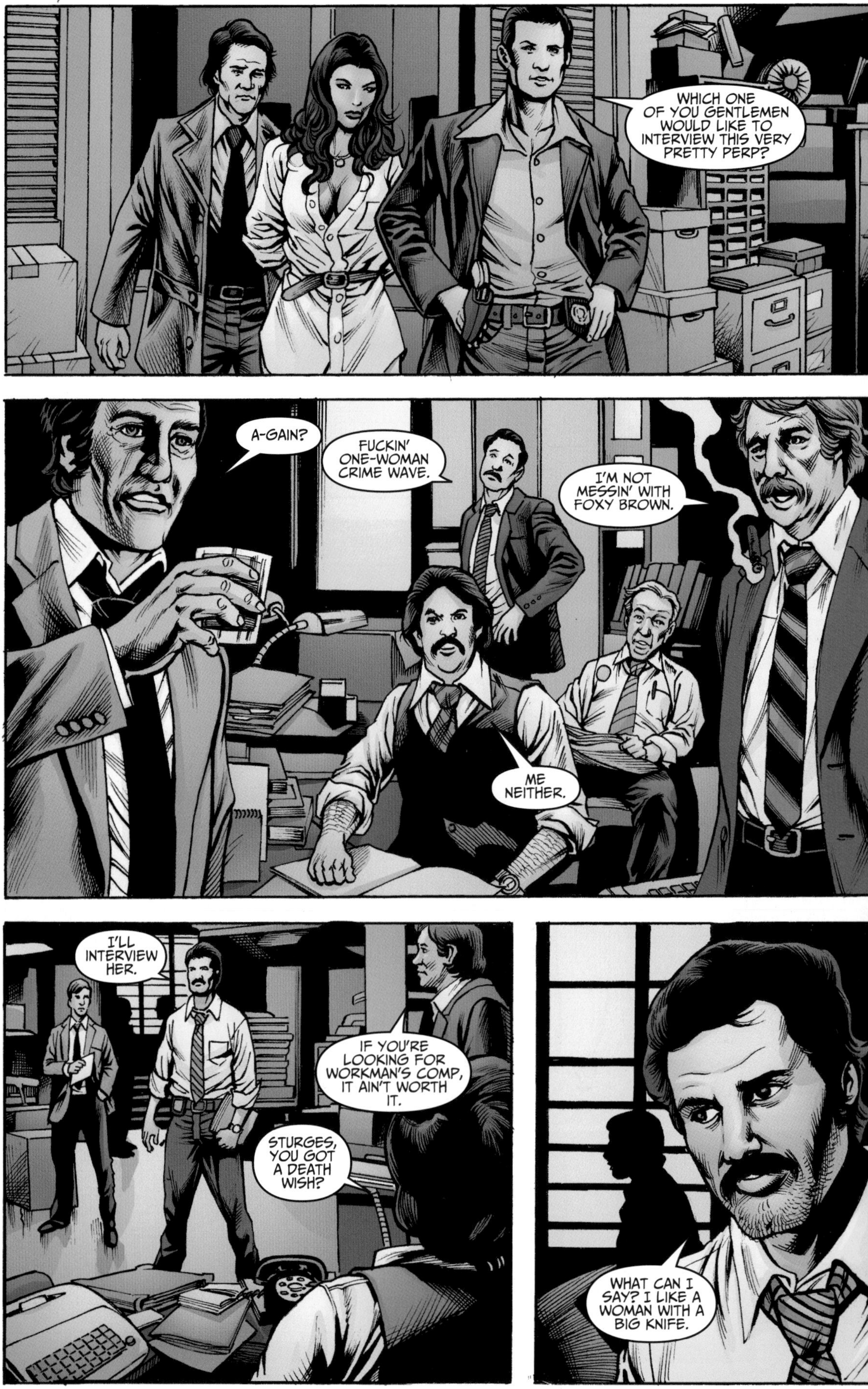
WHICH ONE OF YOU GENTLEMEN WOULD LIKE TO INTERVIEW THIS VERY PRETTY PERP?
A-GAIN?
FUCKIN' ONE-WOMAN CRIME WAVE.
I'M NOT MESSIN' WITH FOXY BROWN.
ME NEITHER.
I'LL INTERVIEW HER.
IF YOU'RE LOOKING FOR WORKMAN'S COMP, IT AIN'T WORTH IT.
STURGES, YOU GOT A DEATH WISH?
WHAT CAN I SAY? I LIKE A WOMAN WITH A BIG KNIFE.

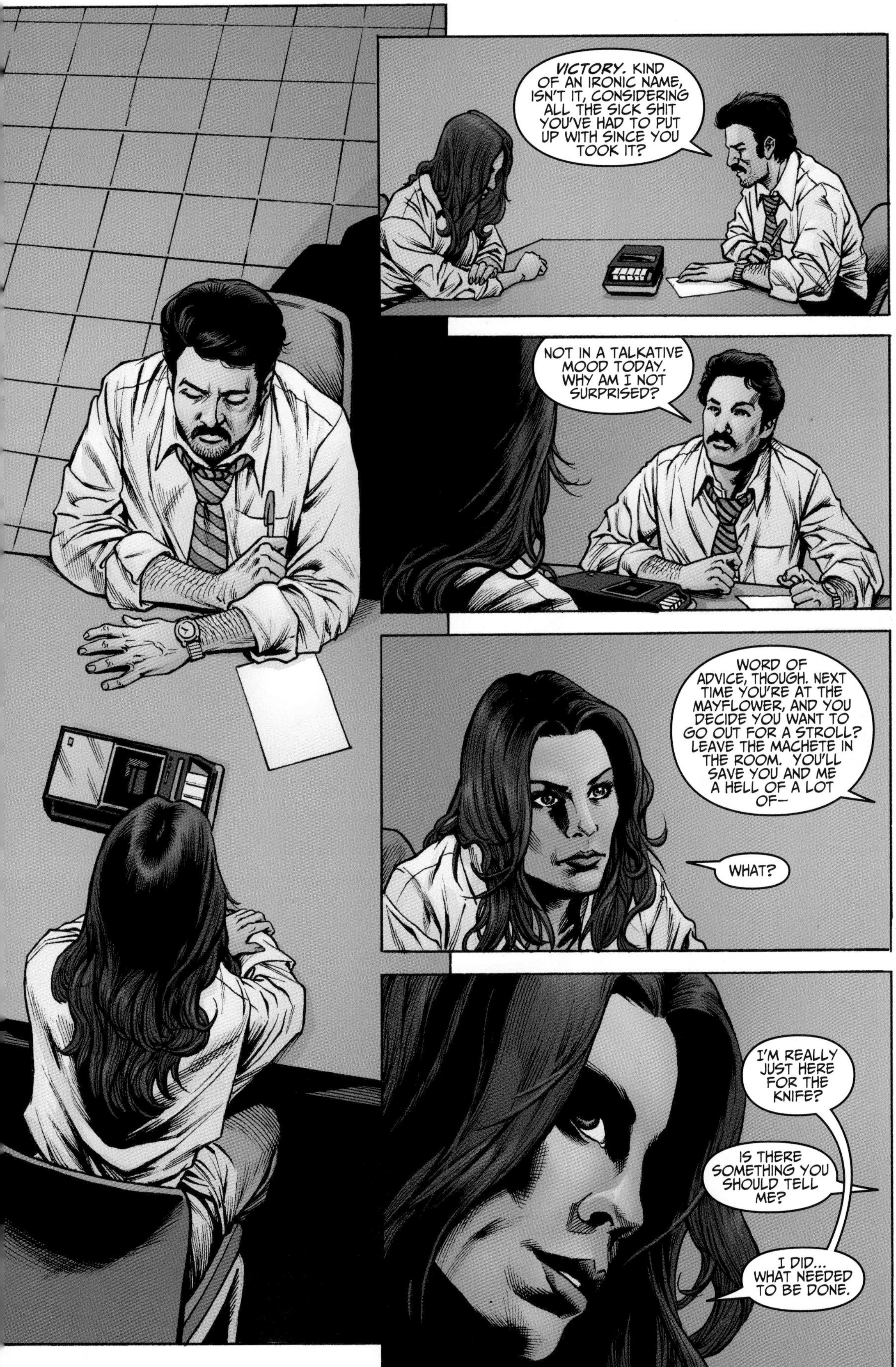
VICTORY. KIND OF AN IRONIC NAME, ISN'T IT, CONSIDERING ALL THE SICK SHIT YOU'VE HAD TO PUT UP WITH SINCE YOU TOOK IT?
NOT IN A TALKATIVE MOOD TODAY. WHY AM I NOT SURPRISED?
WORD OF ADVICE, THOUGH. NEXT TIME YOU'RE AT THE MAYFLOWER, AND YOU DECIDE YOU WANT TO GO OUT FOR A STROLL? LEAVE THE MACHETE IN THE ROOM. YOU'LL SAVE YOU AND ME A HELL OF A LOT OF–
WHAT?
I'M REALLY JUST HERE FOR THE KNIFE?
IS THERE SOMETHING YOU SHOULD TELL ME?
I DID... WHAT NEEDED TO BE DONE.

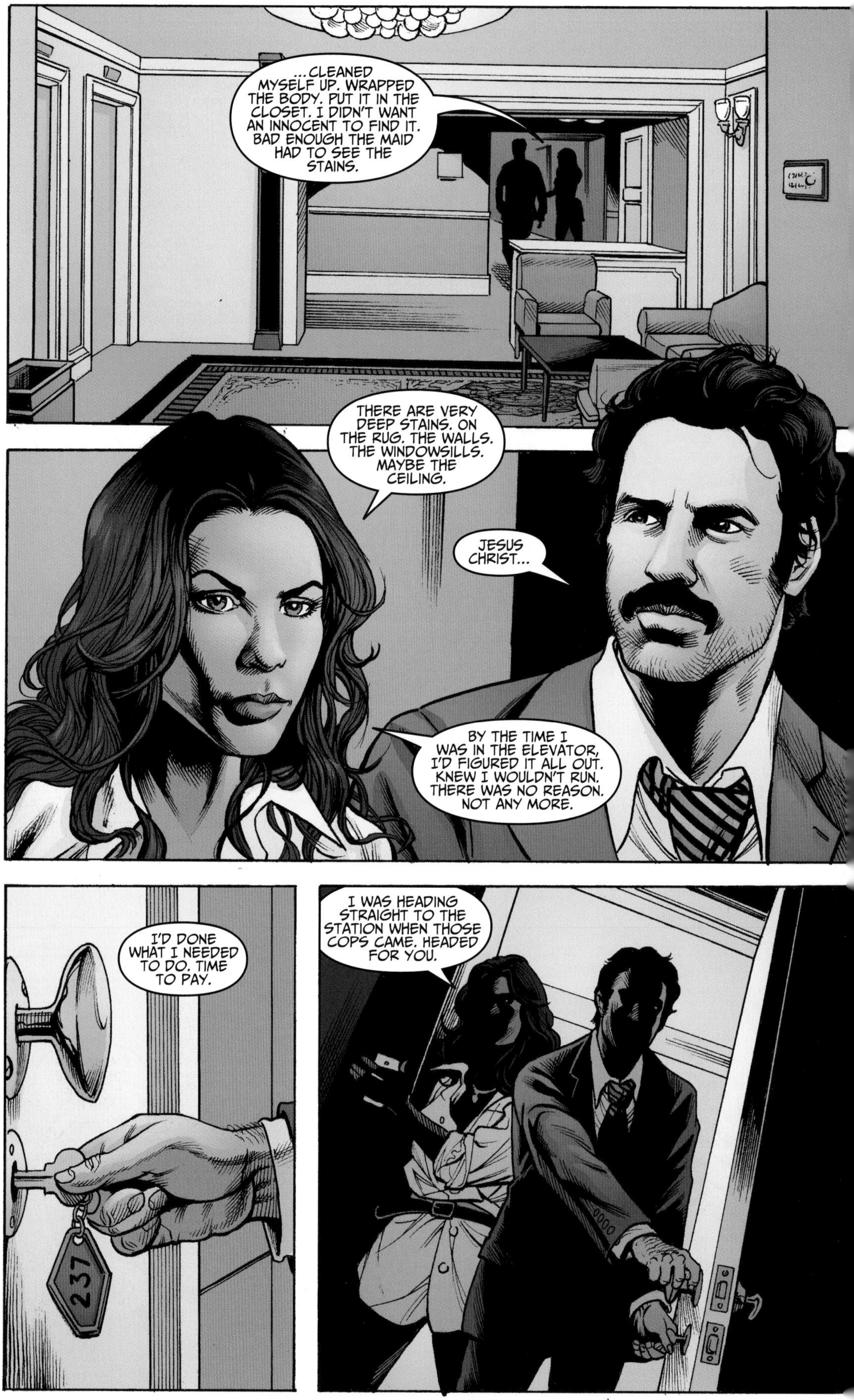
...CLEANED MYSELF UP. WRAPPED THE BODY. PUT IT IN THE CLOSET. I DIDN'T WANT AN INNOCENT TO FIND IT. BAD ENOUGH THE MAID HAD TO SEE THE STAINS.
THERE ARE VERY DEEP STAINS. ON THE RUG. THE WALLS. THE WINDOWSILLS. MAYBE THE CEILING.
JESUS CHRIST...
BY THE TIME I WAS IN THE ELEVATOR, I'D FIGURED IT ALL OUT. KNEW I WOULDN'T RUN. THERE WAS NO REASON. NOT ANY MORE.
I'D DONE WHAT I NEEDED TO DO. TIME TO PAY.
237
I WAS HEADING STRAIGHT TO THE STATION WHEN THOSE COPS CAME. HEADED FOR YOU.

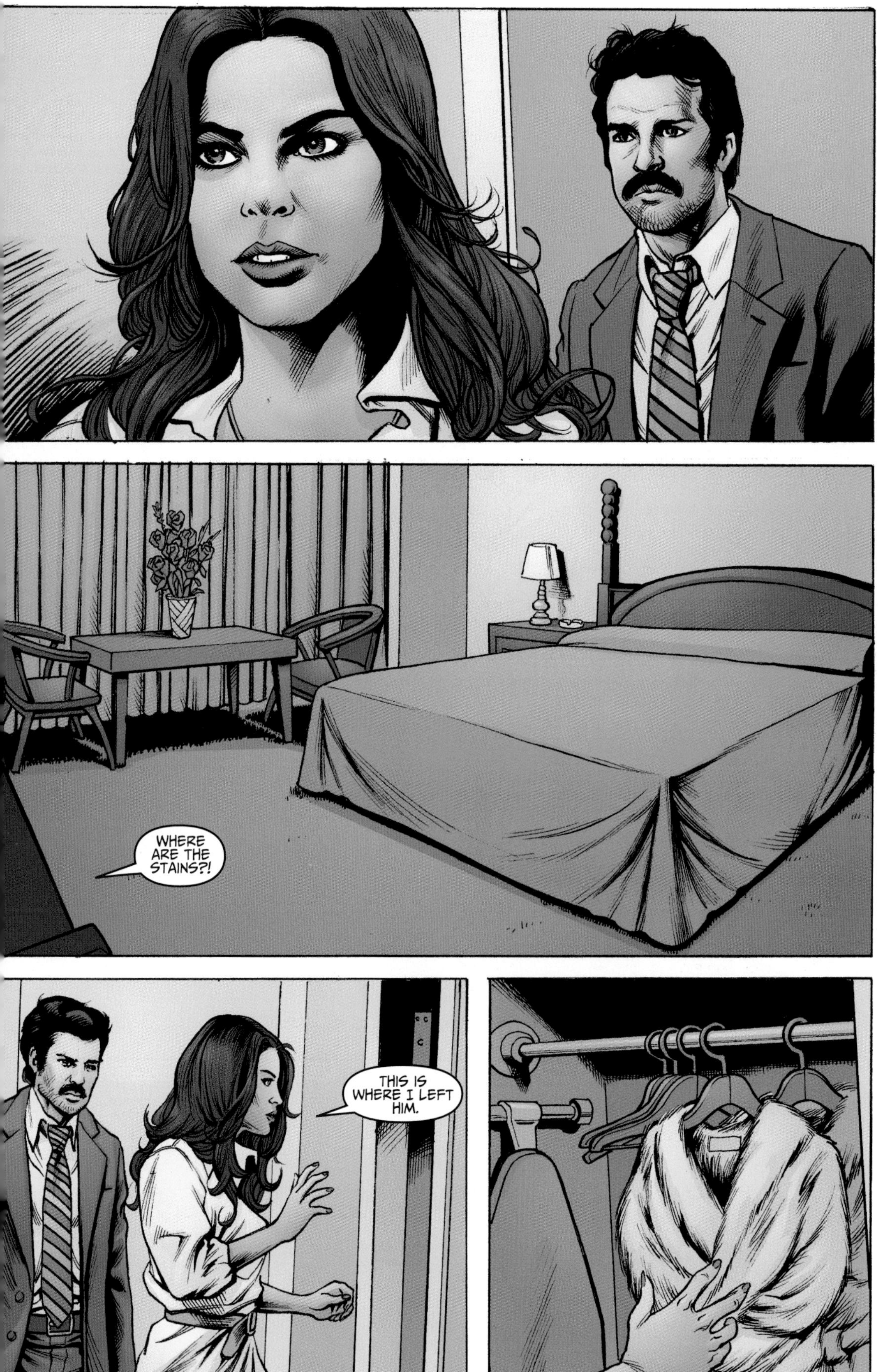
WHERE ARE THE STAINS?!
THIS IS WHERE I LEFT HIM.

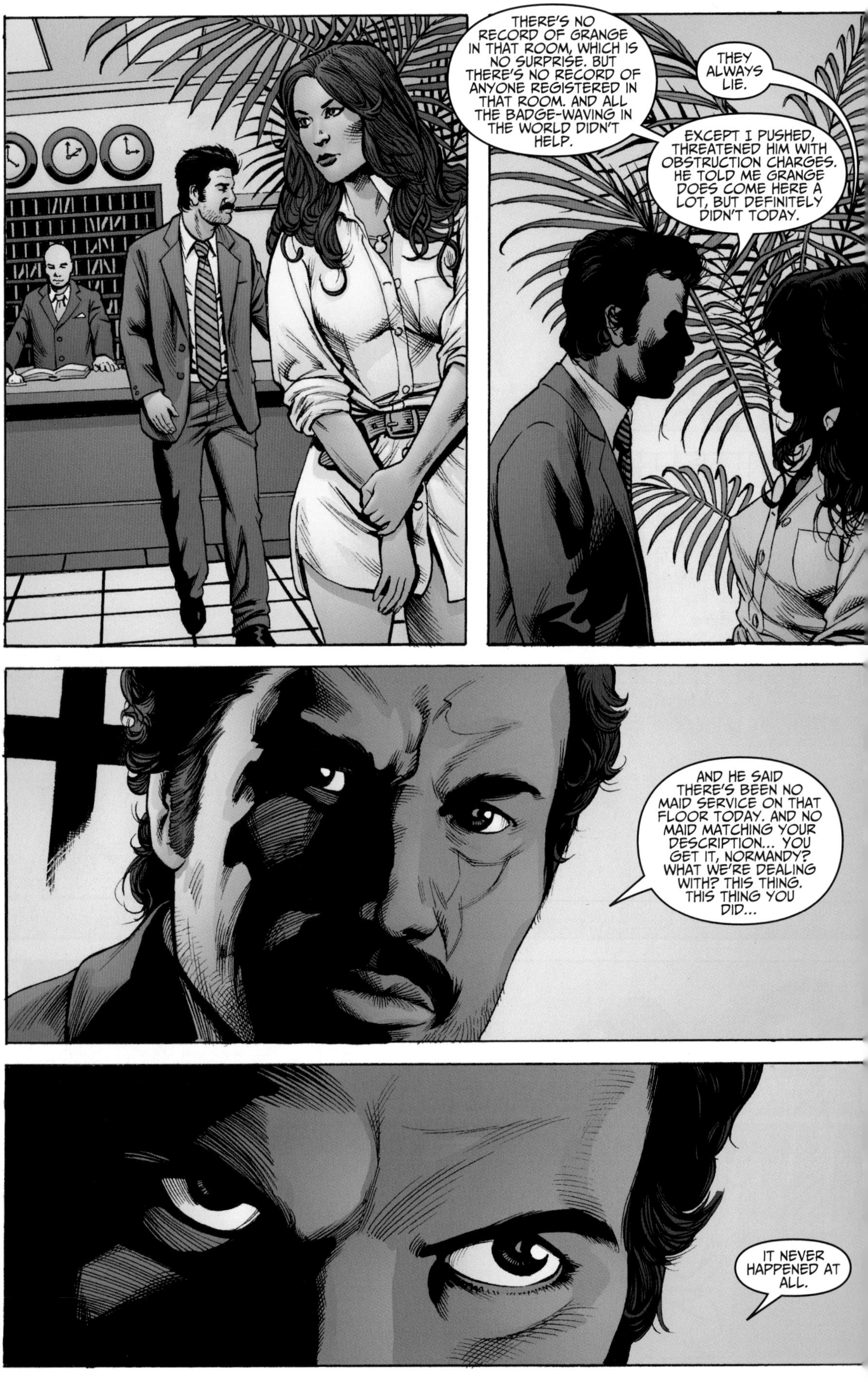
THERE'S NO RECORD OF GRANGE IN THAT ROOM, WHICH IS NO SURPRISE. BUT THERE'S NO RECORD OF ANYONE REGISTERED IN THAT ROOM. AND ALL THE BADGE-WAVING IN THE WORLD DIDN'T HELP.
THEY ALWAYS LIE.
EXCEPT I PUSHED, THREATENED HIM WITH OBSTRUCTION CHARGES. HE TOLD ME GRANGE DOES COME HERE A LOT, BUT DEFINITELY DIDN'T TODAY.
AND HE SAID THERE'S BEEN NO MAID SERVICE ON THAT FLOOR TODAY. AND NO MAID MATCHING YOUR DESCRIPTION... YOU GET IT, NORMANDY? WHAT WE'RE DEALING WITH? THIS THING. THIS THING YOU DID...
IT NEVER HAPPENED AT ALL.

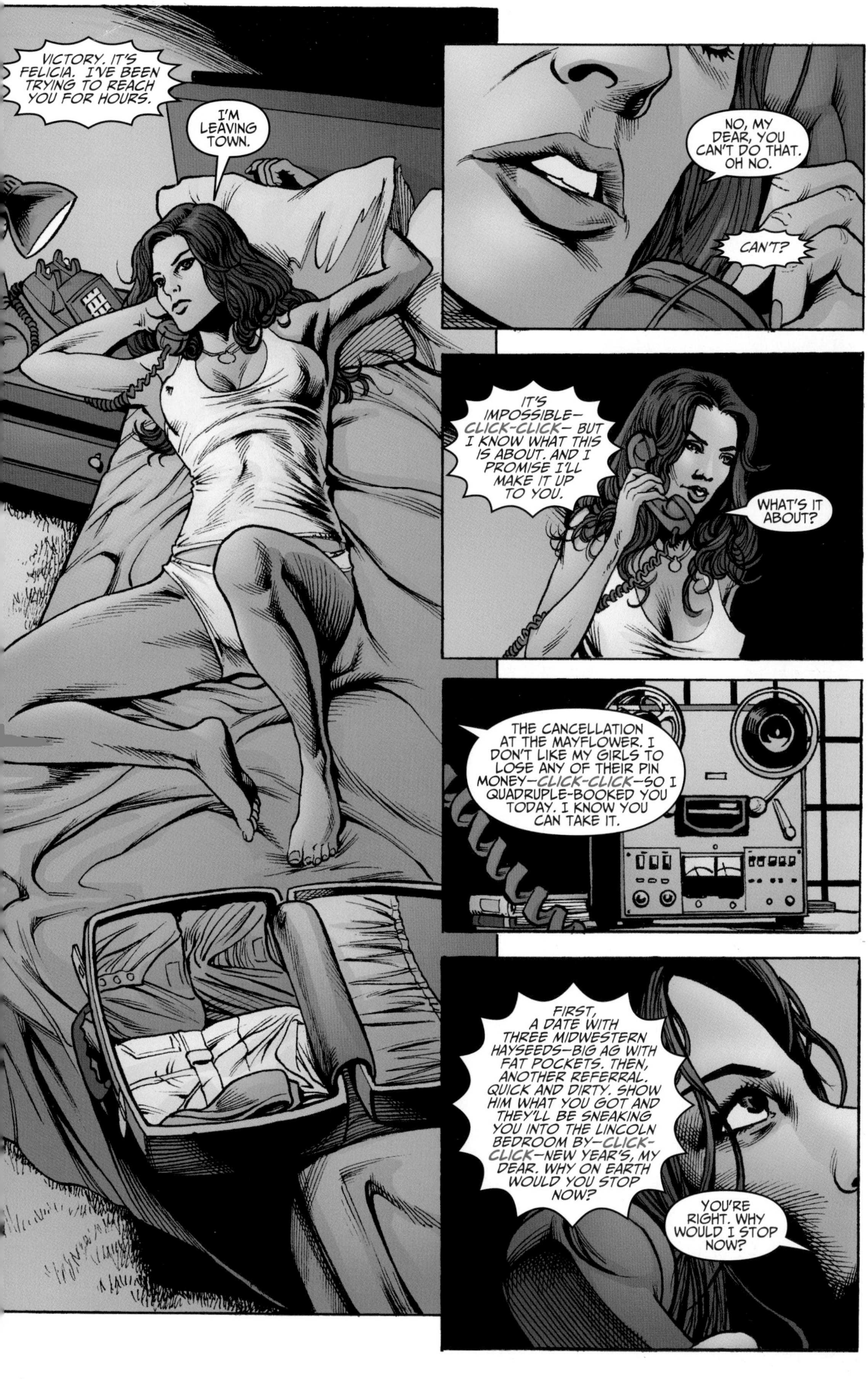
VICTORY. IT'S FELICIA. I'VE BEEN TRYING TO REACH YOU FOR HOURS.
I'M LEAVING TOWN.
NO, MY DEAR, YOU CAN'T DO THAT. OH NO.
CAN'T?
IT'S IMPOSSIBLE— CLICK-CLICK— BUT I KNOW WHAT THIS IS ABOUT. AND I PROMISE I'LL MAKE IT UP TO YOU.
WHAT'S IT ABOUT?
THE CANCELLATION AT THE MAYFLOWER. I DON'T LIKE MY GIRLS TO LOSE ANY OF THEIR PIN MONEY—CLICK-CLICK—SO I QUADRUPLE-BOOKED YOU TODAY. I KNOW YOU CAN TAKE IT.
FIRST, A DATE WITH THREE MIDWESTERN HAYSEEDS—BIG AG WITH FAT POCKETS. THEN, ANOTHER REFERRAL. QUICK AND DIRTY. SHOW HIM WHAT YOU GOT AND THEY'LL BE SNEAKING YOU INTO THE LINCOLN BEDROOM BY—CLICK-CLICK—NEW YEAR'S, MY DEAR. WHY ON EARTH WOULD YOU STOP NOW?
YOU'RE RIGHT. WHY WOULD I STOP NOW?

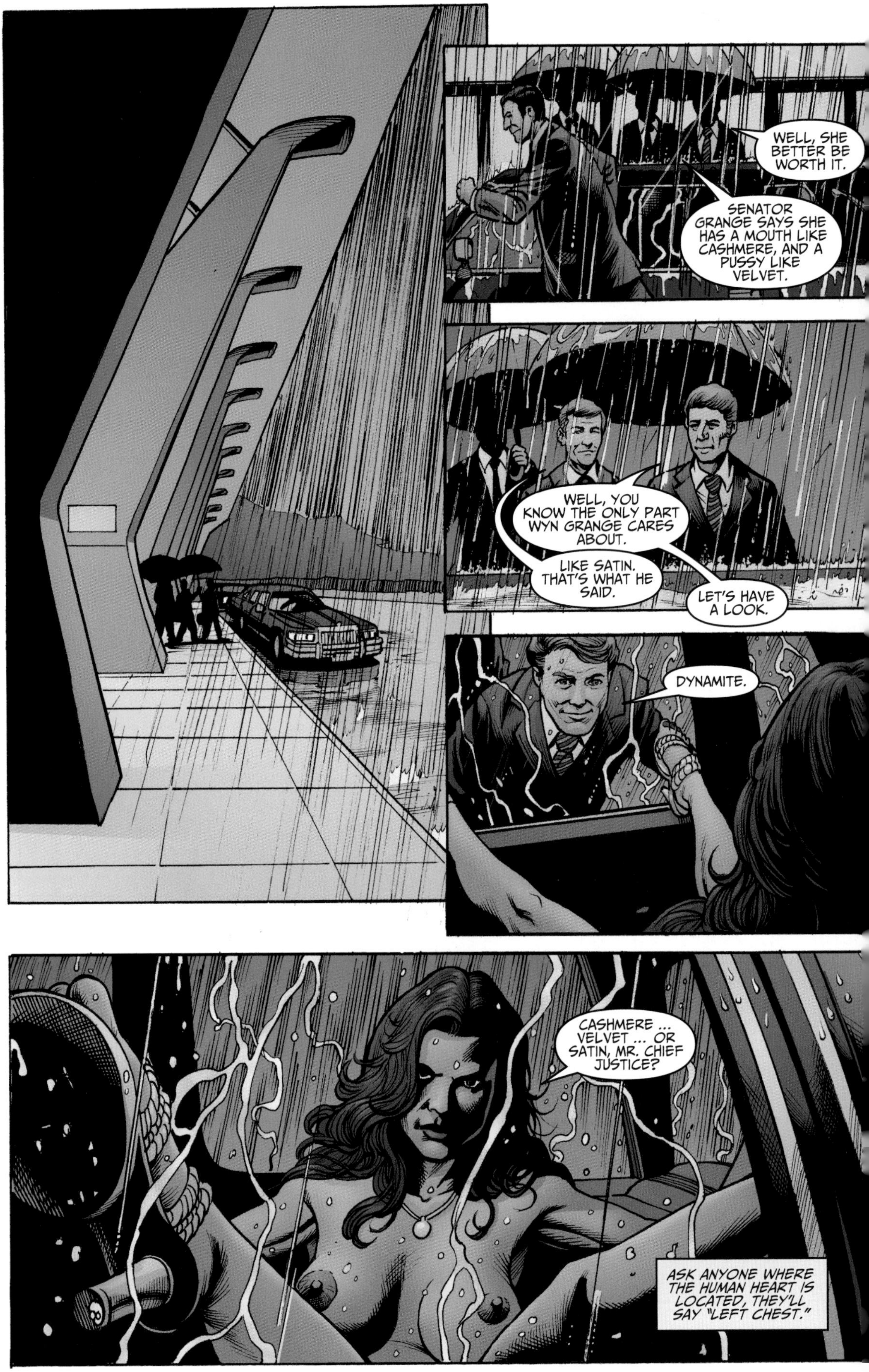
WELL, SHE BETTER BE WORTH IT.
SENATOR GRANGE SAYS SHE HAS A MOUTH LIKE CASHMERE, AND A PUSSY LIKE VELVET.
WELL, YOU KNOW THE ONLY PART WYN GRANGE CARES ABOUT.
LIKE SATIN. THAT'S WHAT HE SAID.
LET'S HAVE A LOOK.
DYNAMITE.
CASHMERE ... VELVET ... OR SATIN, MR. CHIEF JUSTICE?
ASK ANYONE WHERE THE HUMAN HEART IS LOCATED, THEY'LL SAY "LEFT CHEST."

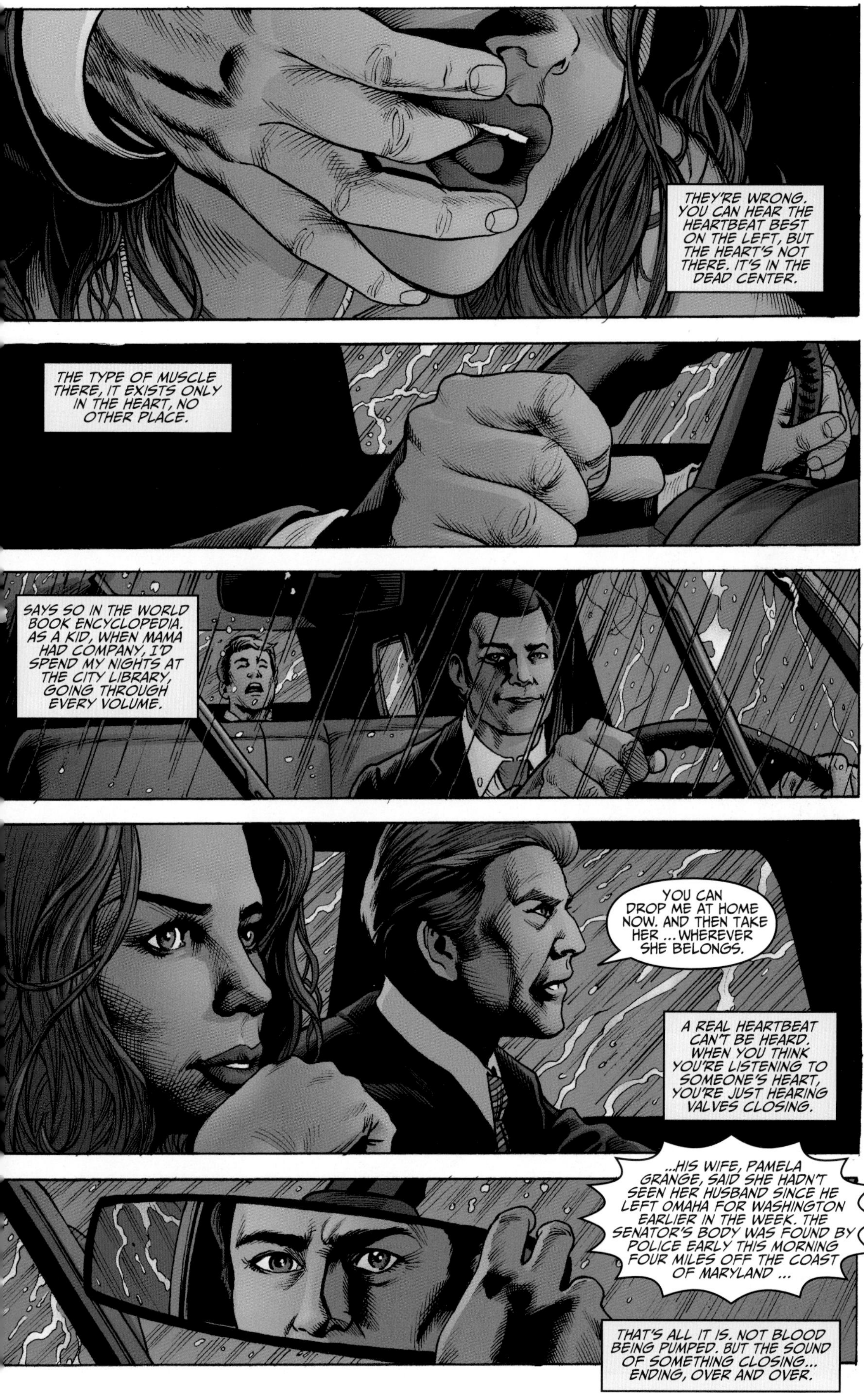
THEY'RE WRONG. YOU CAN HEAR THE HEARTBEAT BEST ON THE LEFT, BUT THE HEART'S NOT THERE. IT'S IN THE DEAD CENTER.
THE TYPE OF MUSCLE THERE, IT EXISTS ONLY IN THE HEART, NO OTHER PLACE.
SAYS SO IN THE WORLD BOOK ENCYCLOPEDIA. AS A KID, WHEN MAMA HAD COMPANY, I'D SPEND MY NIGHTS AT THE CITY LIBRARY, GOING THROUGH EVERY VOLUME.
YOU CAN DROP ME AT HOME NOW. AND THEN TAKE HER ...WHEREVER SHE BELONGS.
A REAL HEARTBEAT CAN'T BE HEARD. WHEN YOU THINK YOU'RE LISTENING TO SOMEONE'S HEART, YOU'RE JUST HEARING VALVES CLOSING.
...HIS WIFE, PAMELA GRANGE, SAID SHE HADN'T SEEN HER HUSBAND SINCE HE LEFT OMAHA FOR WASHINGTON EARLIER IN THE WEEK. THE SENATOR'S BODY WAS FOUND BY POLICE EARLY THIS MORNING FOUR MILES OFF THE COAST OF MARYLAND ...
THAT'S ALL IT IS. NOT BLOOD BEING PUMPED. BUT THE SOUND OF SOMETHING CLOSING... ENDING, OVER AND OVER.

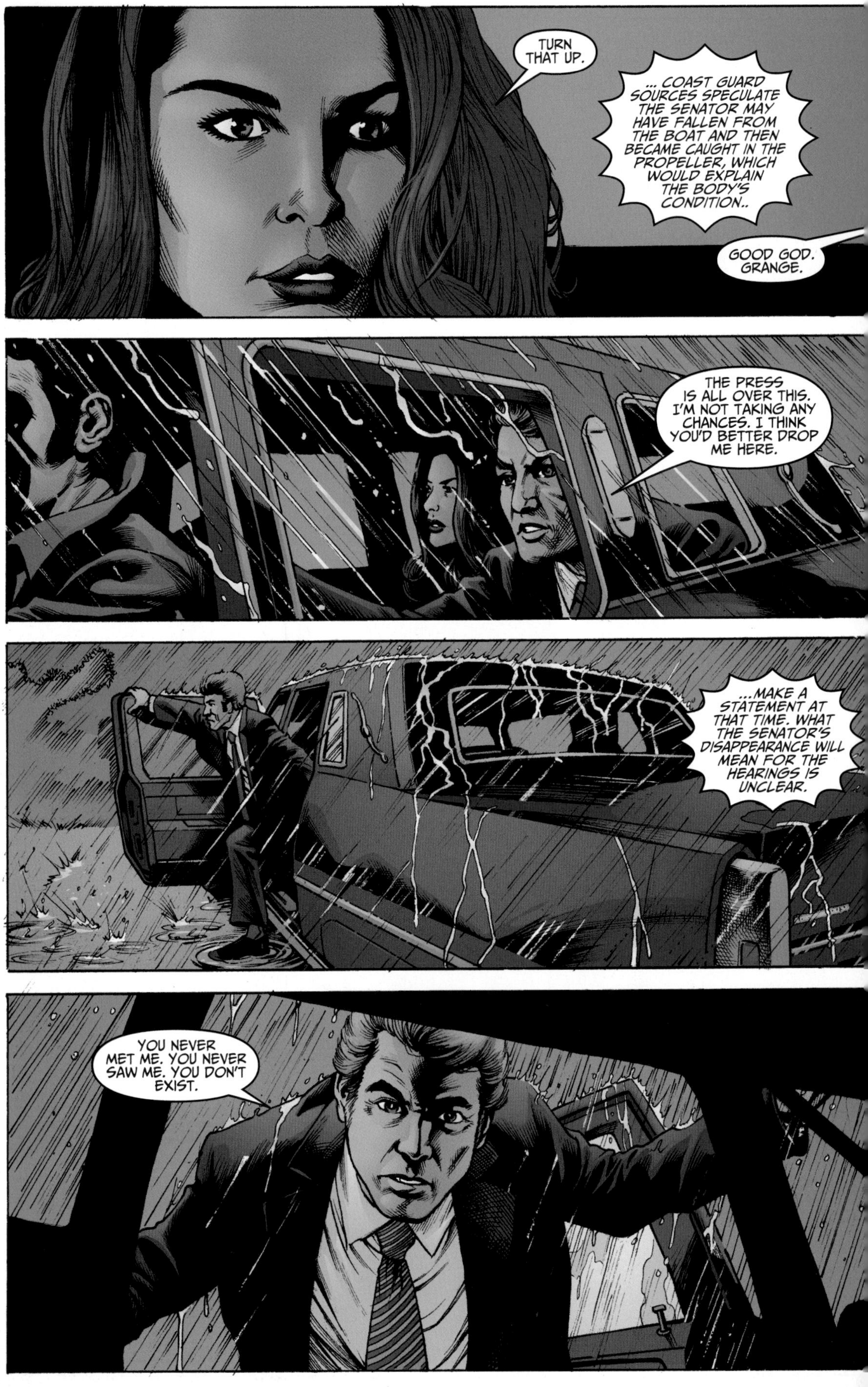
TURN THAT UP.
... COAST GUARD SOURCES SPECULATE THE SENATOR MAY HAVE FALLEN FROM THE BOAT AND THEN BECAME CAUGHT IN THE PROPELLER, WHICH WOULD EXPLAIN THE BODY'S CONDITION..
GOOD GOD. GRANGE.
THE PRESS IS ALL OVER THIS. I'M NOT TAKING ANY CHANCES. I THINK YOU'D BETTER DROP ME HERE.
...MAKE A STATEMENT AT THAT TIME. WHAT THE SENATOR'S DISAPPEARANCE WILL MEAN FOR THE HEARINGS IS UNCLEAR.
YOU NEVER MET ME. YOU NEVER SAW ME. YOU DON'T EXIST.

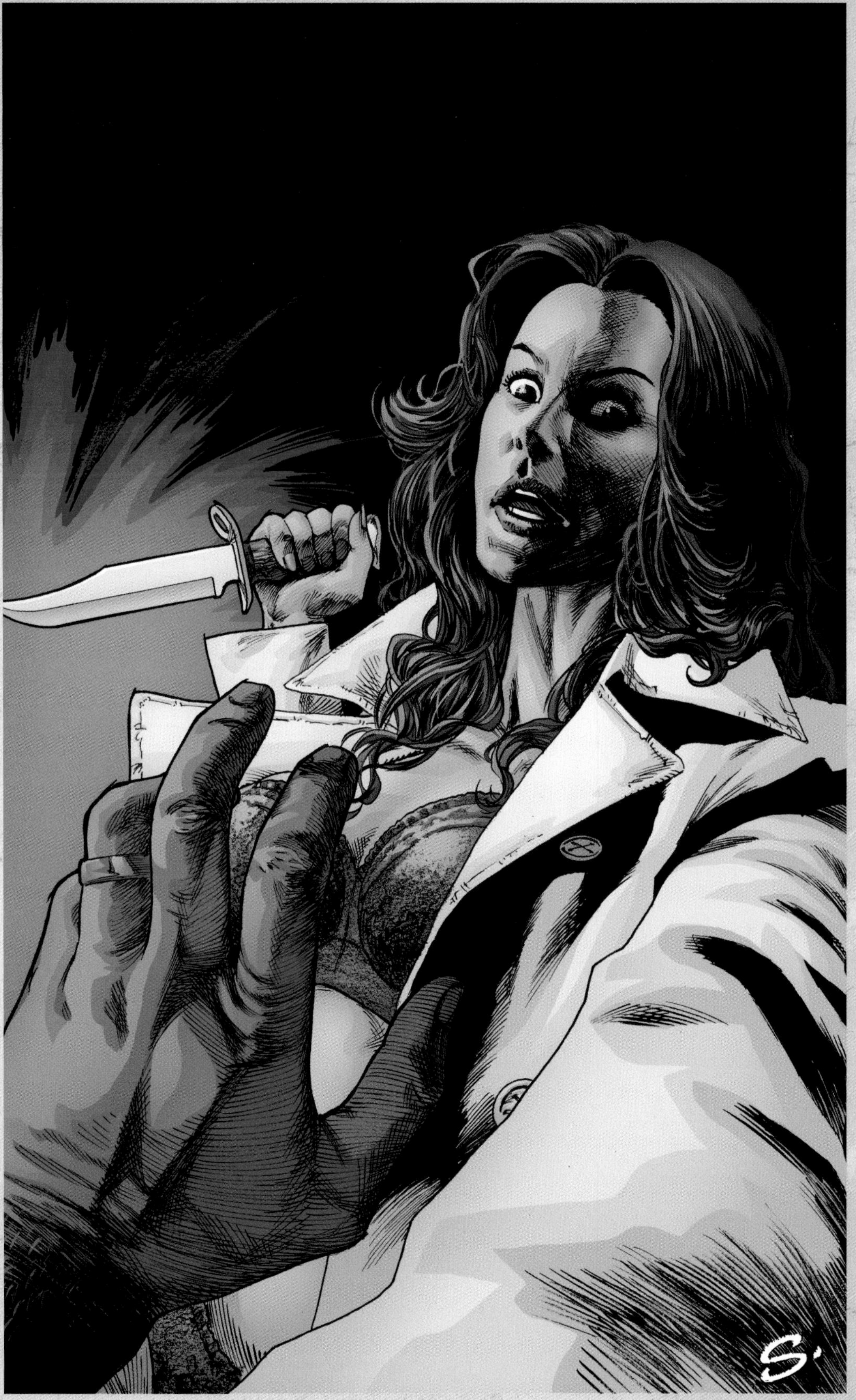

ILLUSTRATED BY **STEVE SCOTT**

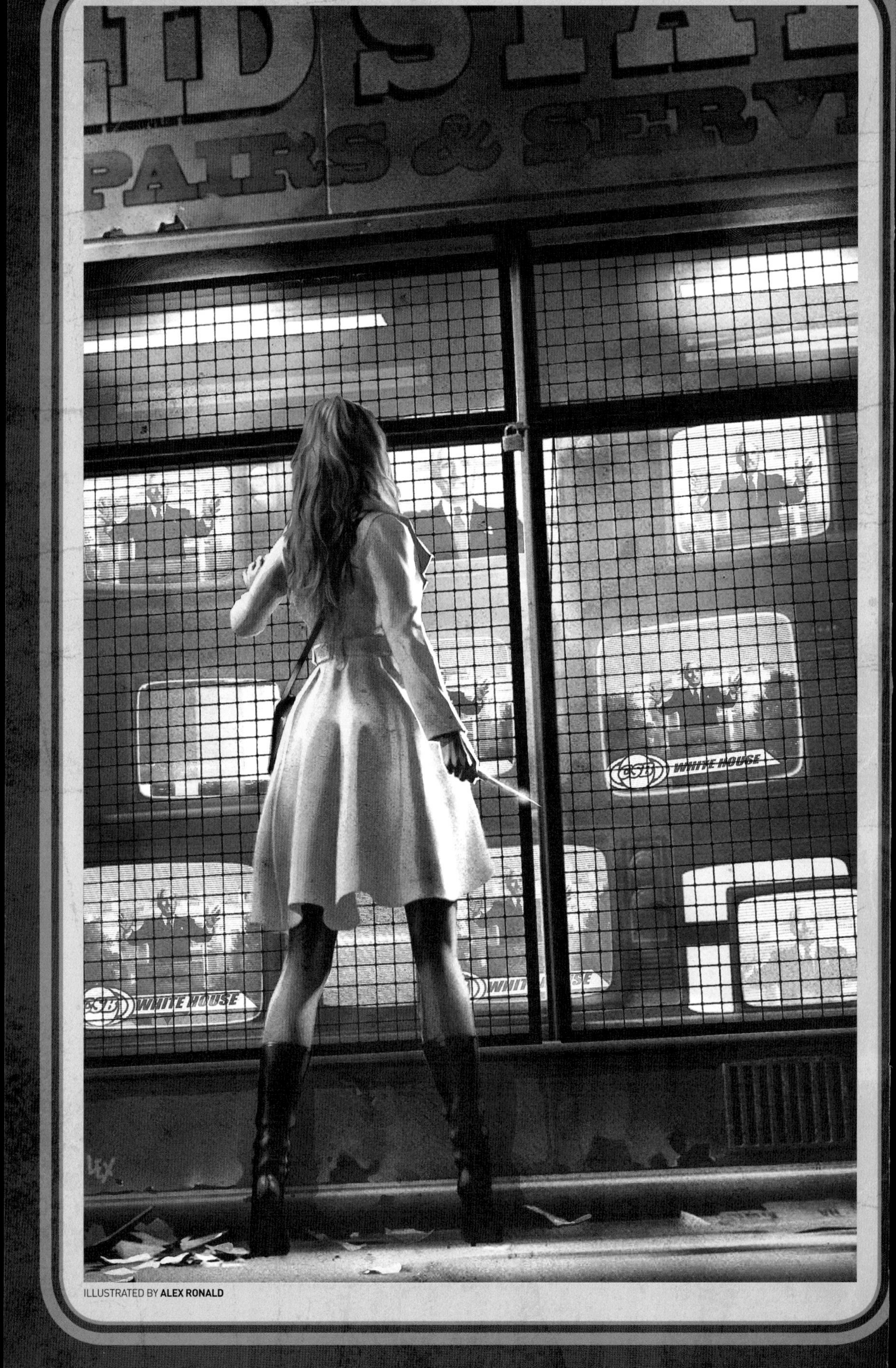
WHITE HOUSE
WHITE HOUSE

ILLUSTRATED BY **ALEX RONALD**

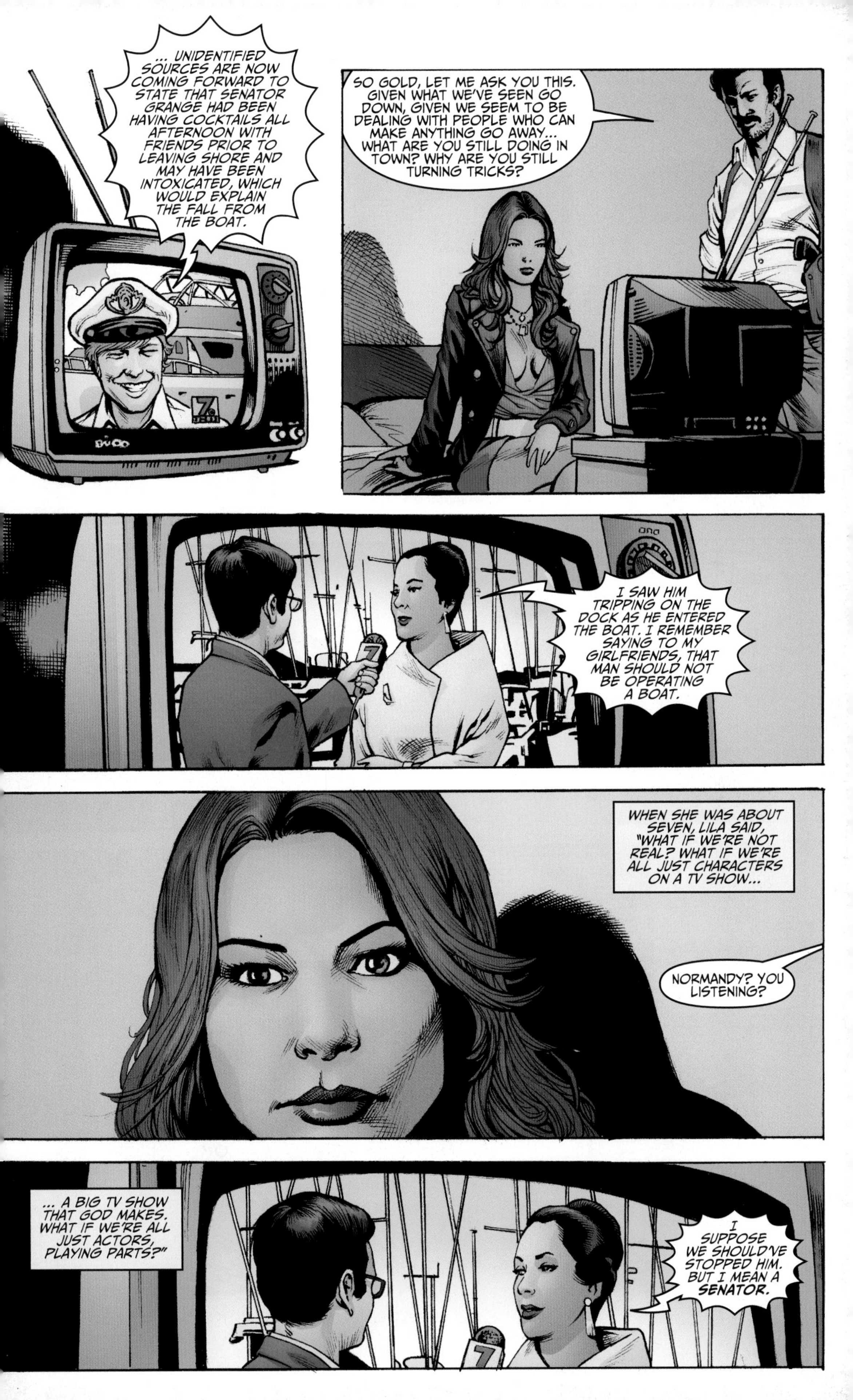

... UNIDENTIFIED SOURCES ARE NOW COMING FORWARD TO STATE THAT SENATOR GRANGE HAD BEEN HAVING COCKTAILS ALL AFTERNOON WITH FRIENDS PRIOR TO LEAVING SHORE AND MAY HAVE BEEN INTOXICATED, WHICH WOULD EXPLAIN THE FALL FROM THE BOAT.
SO GOLD, LET ME ASK YOU THIS. GIVEN WHAT WE'VE SEEN GO DOWN, GIVEN WE SEEM TO BE DEALING WITH PEOPLE WHO CAN MAKE ANYTHING GO AWAY... WHAT ARE YOU STILL DOING IN TOWN? WHY ARE YOU STILL TURNING TRICKS?
I SAW HIM TRIPPING ON THE DOCK AS HE ENTERED THE BOAT. I REMEMBER SAYING TO MY GIRLFRIENDS, THAT MAN SHOULD NOT BE OPERATING A BOAT.
WHEN SHE WAS ABOUT SEVEN, LILA SAID, "WHAT IF WE'RE NOT REAL? WHAT IF WE'RE ALL JUST CHARACTERS ON A TV SHOW...
NORMANDY? YOU LISTENING?
... A BIG TV SHOW THAT GOD MAKES. WHAT IF WE'RE ALL JUST ACTORS, PLAYING PARTS?"
I SUPPOSE WE SHOULD'VE STOPPED HIM. BUT I MEAN A **SENATOR**.

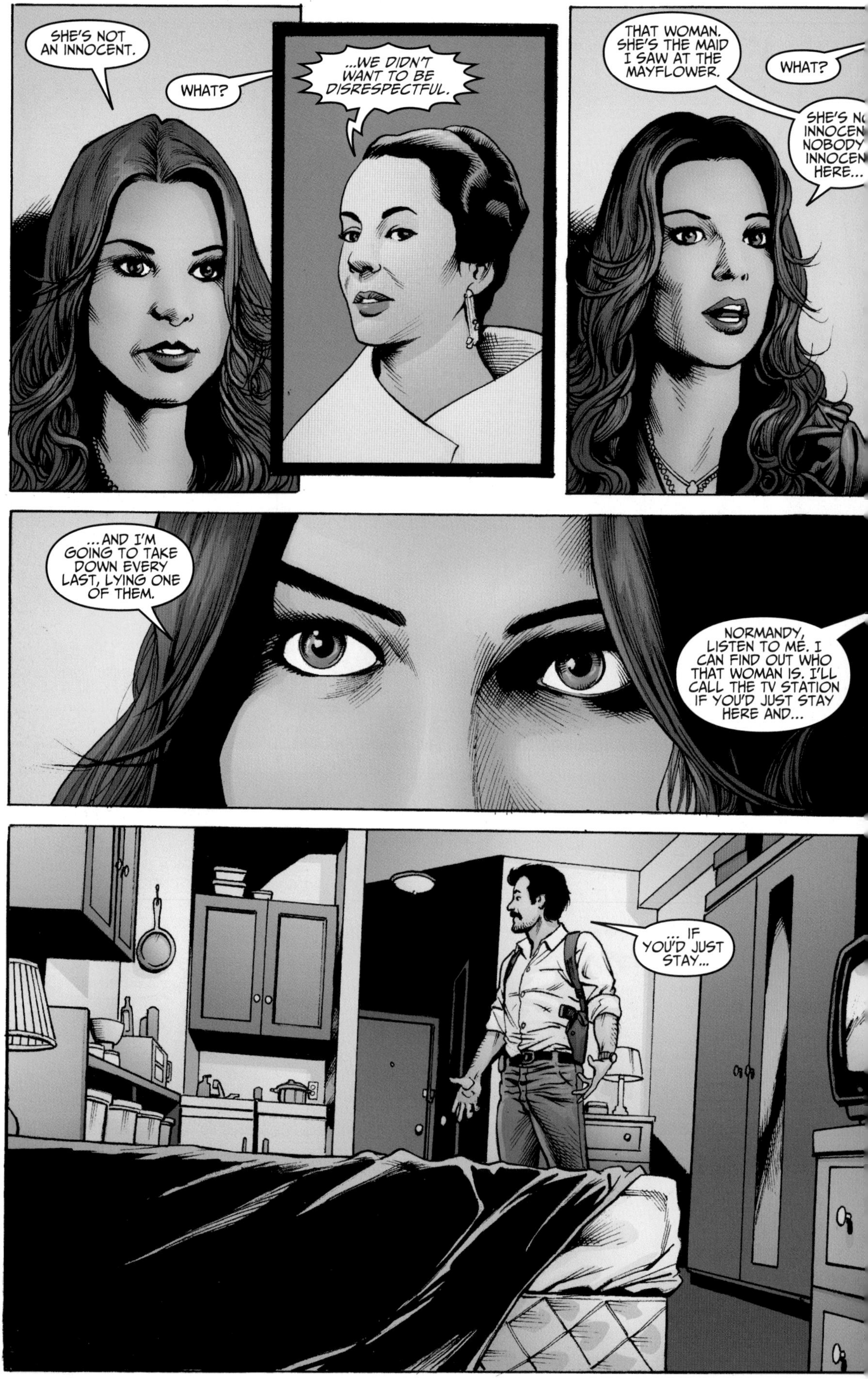
SHE'S NOT AN INNOCENT.
WHAT?
...WE DIDN'T WANT TO BE DISRESPECTFUL.
THAT WOMAN. SHE'S THE MAID I SAW AT THE MAYFLOWER.
WHAT?
SHE'S NO INNOCEN NOBODY INNOCEN HERE...
...AND I'M GOING TO TAKE DOWN EVERY LAST, LYING ONE OF THEM.
NORMANDY, LISTEN TO ME. I CAN FIND OUT WHO THAT WOMAN IS. I'LL CALL THE TV STATION IF YOU'D JUST STAY HERE AND...
... IF YOU'D JUST STAY...

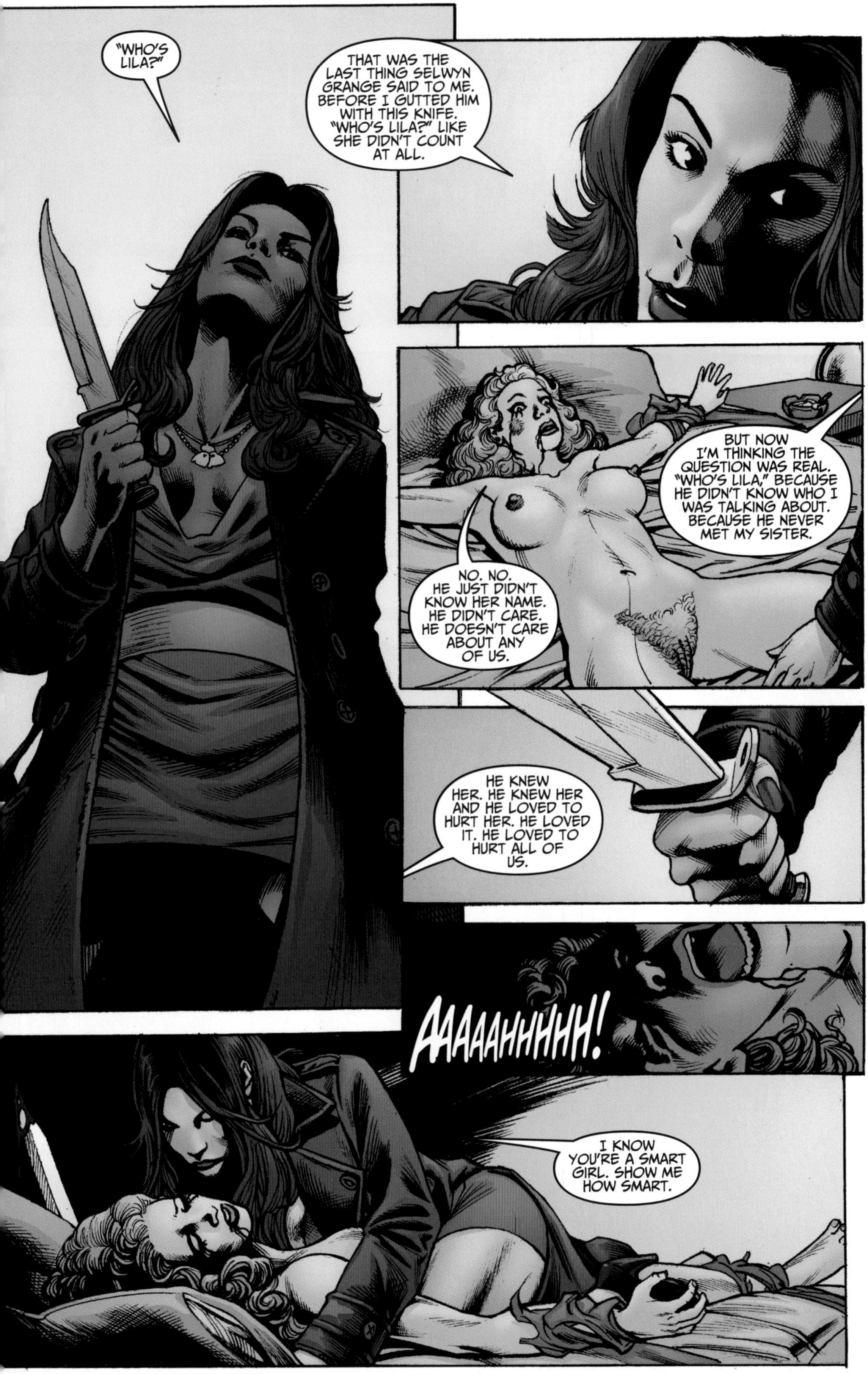
"WHO'S LILA?"
THAT WAS THE LAST THING SELWYN GRANGE SAID TO ME. BEFORE I GUTTED HIM WITH THIS KNIFE. "WHO'S LILA?" LIKE SHE DIDN'T COUNT AT ALL.
BUT NOW I'M THINKING THE QUESTION WAS REAL. "WHO'S LILA," BECAUSE HE DIDN'T KNOW WHO I WAS TALKING ABOUT. BECAUSE HE NEVER MET MY SISTER.
NO. NO. HE JUST DIDN'T KNOW HER NAME. HE DIDN'T CARE. HE DOESN'T CARE ABOUT ANY OF US.
HE KNEW HER. HE KNEW HER AND HE LOVED TO HURT HER. HE LOVED IT. HE LOVED TO HURT ALL OF US.
AAAAAHHHHH!
I KNOW YOU'RE A SMART GIRL. SHOW ME HOW SMART.

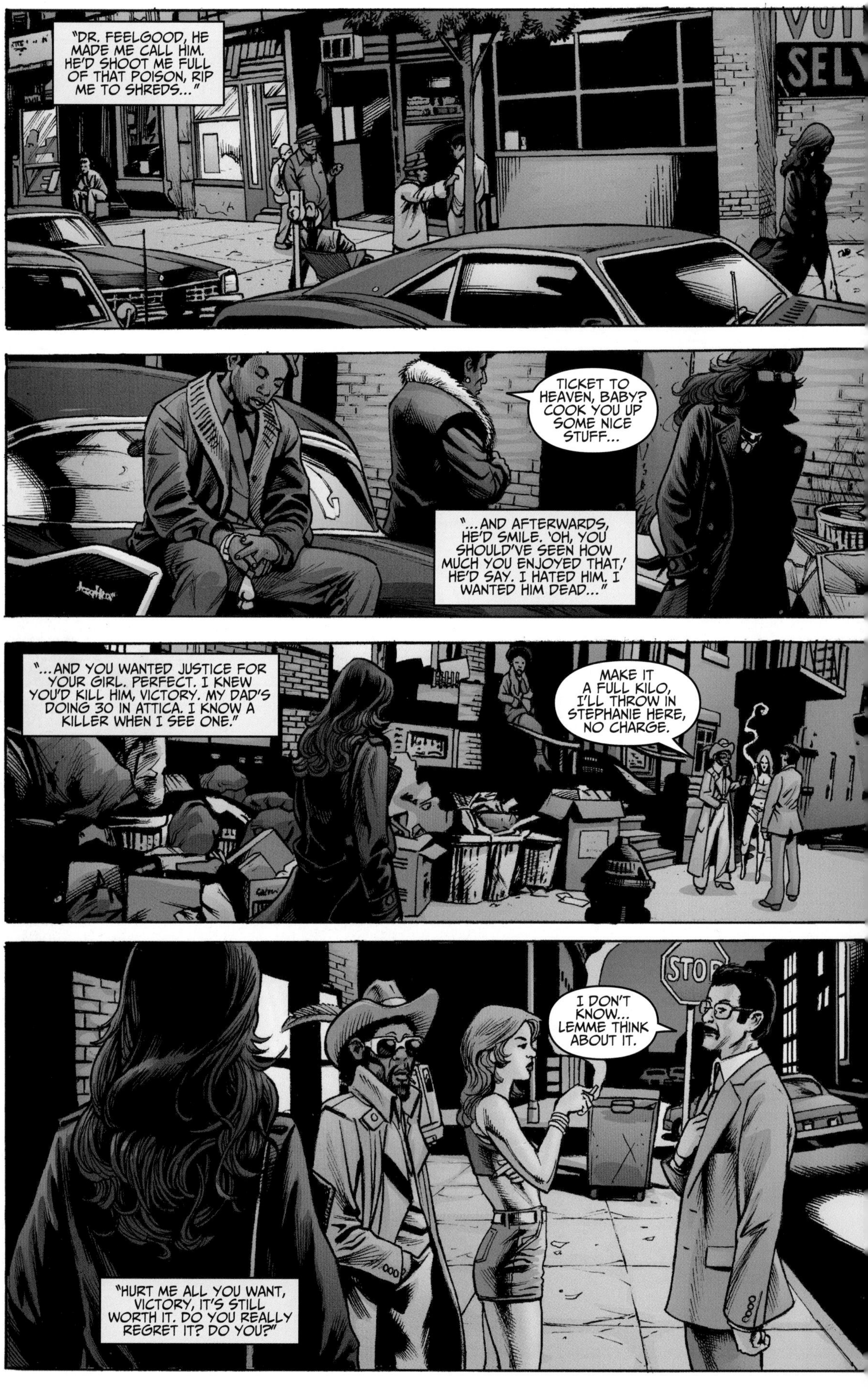
"DR. FEELGOOD, HE MADE ME CALL HIM. HE'D SHOOT ME FULL OF THAT POISON, RIP ME TO SHREDS..."
TICKET TO HEAVEN, BABY? COOK YOU UP SOME NICE STUFF...
"...AND AFTERWARDS, HE'D SMILE. 'OH, YOU SHOULD'VE SEEN HOW MUCH YOU ENJOYED THAT,' HE'D SAY. I HATED HIM. I WANTED HIM DEAD..."
"...AND YOU WANTED JUSTICE FOR YOUR GIRL. PERFECT. I KNEW YOU'D KILL HIM, VICTORY. MY DAD'S DOING 30 IN ATTICA. I KNOW A KILLER WHEN I SEE ONE."
MAKE IT A FULL KILO, I'LL THROW IN STEPHANIE HERE, NO CHARGE.
I DON'T KNOW... LEMME THINK ABOUT IT.
"HURT ME ALL YOU WANT, VICTORY, IT'S STILL WORTH IT. DO YOU REALLY REGRET IT? DO YOU?"

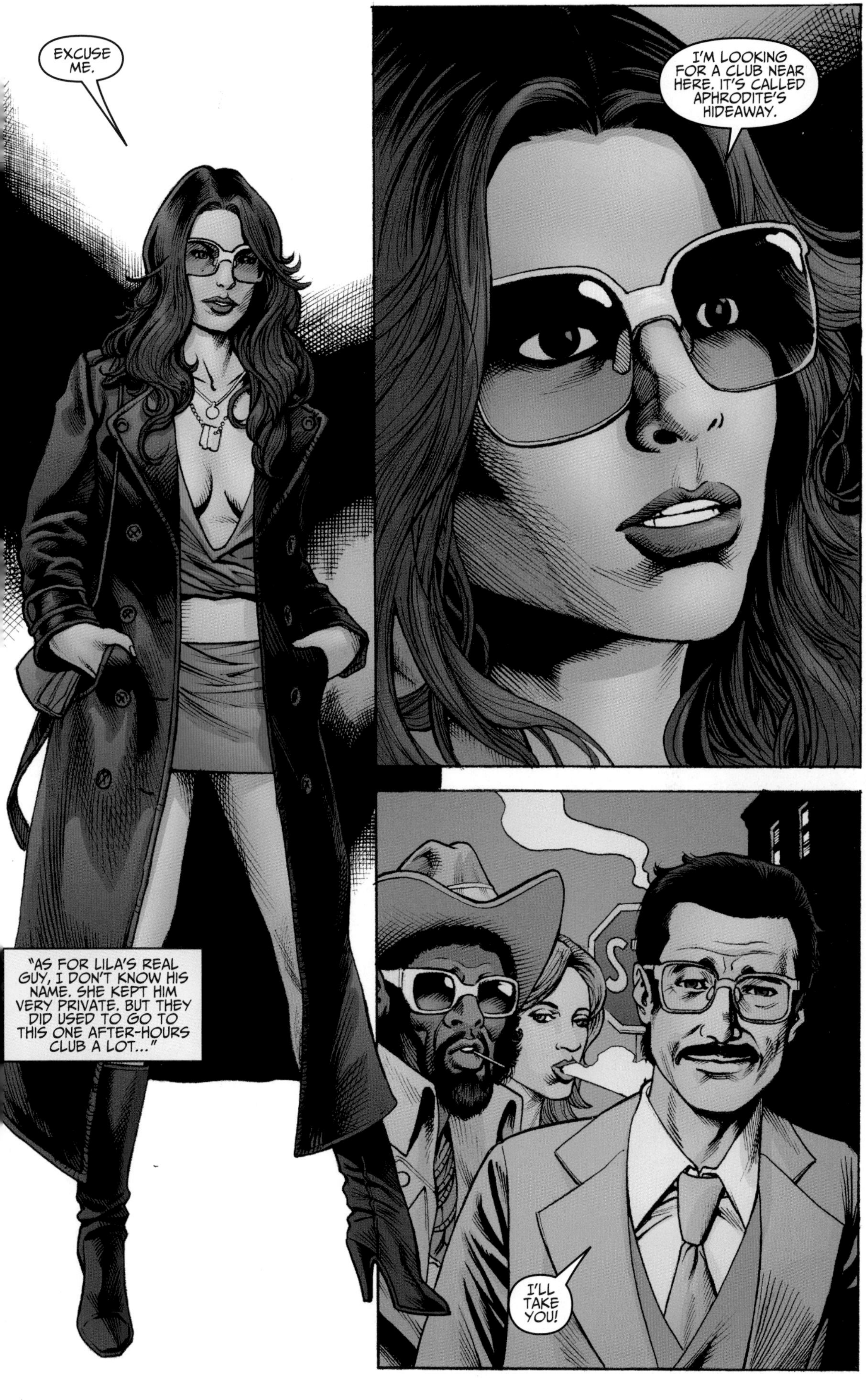
EXCUSE ME.
I'M LOOKING FOR A CLUB NEAR HERE. IT'S CALLED APHRODITE'S HIDEAWAY.
"AS FOR LILA'S REAL GUY, I DON'T KNOW HIS NAME. SHE KEPT HIM VERY PRIVATE. BUT THEY DID USED TO GO TO THIS ONE AFTER-HOURS CLUB A LOT..."
I'LL TAKE YOU!

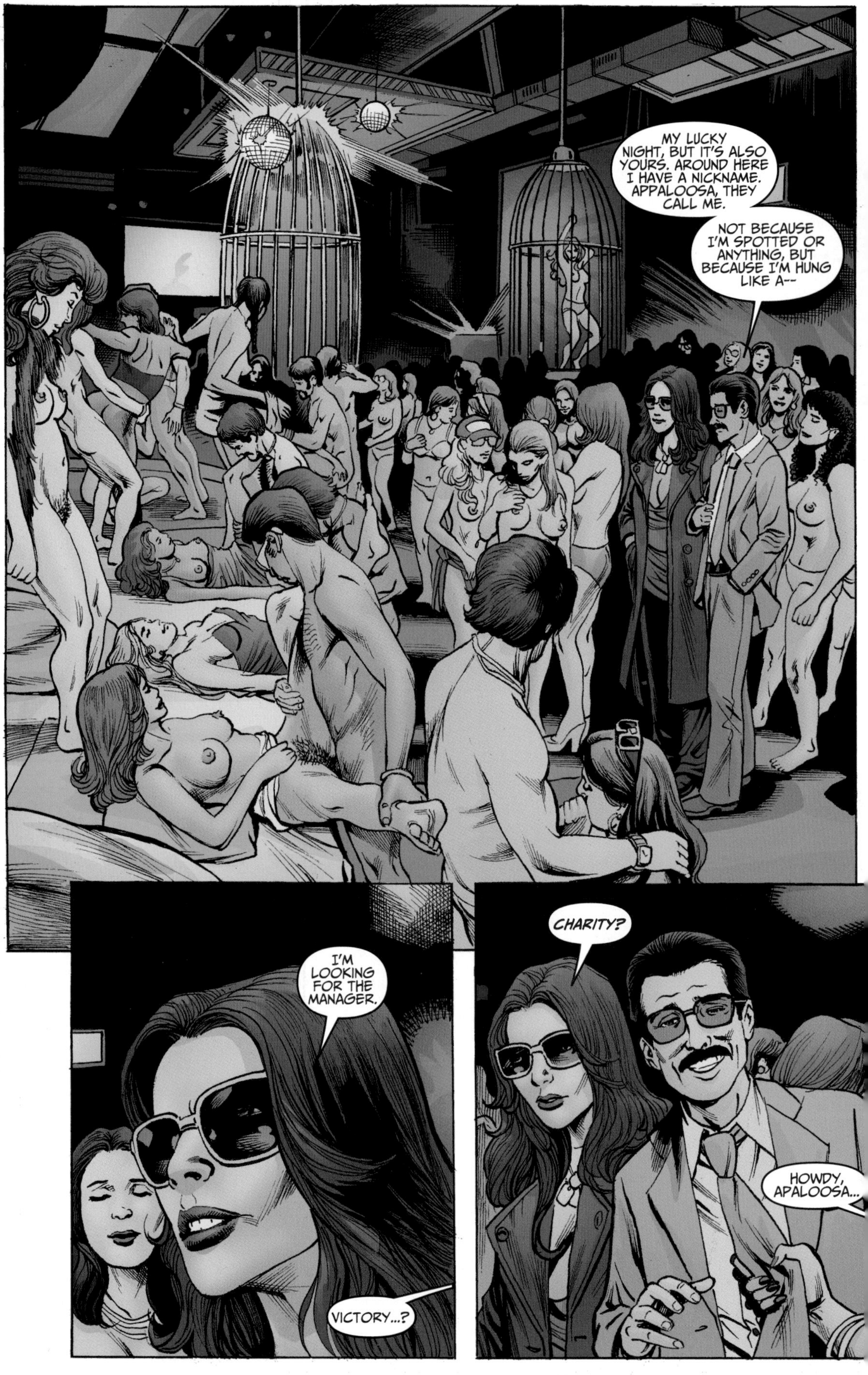

MY LUCKY NIGHT, BUT IT'S ALSO YOURS. AROUND HERE I HAVE A NICKNAME. APPALOOSA, THEY CALL ME.
NOT BECAUSE I'M SPOTTED OR ANYTHING, BUT BECAUSE I'M HUNG LIKE A--
I'M LOOKING FOR THE MANAGER.
VICTORY...?
CHARITY?
HOWDY, APALOOSA...

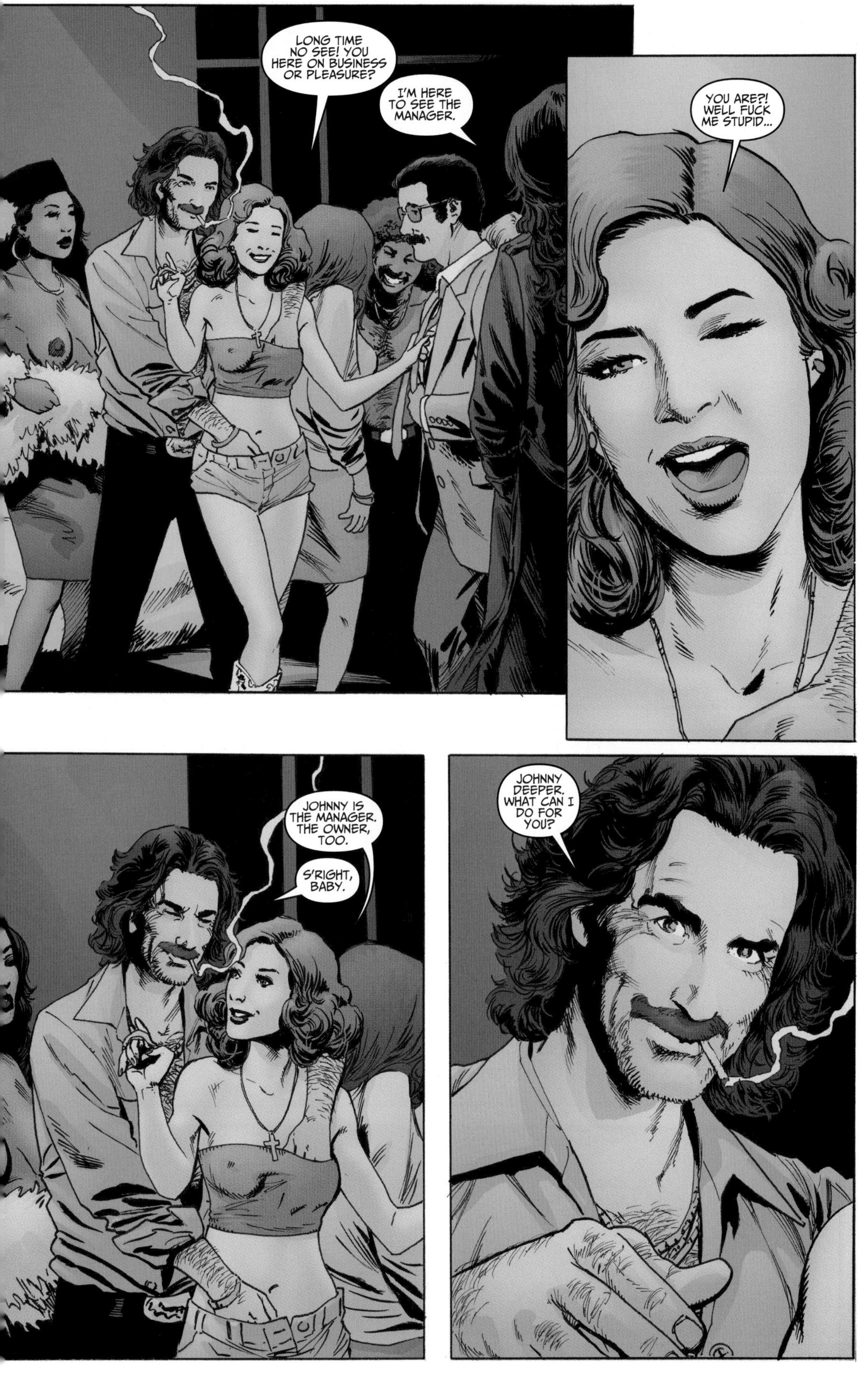
LONG TIME NO SEE! YOU HERE ON BUSINESS OR PLEASURE?
I'M HERE TO SEE THE MANAGER.
YOU ARE?! WELL FUCK ME STUPID...
JOHNNY IS THE MANAGER. THE OWNER, TOO.
S'RIGHT, BABY.
JOHNNY DEEPER. WHAT CAN I DO FOR YOU?

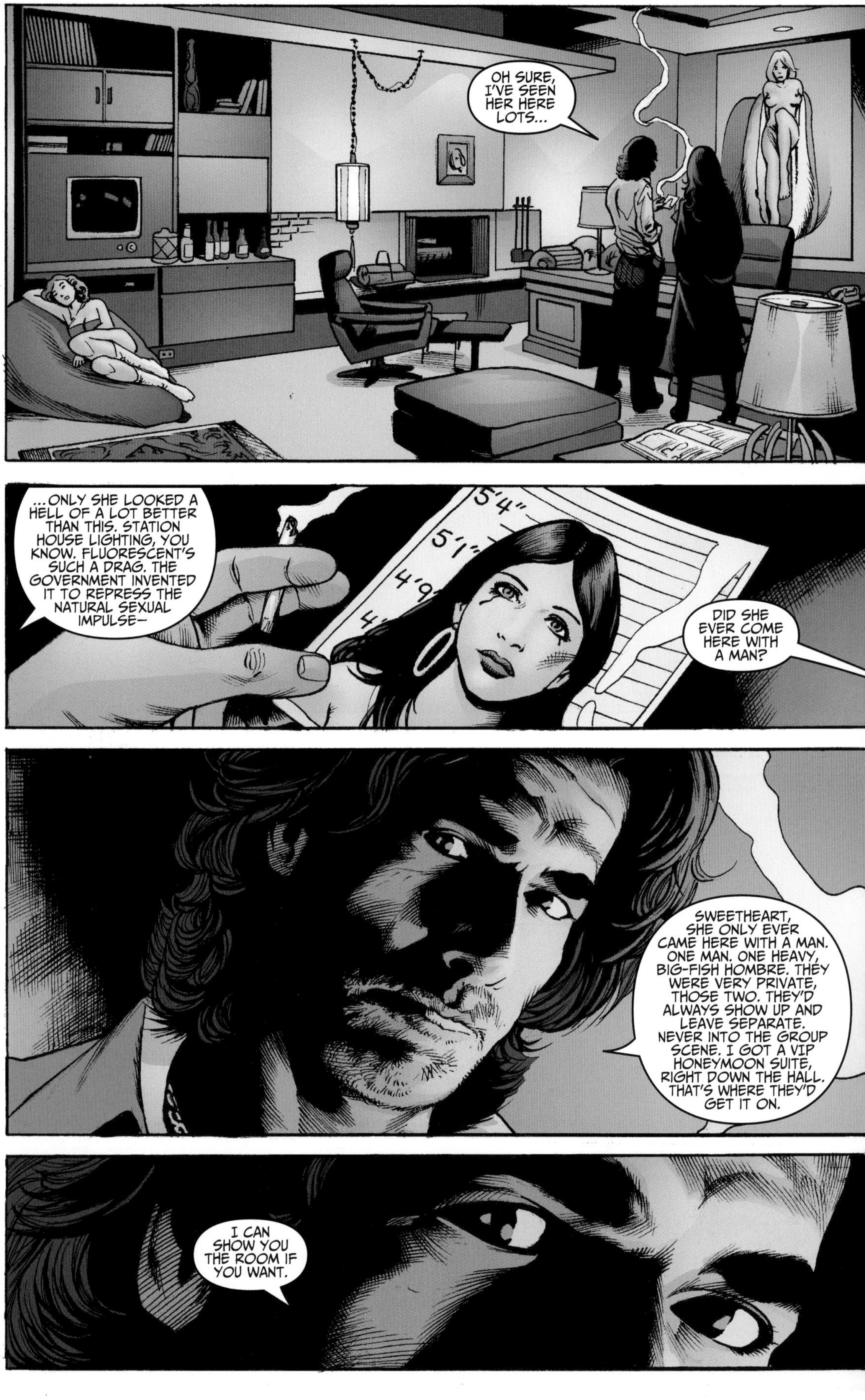
OH SURE, I'VE SEEN HER HERE LOTS...
...ONLY SHE LOOKED A HELL OF A LOT BETTER THAN THIS. STATION HOUSE LIGHTING, YOU KNOW. FLUORESCENT'S SUCH A DRAG. THE GOVERNMENT INVENTED IT TO REPRESS THE NATURAL SEXUAL IMPULSE–
DID SHE EVER COME HERE WITH A MAN?
SWEETHEART, SHE ONLY EVER CAME HERE WITH A MAN. ONE MAN. ONE HEAVY, BIG-FISH HOMBRE. THEY WERE VERY PRIVATE, THOSE TWO. THEY'D ALWAYS SHOW UP AND LEAVE SEPARATE. NEVER INTO THE GROUP SCENE. I GOT A VIP HONEYMOON SUITE, RIGHT DOWN THE HALL. THAT'S WHERE THEY'D GET IT ON.
I CAN SHOW YOU THE ROOM IF YOU WANT.

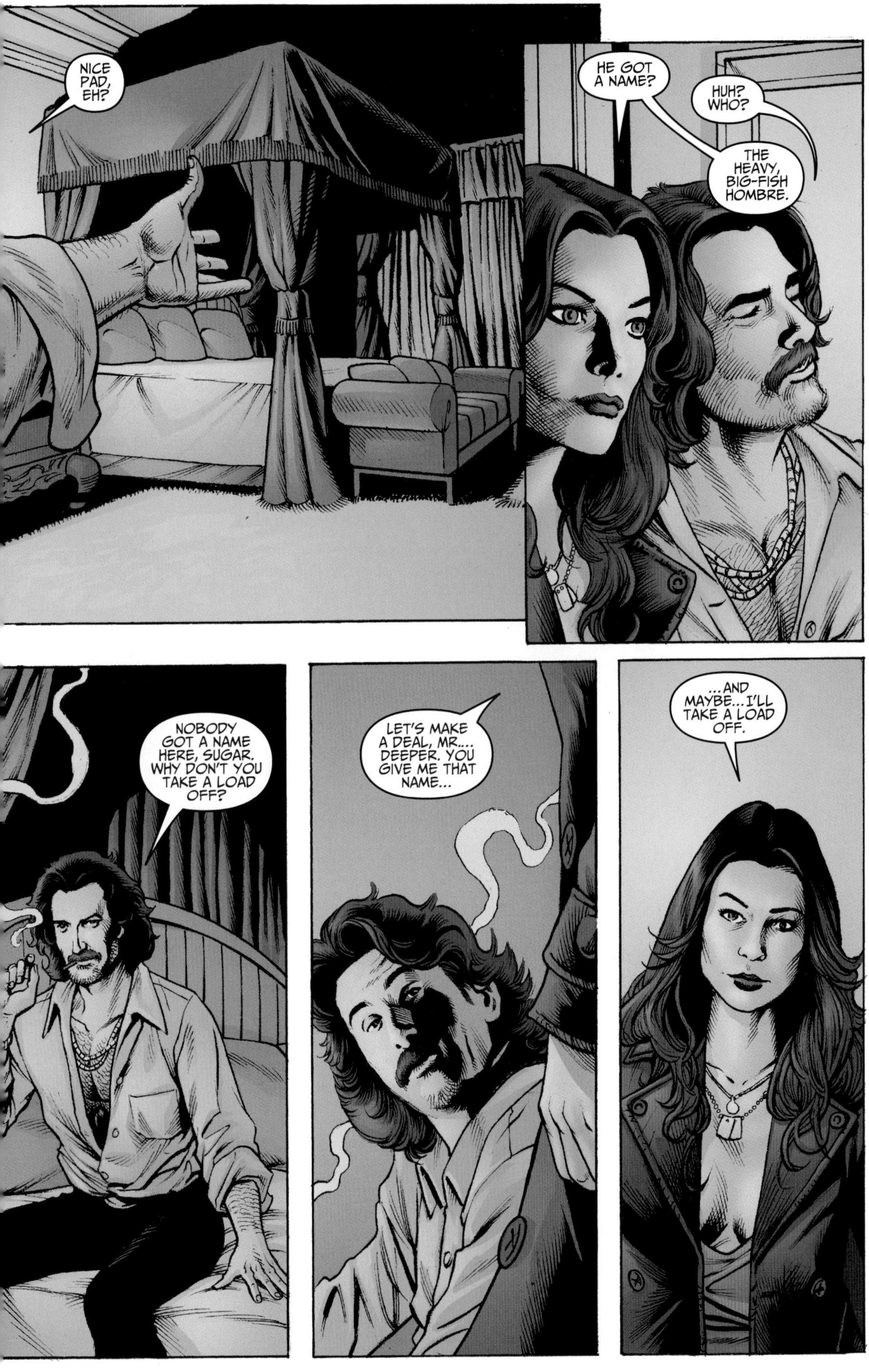
NICE PAD, EH?
HE GOT A NAME?
HUH? WHO?
THE HEAVY, BIG-FISH HOMBRE.
NOBODY GOT A NAME HERE, SUGAR. WHY DON'T YOU TAKE A LOAD OFF?
LET'S MAKE A DEAL, MR.... DEEPER. YOU GIVE ME THAT NAME...
...AND MAYBE...I'LL TAKE A LOAD OFF.

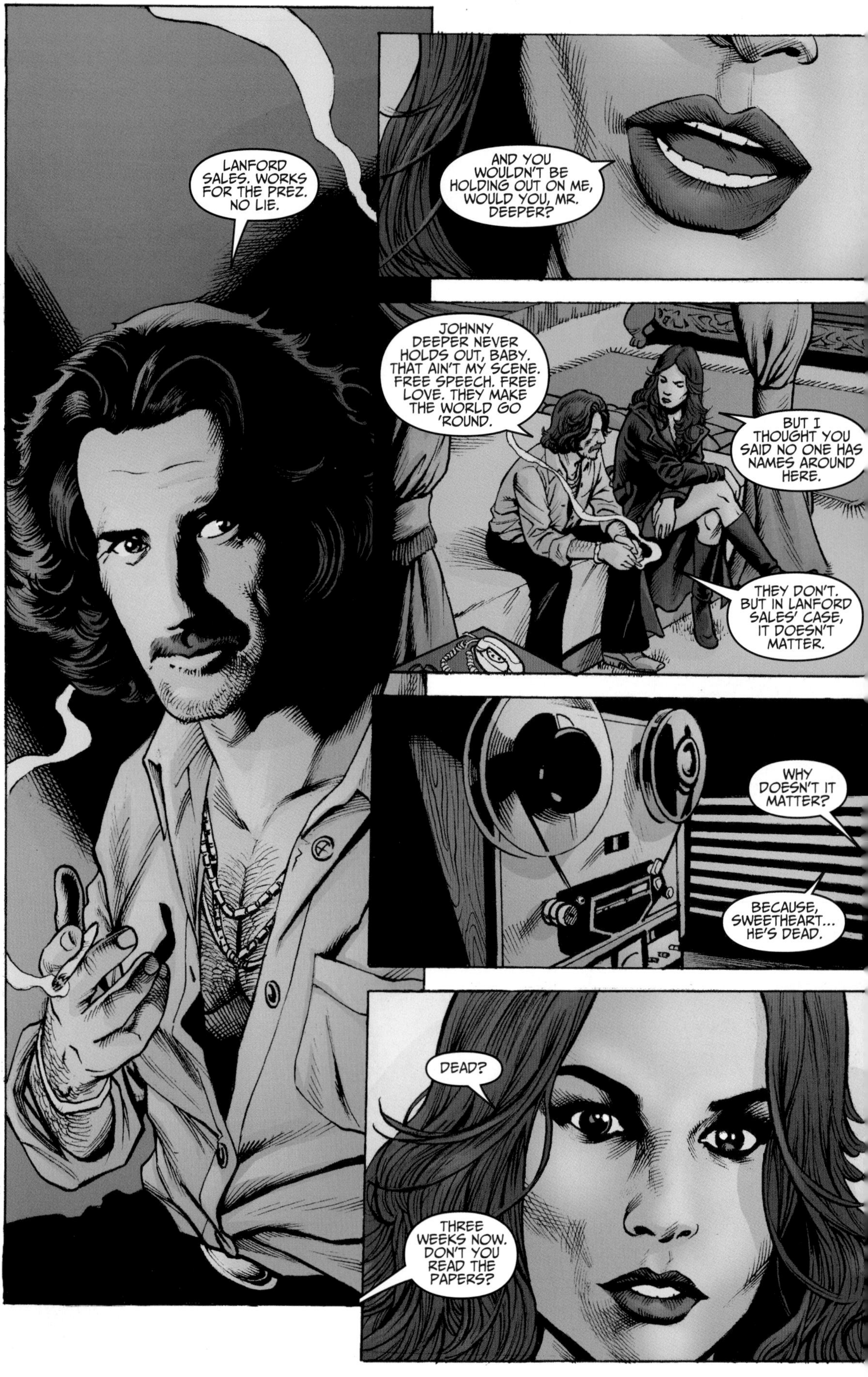
LANFORD SALES. WORKS FOR THE PREZ. NO LIE.
AND YOU WOULDN'T BE HOLDING OUT ON ME, WOULD YOU, MR. DEEPER?
JOHNNY DEEPER NEVER HOLDS OUT, BABY. THAT AIN'T MY SCENE. FREE SPEECH. FREE LOVE. THEY MAKE THE WORLD GO 'ROUND.
BUT I THOUGHT YOU SAID NO ONE HAS NAMES AROUND HERE.
THEY DON'T. BUT IN LANFORD SALES' CASE, IT DOESN'T MATTER.
WHY DOESN'T IT MATTER?
BECAUSE, SWEETHEART... HE'S DEAD.
DEAD?
THREE WEEKS NOW. DON'T YOU READ THE PAPERS?

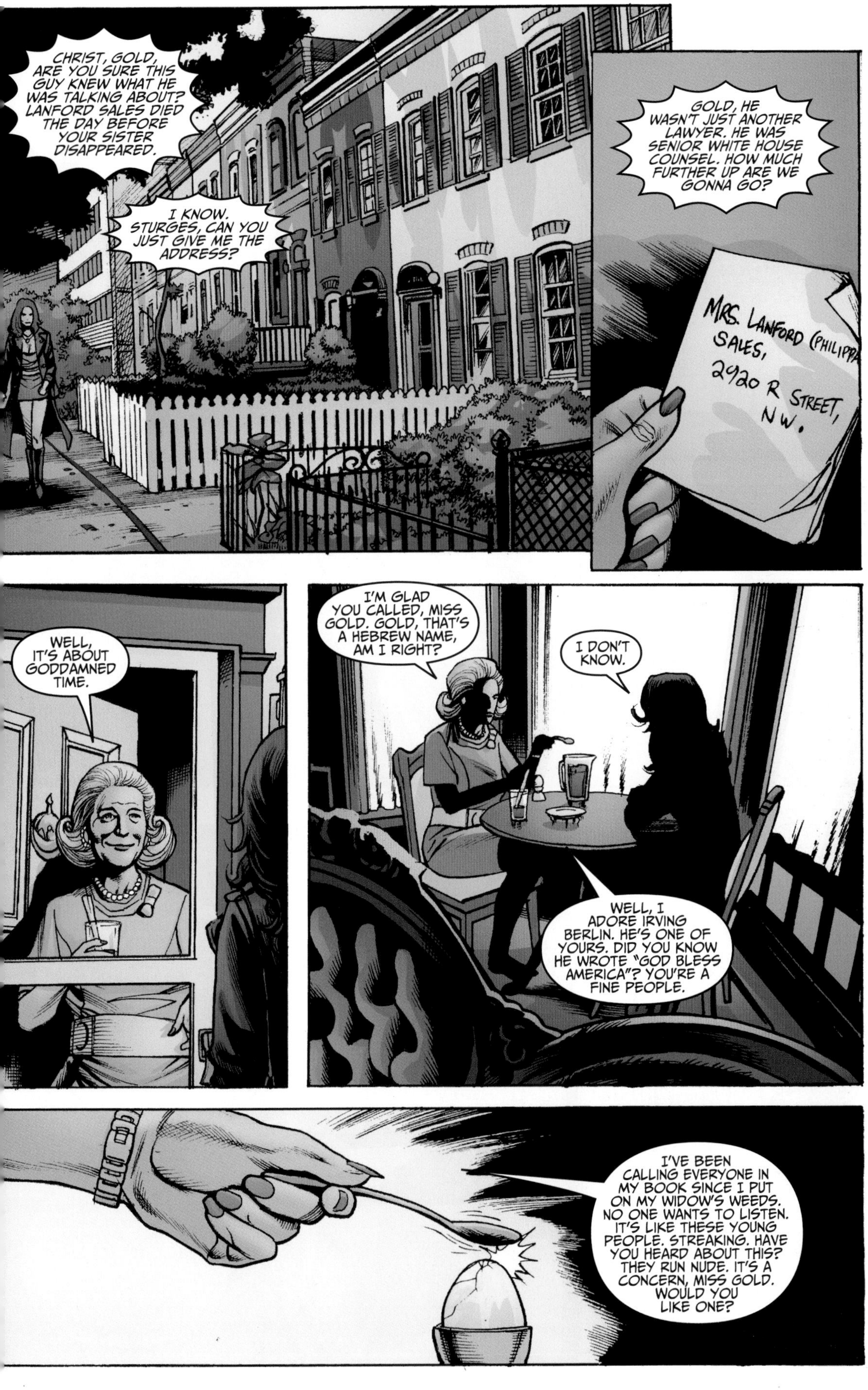
CHRIST, GOLD, ARE YOU SURE THIS GUY KNEW WHAT HE WAS TALKING ABOUT? LANFORD SALES DIED THE DAY BEFORE YOUR SISTER DISAPPEARED.
I KNOW. STURGES, CAN YOU JUST GIVE ME THE ADDRESS?
GOLD, HE WASN'T JUST ANOTHER LAWYER. HE WAS SENIOR WHITE HOUSE COUNSEL. HOW MUCH FURTHER UP ARE WE GONNA GO?
MRS. LANFORD (PHILIPPA
SALES,
2920 R STREET,
NW.
WELL, IT'S ABOUT GODDAMNED TIME.
I'M GLAD YOU CALLED, MISS GOLD. GOLD, THAT'S A HEBREW NAME, AM I RIGHT?
I DON'T KNOW.
WELL, I ADORE IRVING BERLIN. HE'S ONE OF YOURS. DID YOU KNOW HE WROTE "GOD BLESS AMERICA"? YOU'RE A FINE PEOPLE.
I'VE BEEN CALLING EVERYONE IN MY BOOK SINCE I PUT ON MY WIDOW'S WEEDS. NO ONE WANTS TO LISTEN. IT'S LIKE THESE YOUNG PEOPLE. STREAKING. HAVE YOU HEARD ABOUT THIS? THEY RUN NUDE. IT'S A CONCERN, MISS GOLD. WOULD YOU LIKE ONE?

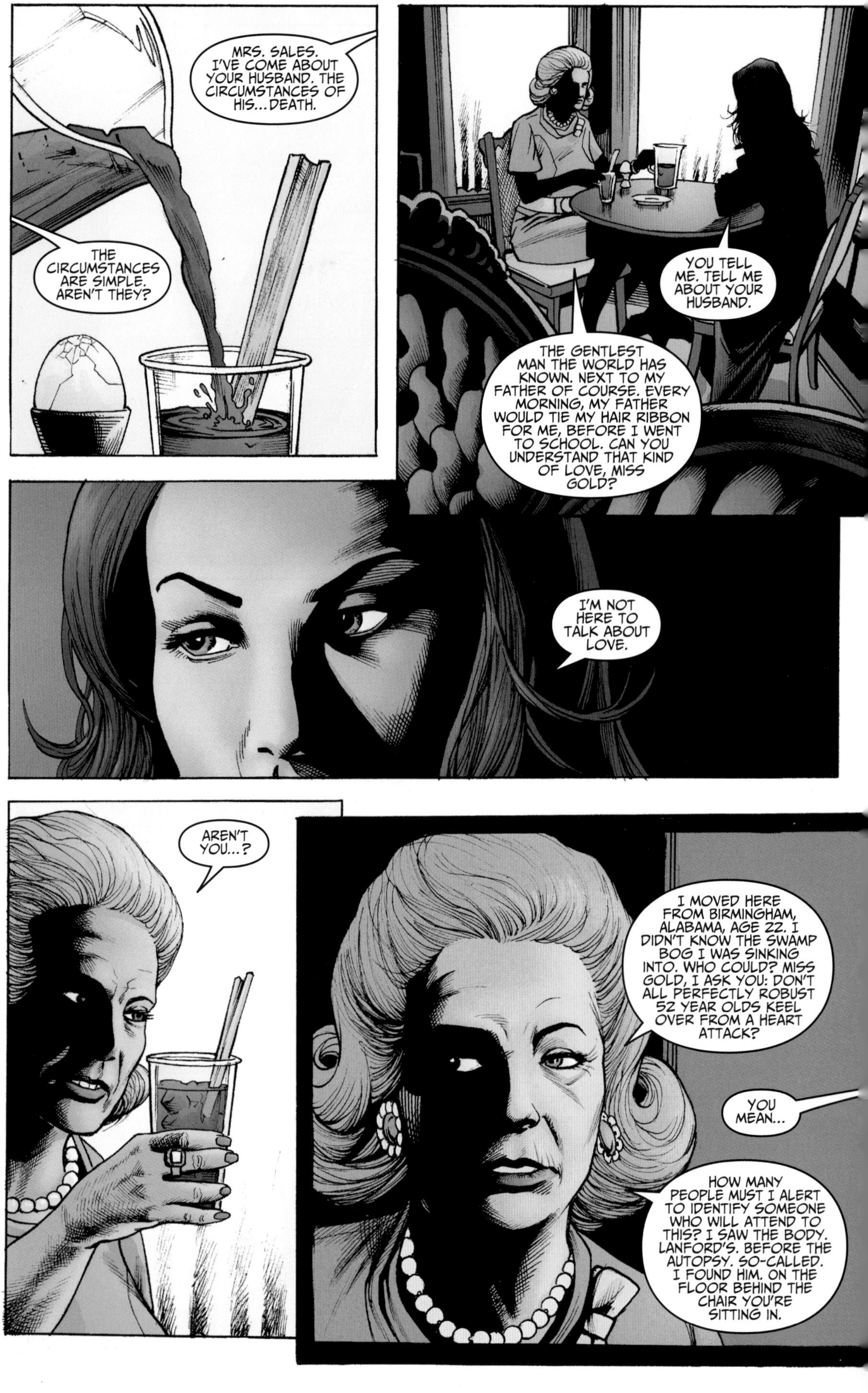
MRS. SALES. I'VE COME ABOUT YOUR HUSBAND. THE CIRCUMSTANCES OF HIS... DEATH.
THE CIRCUMSTANCES ARE SIMPLE. AREN'T THEY?
YOU TELL ME. TELL ME ABOUT YOUR HUSBAND.
THE GENTLEST MAN THE WORLD HAS KNOWN. NEXT TO MY FATHER OF COURSE. EVERY MORNING, MY FATHER WOULD TIE MY HAIR RIBBON FOR ME, BEFORE I WENT TO SCHOOL. CAN YOU UNDERSTAND THAT KIND OF LOVE, MISS GOLD?
I'M NOT HERE TO TALK ABOUT LOVE.
AREN'T YOU...?
I MOVED HERE FROM BIRMINGHAM, ALABAMA, AGE 22. I DIDN'T KNOW THE SWAMP BOG I WAS SINKING INTO. WHO COULD? MISS GOLD, I ASK YOU: DON'T ALL PERFECTLY ROBUST 52 YEAR OLDS KEEL OVER FROM A HEART ATTACK?
YOU MEAN...
HOW MANY PEOPLE MUST I ALERT TO IDENTIFY SOMEONE WHO WILL ATTEND TO THIS? I SAW THE BODY. LANFORD'S. BEFORE THE AUTOPSY. SO-CALLED. I FOUND HIM. ON THE FLOOR BEHIND THE CHAIR YOU'RE SITTING IN.

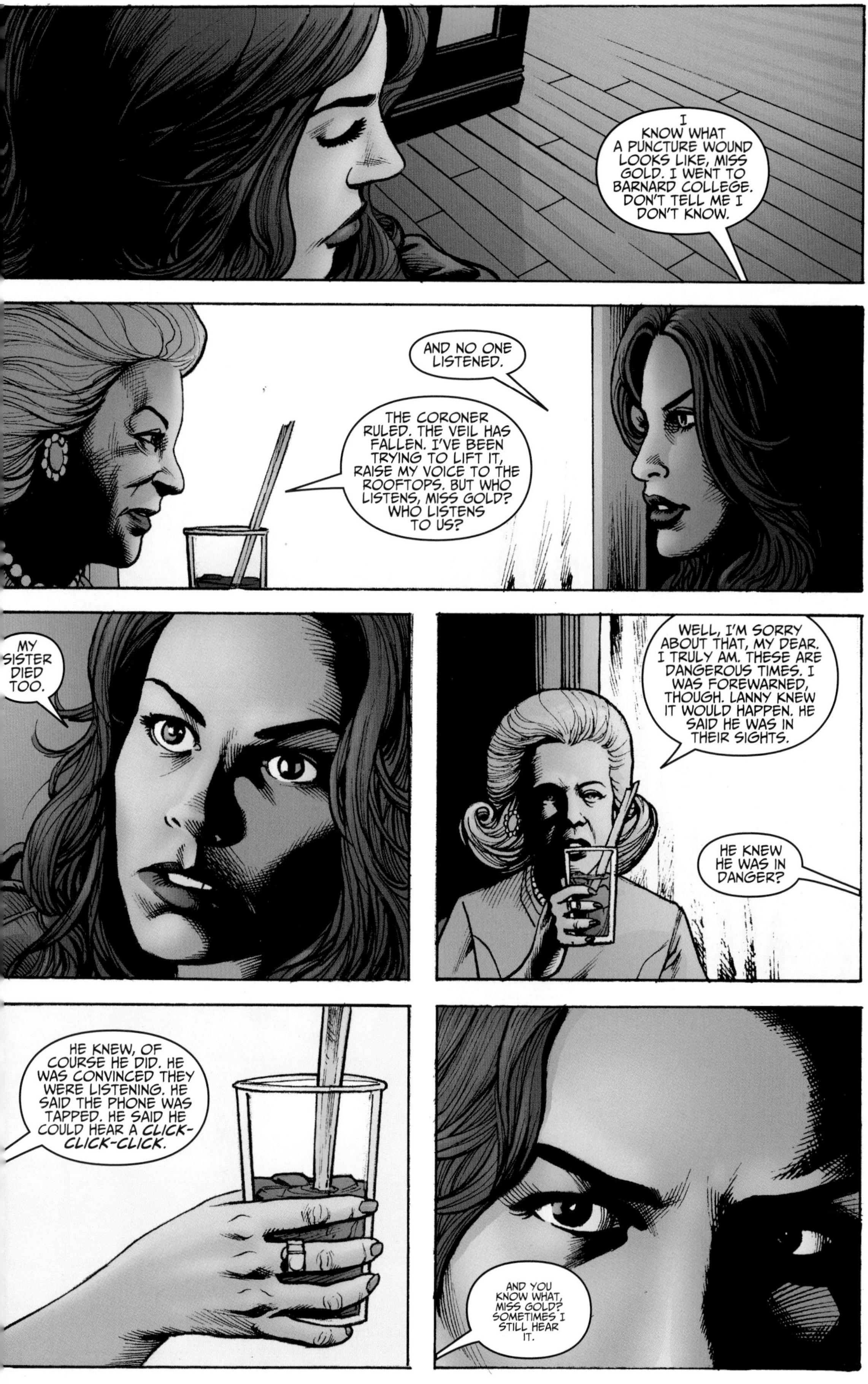
I KNOW WHAT A PUNCTURE WOUND LOOKS LIKE, MISS GOLD. I WENT TO BARNARD COLLEGE. DON'T TELL ME I DON'T KNOW.
AND NO ONE LISTENED.
THE CORONER RULED. THE VEIL HAS FALLEN. I'VE BEEN TRYING TO LIFT IT, RAISE MY VOICE TO THE ROOFTOPS. BUT WHO LISTENS, MISS GOLD? WHO LISTENS TO US?
MY SISTER DIED TOO.
WELL, I'M SORRY ABOUT THAT, MY DEAR. I TRULY AM. THESE ARE DANGEROUS TIMES. I WAS FOREWARNED, THOUGH. LANNY KNEW IT WOULD HAPPEN. HE SAID HE WAS IN THEIR SIGHTS.
HE KNEW HE WAS IN DANGER?
HE KNEW, OF COURSE HE DID. HE WAS CONVINCED THEY WERE LISTENING. HE SAID THE PHONE WAS TAPPED. HE SAID HE COULD HEAR A CLICK-CLICK-CLICK.
AND YOU KNOW WHAT, MISS GOLD? SOMETIMES I STILL HEAR IT.

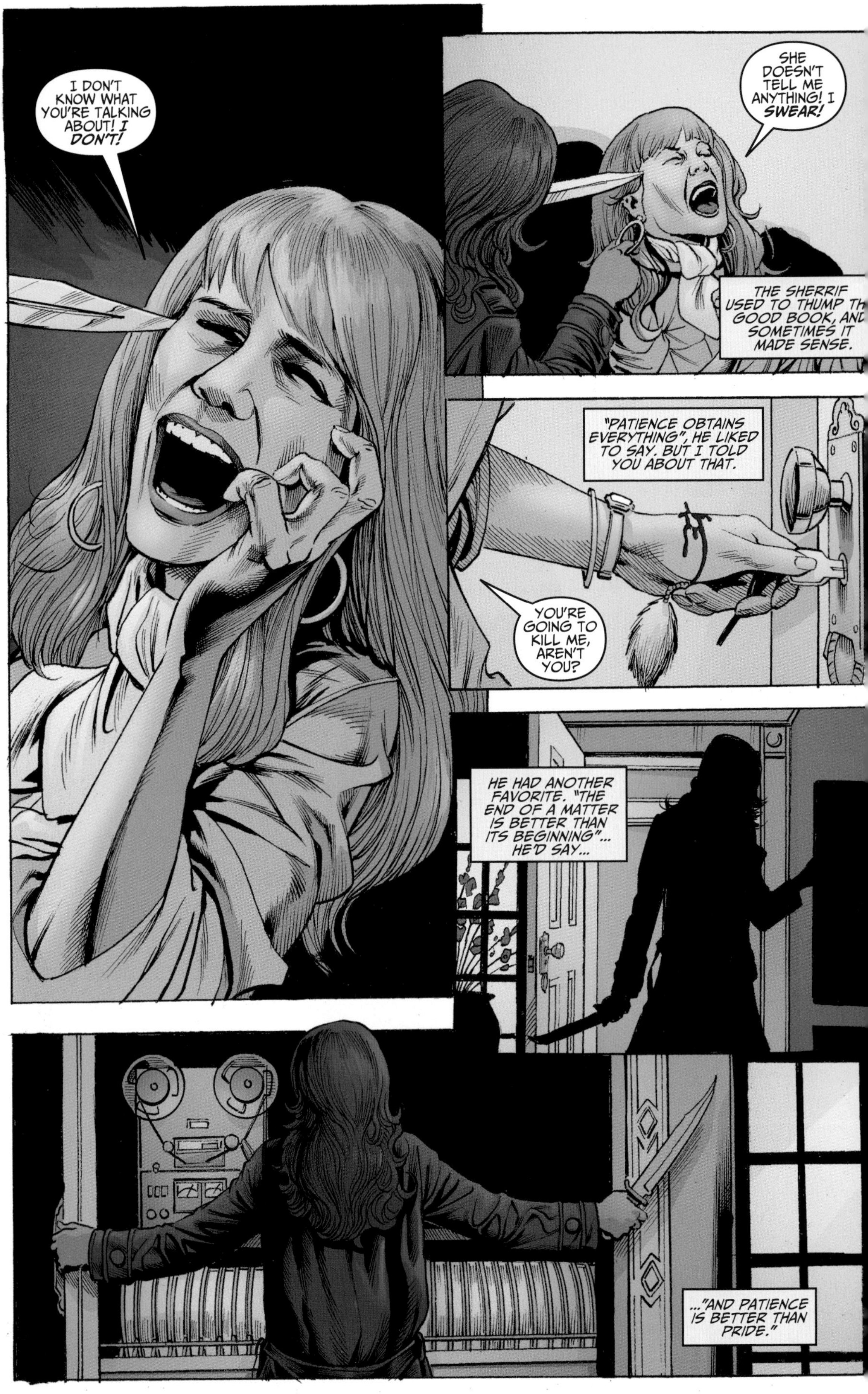
I DON'T KNOW WHAT YOU'RE TALKING ABOUT! I DON'T!
SHE DOESN'T TELL ME ANYTHING! I SWEAR!
THE SHERRIF USED TO THUMP TH GOOD BOOK, AND SOMETIMES IT MADE SENSE.
"PATIENCE OBTAINS EVERYTHING", HE LIKED TO SAY. BUT I TOLD YOU ABOUT THAT.
YOU'RE GOING TO KILL ME, AREN'T YOU?
HE HAD ANOTHER FAVORITE. "THE END OF A MATTER IS BETTER THAN ITS BEGINNING"... HE'D SAY...
..."AND PATIENCE IS BETTER THAN PRIDE."

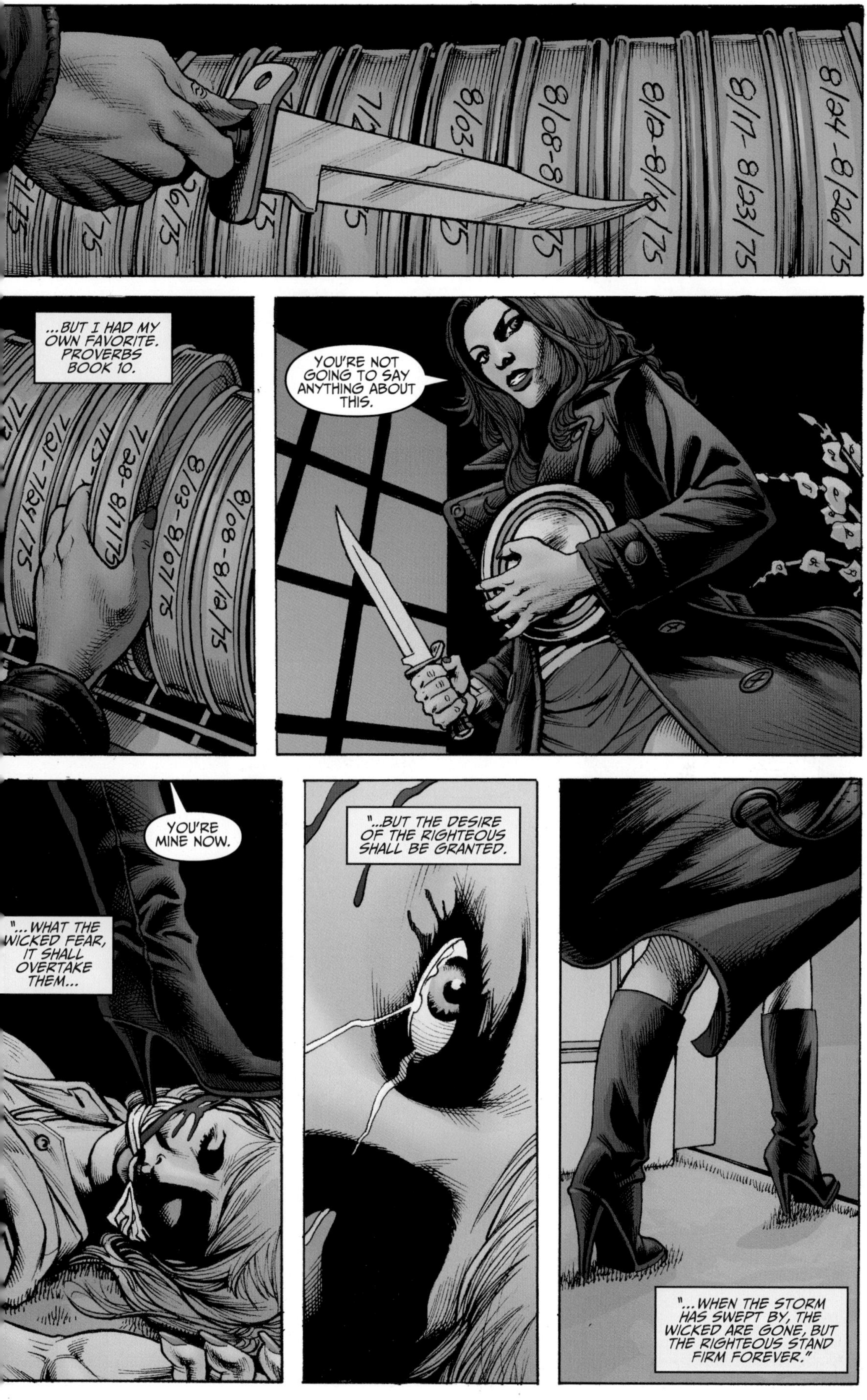
...BUT I HAD MY OWN FAVORITE. PROVERBS BOOK 10.
YOU'RE NOT GOING TO SAY ANYTHING ABOUT THIS.
YOU'RE MINE NOW.
"...WHAT THE WICKED FEAR, IT SHALL OVERTAKE THEM...
"...BUT THE DESIRE OF THE RIGHTEOUS SHALL BE GRANTED.
"...WHEN THE STORM HAS SWEPT BY, THE WICKED ARE GONE, BUT THE RIGHTEOUS STAND FIRM FOREVER."

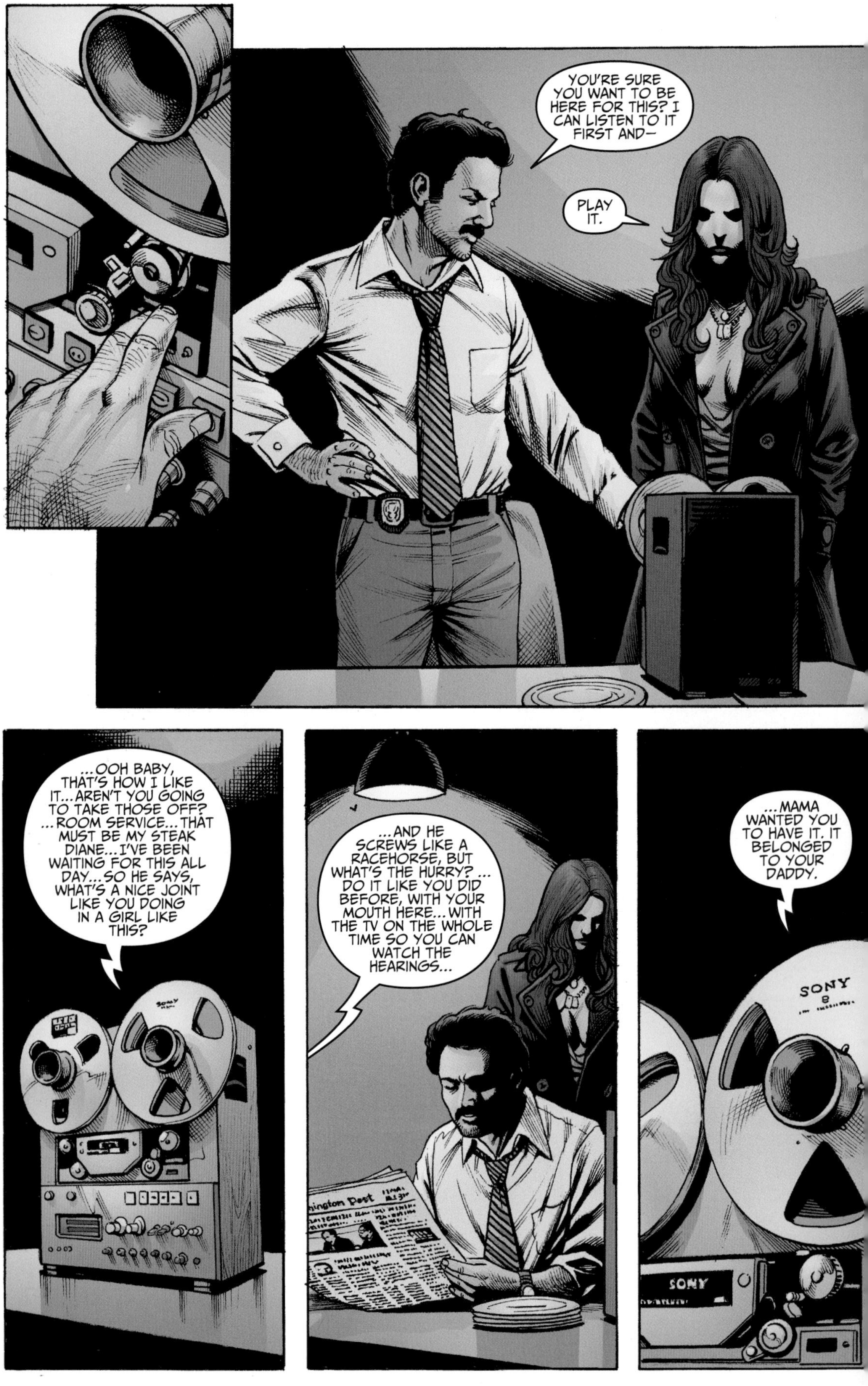

YOU'RE SURE YOU WANT TO BE HERE FOR THIS? I CAN LISTEN TO IT FIRST AND—
PLAY IT.
...OOH BABY, THAT'S HOW I LIKE IT...AREN'T YOU GOING TO TAKE THOSE OFF? ...ROOM SERVICE... THAT MUST BE MY STEAK DIANE...I'VE BEEN WAITING FOR THIS ALL DAY...SO HE SAYS, WHAT'S A NICE JOINT LIKE YOU DOING IN A GIRL LIKE THIS?
...AND HE SCREWS LIKE A RACEHORSE, BUT WHAT'S THE HURRY? ... DO IT LIKE YOU DID BEFORE, WITH YOUR MOUTH HERE...WITH THE TV ON THE WHOLE TIME SO YOU CAN WATCH THE HEARINGS...
...MAMA WANTED YOU TO HAVE IT. IT BELONGED TO YOUR DADDY.
SONY
SONY

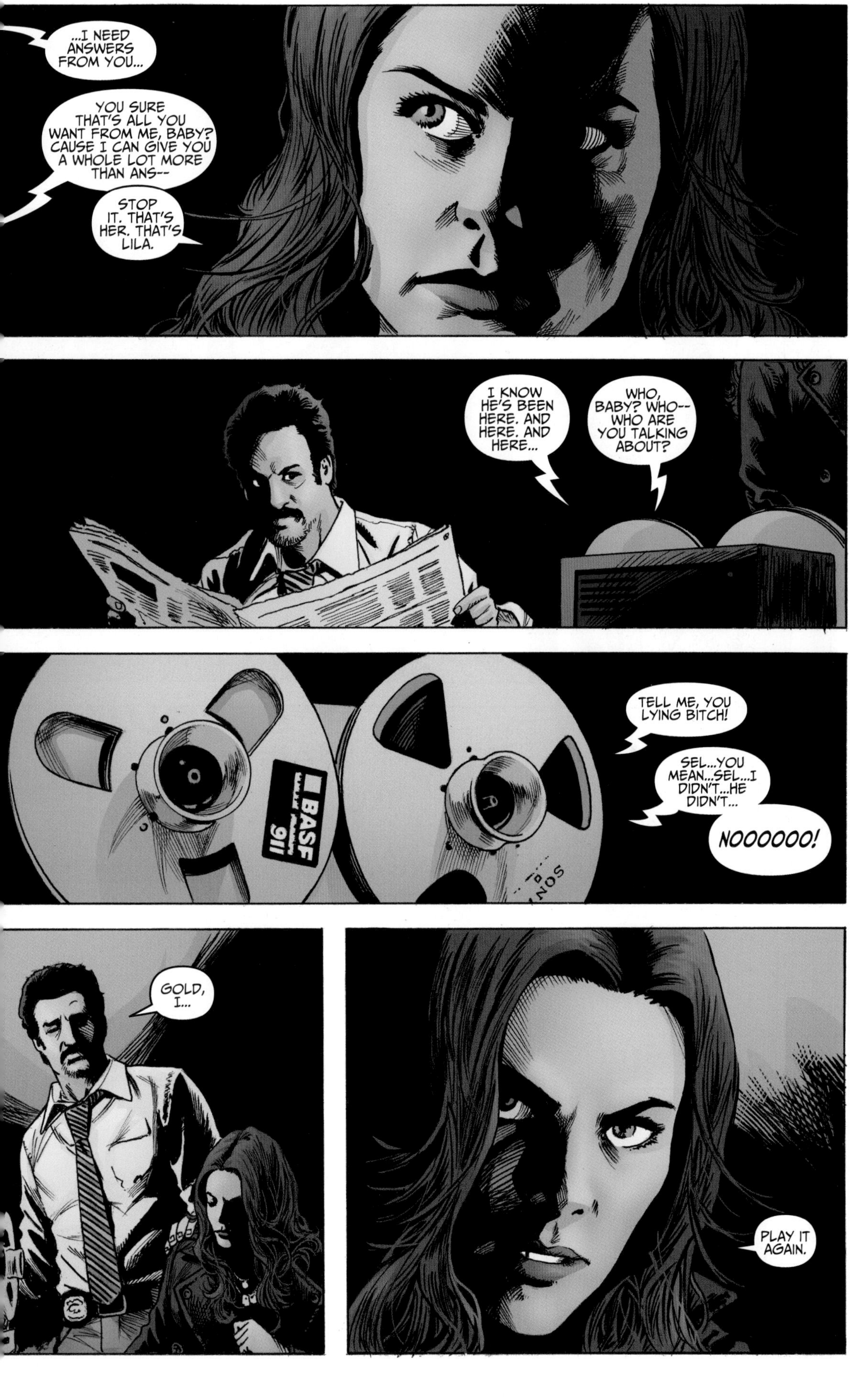
...I NEED ANSWERS FROM YOU...
YOU SURE THAT'S ALL YOU WANT FROM ME, BABY? CAUSE I CAN GIVE YOU A WHOLE LOT MORE THAN ANS--
STOP IT. THAT'S HER. THAT'S LILA.
I KNOW HE'S BEEN HERE. AND HERE. AND HERE...
WHO, BABY? WHO-- WHO ARE YOU TALKING ABOUT?
BASF
TELL ME, YOU LYING BITCH!
SEL...YOU MEAN...SEL...I DIDN'T...HE DIDN'T...
NOOOOOO!
GOLD, I...
PLAY IT AGAIN.

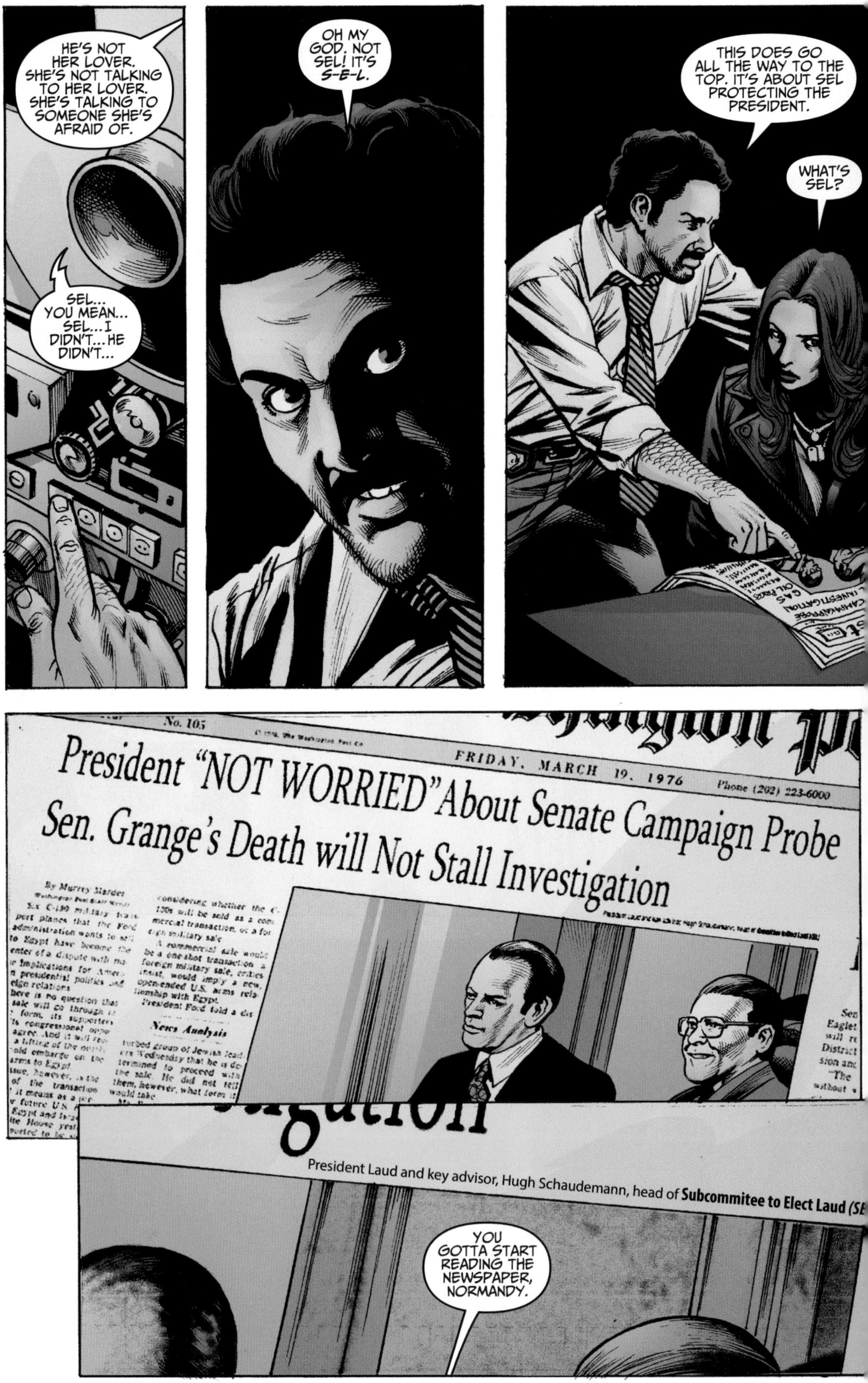
HE'S NOT HER LOVER. SHE'S NOT TALKING TO HER LOVER. SHE'S TALKING TO SOMEONE SHE'S AFRAID OF.
SEL... YOU MEAN... SEL... I DIDN'T... HE DIDN'T...
OH MY GOD. NOT SEL! IT'S S-E-L.
THIS DOES GO ALL THE WAY TO THE TOP. IT'S ABOUT SEL PROTECTING THE PRESIDENT.
WHAT'S SEL?
No. 105
FRIDAY, MARCH 19, 1976
Phone (202) 223-6000
President "NOT WORRIED" About Senate Campaign Probe
Sen. Grange's Death will Not Stall Investigation
News Analysis
President Laud and key advisor, Hugh Schaudemann, head of **Subcommitee to Elect Laud**
YOU GOTTA START READING THE NEWSPAPER, NORMANDY.

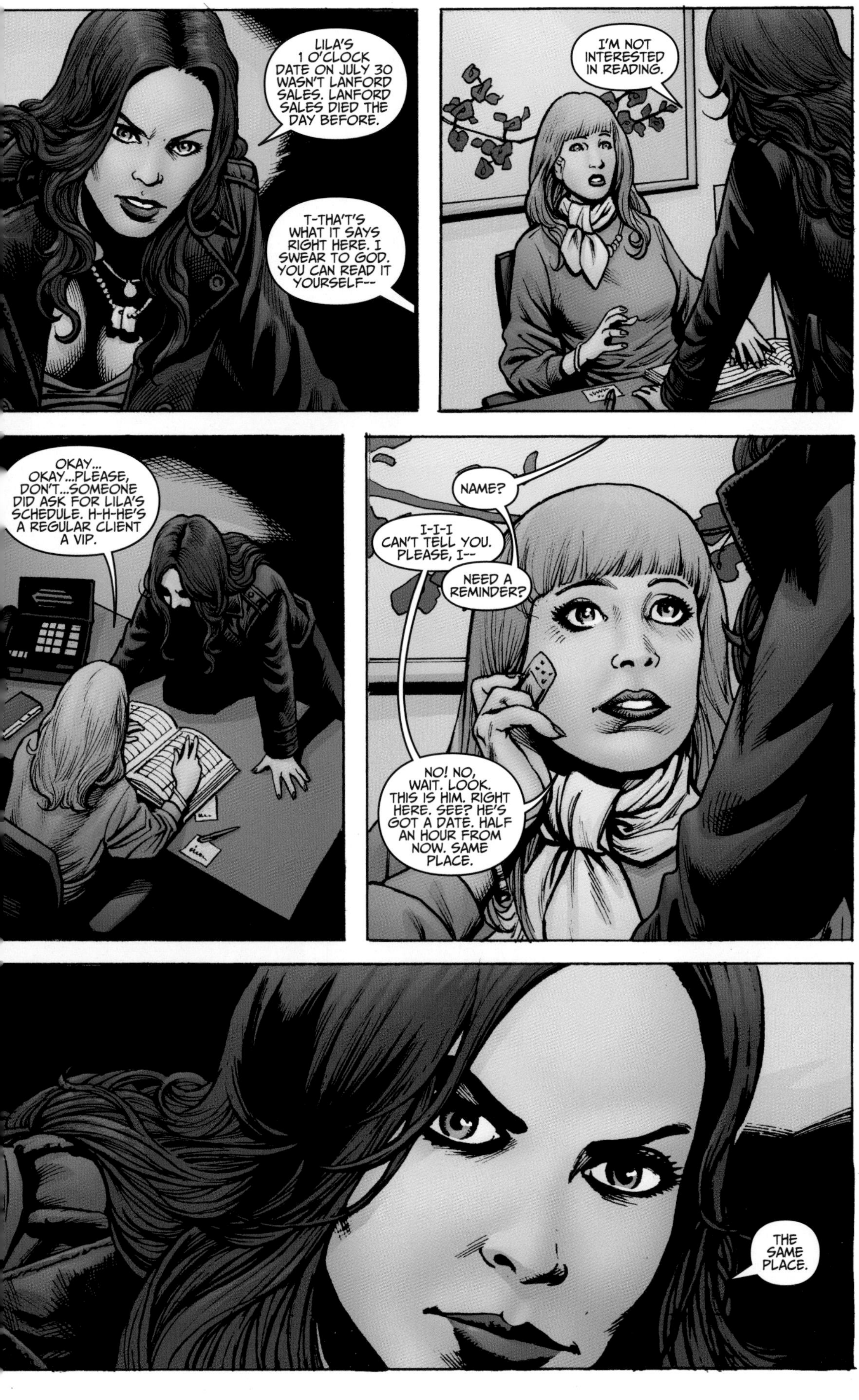
LILA'S 1 O'CLOCK DATE ON JULY 30 WASN'T LANFORD SALES. LANFORD SALES DIED THE DAY BEFORE.
T-THA'T'S WHAT IT SAYS RIGHT HERE. I SWEAR TO GOD. YOU CAN READ IT YOURSELF--
I'M NOT INTERESTED IN READING.
OKAY... OKAY...PLEASE, DON'T...SOMEONE DID ASK FOR LILA'S SCHEDULE. H-H-HE'S A REGULAR CLIENT A VIP.
NAME?
I-I-I CAN'T TELL YOU. PLEASE, I--
NEED A REMINDER?
NO! NO, WAIT. LOOK. THIS IS HIM. RIGHT HERE. SEE? HE'S GOT A DATE. HALF AN HOUR FROM NOW. SAME PLACE.
THE SAME PLACE.

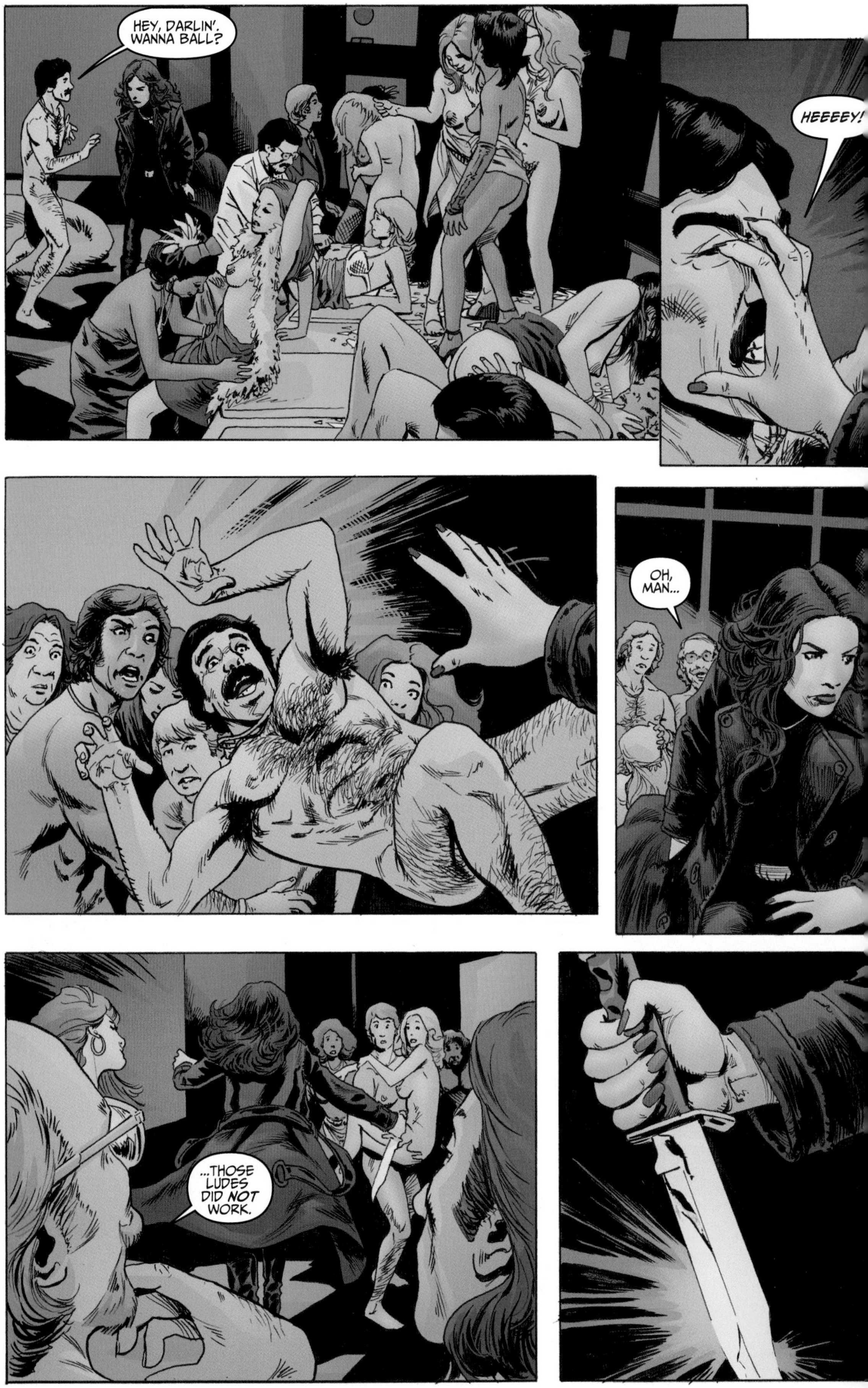
HEY, DARLIN'. WANNA BALL?
HEEEEY!
OH, MAN...
...THOSE LUDES DID NOT WORK.

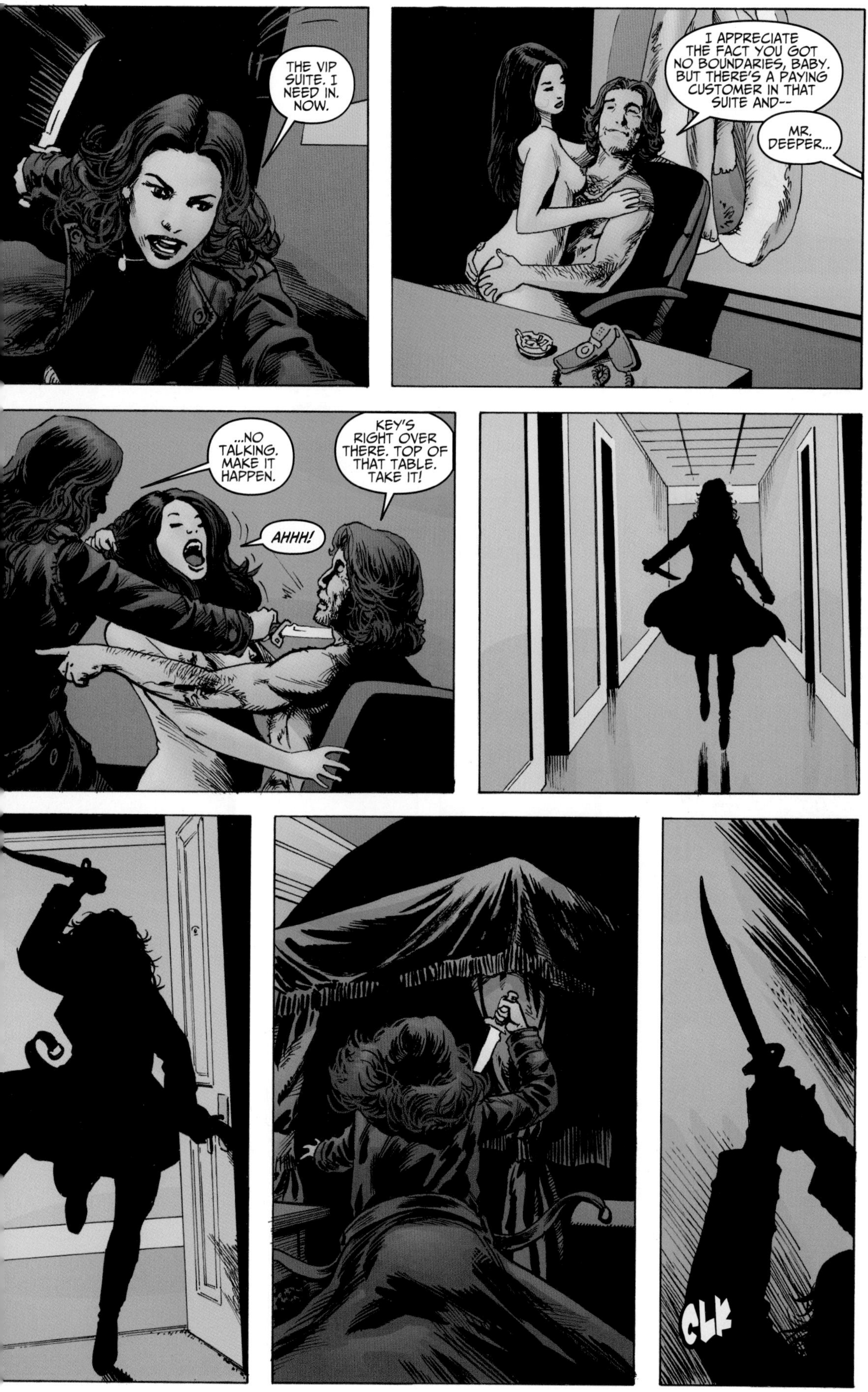
THE VIP SUITE. I NEED IN. NOW.
I APPRECIATE THE FACT YOU GOT NO BOUNDARIES, BABY. BUT THERE'S A PAYING CUSTOMER IN THAT SUITE AND--
MR. DEEPER...
...NO TALKING. MAKE IT HAPPEN.
KEY'S RIGHT OVER THERE. TOP OF THAT TABLE. TAKE IT!
AHHH!
CLK

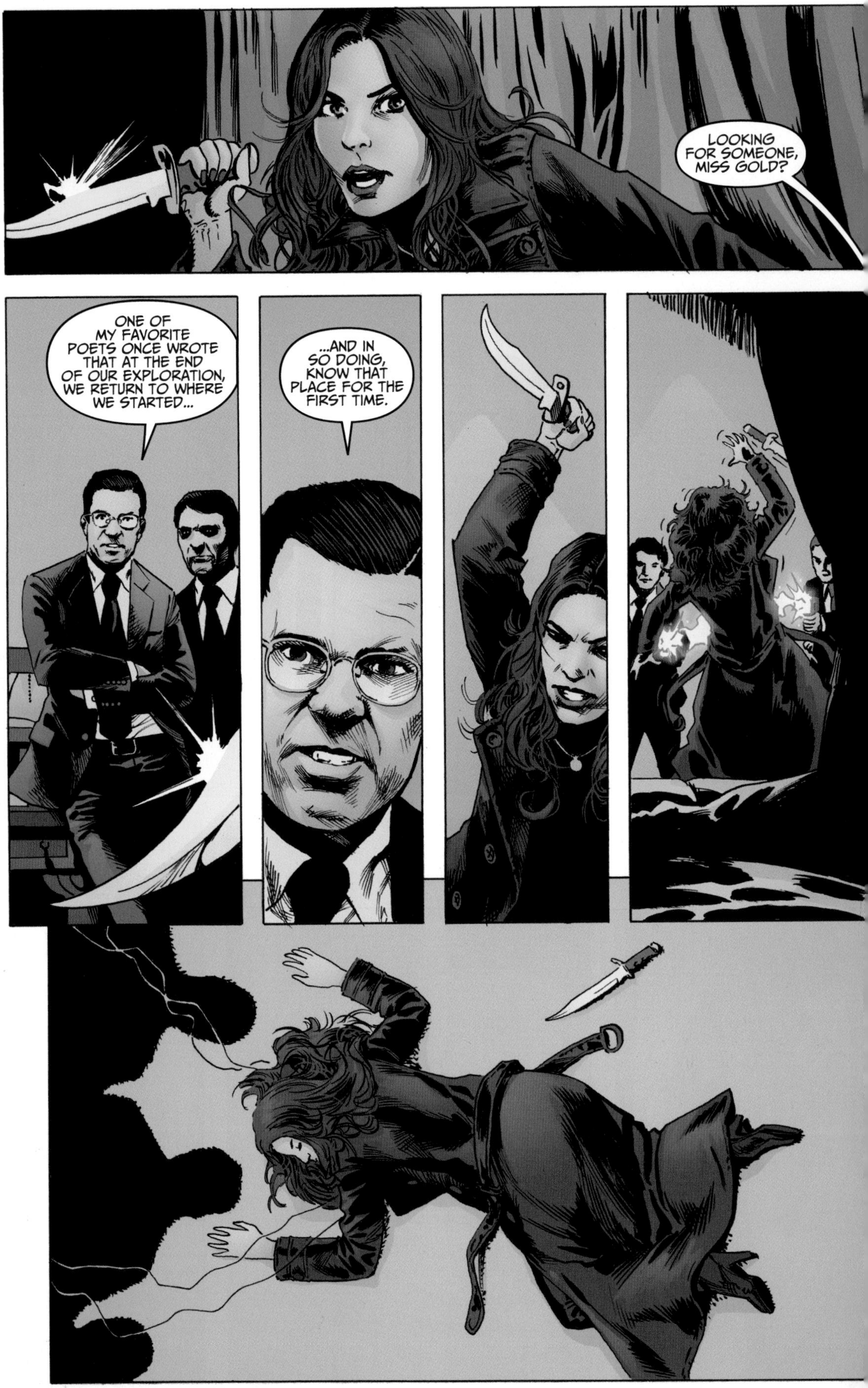
LOOKING FOR SOMEONE, MISS GOLD?
ONE OF MY FAVORITE POETS ONCE WROTE THAT AT THE END OF OUR EXPLORATION, WE RETURN TO WHERE WE STARTED...
...AND IN SO DOING, KNOW THAT PLACE FOR THE FIRST TIME.

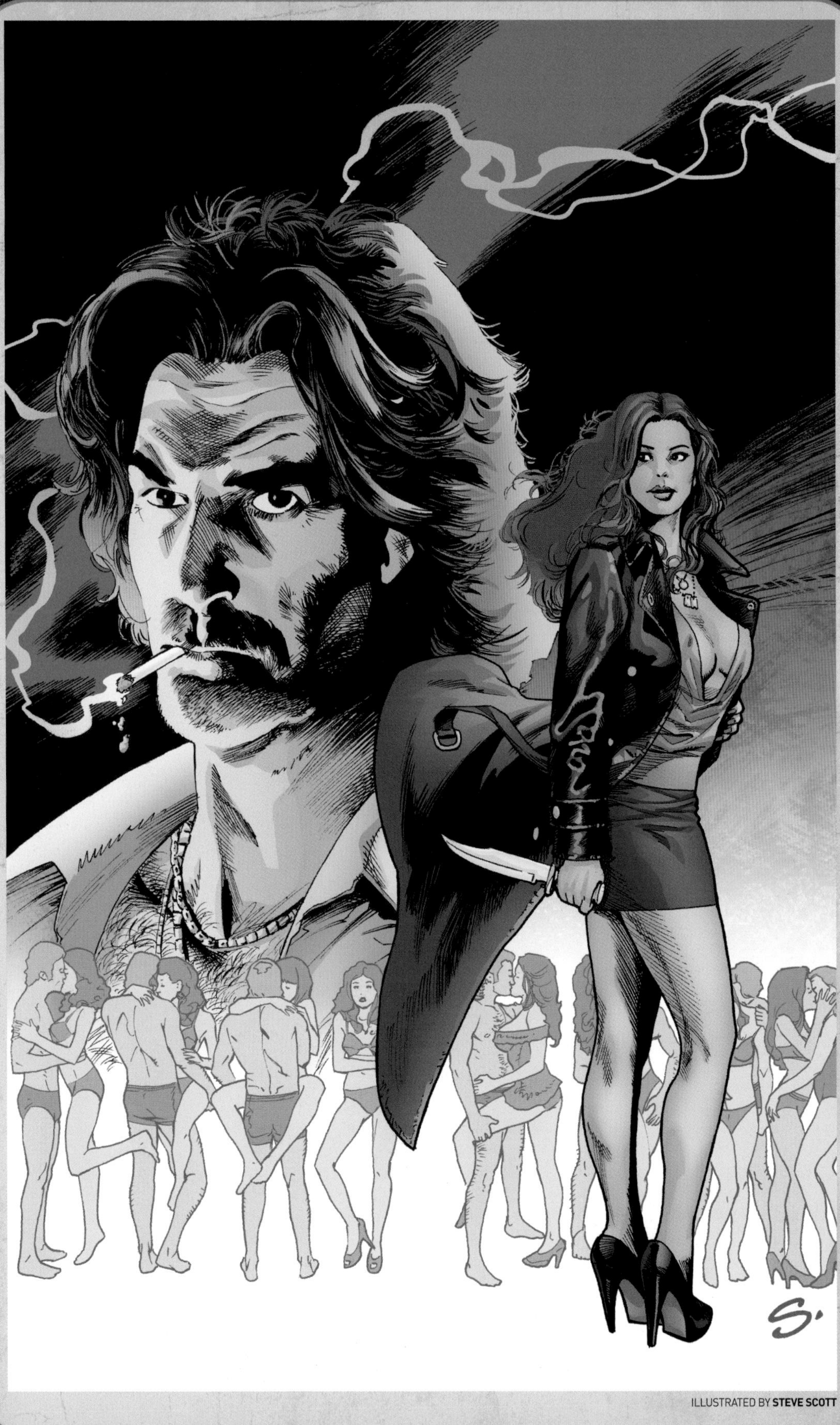

ILLUSTRATED BY **STEVE SCOTT**

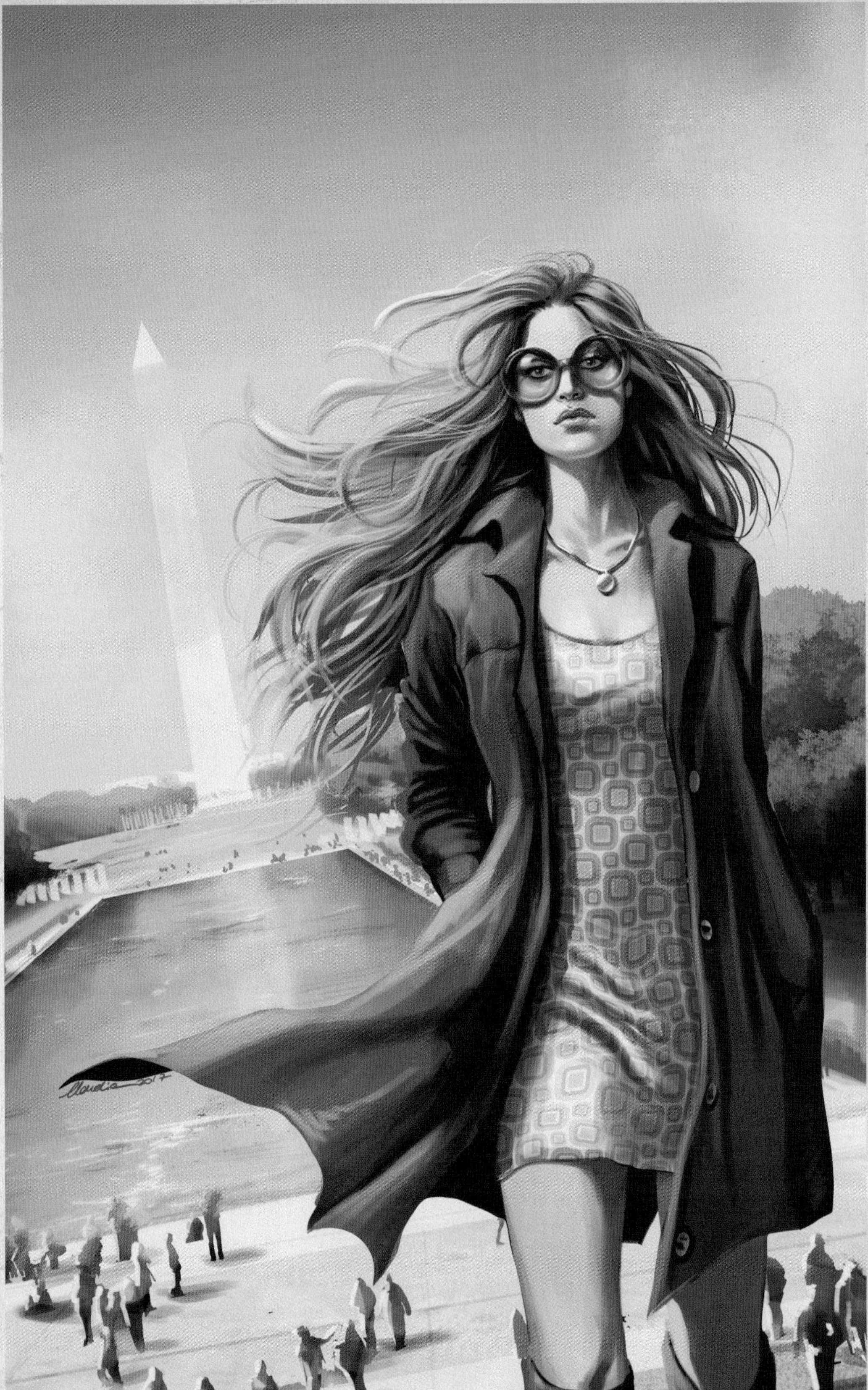
Claudia 2017

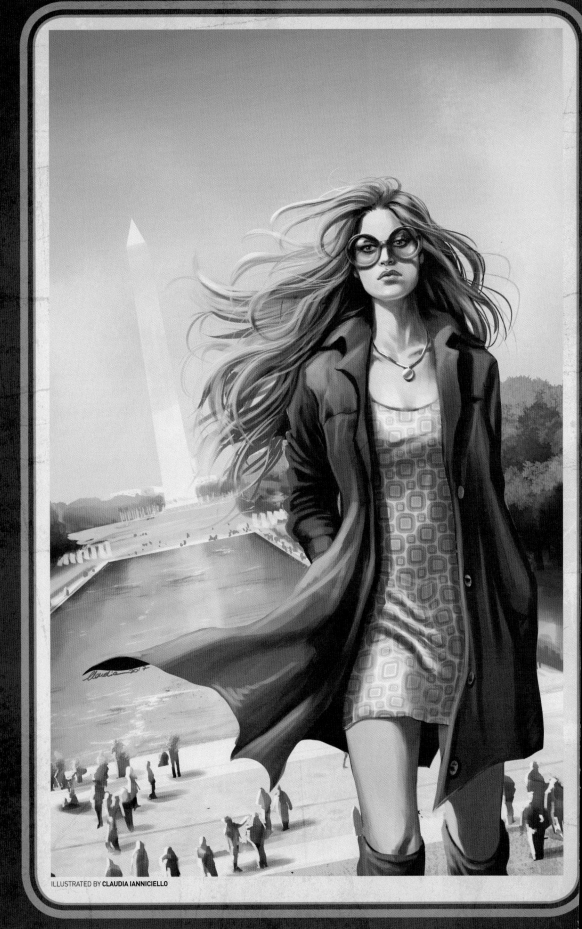

ILLUSTRATED BY **CLAUDIA IANNICIELLO**

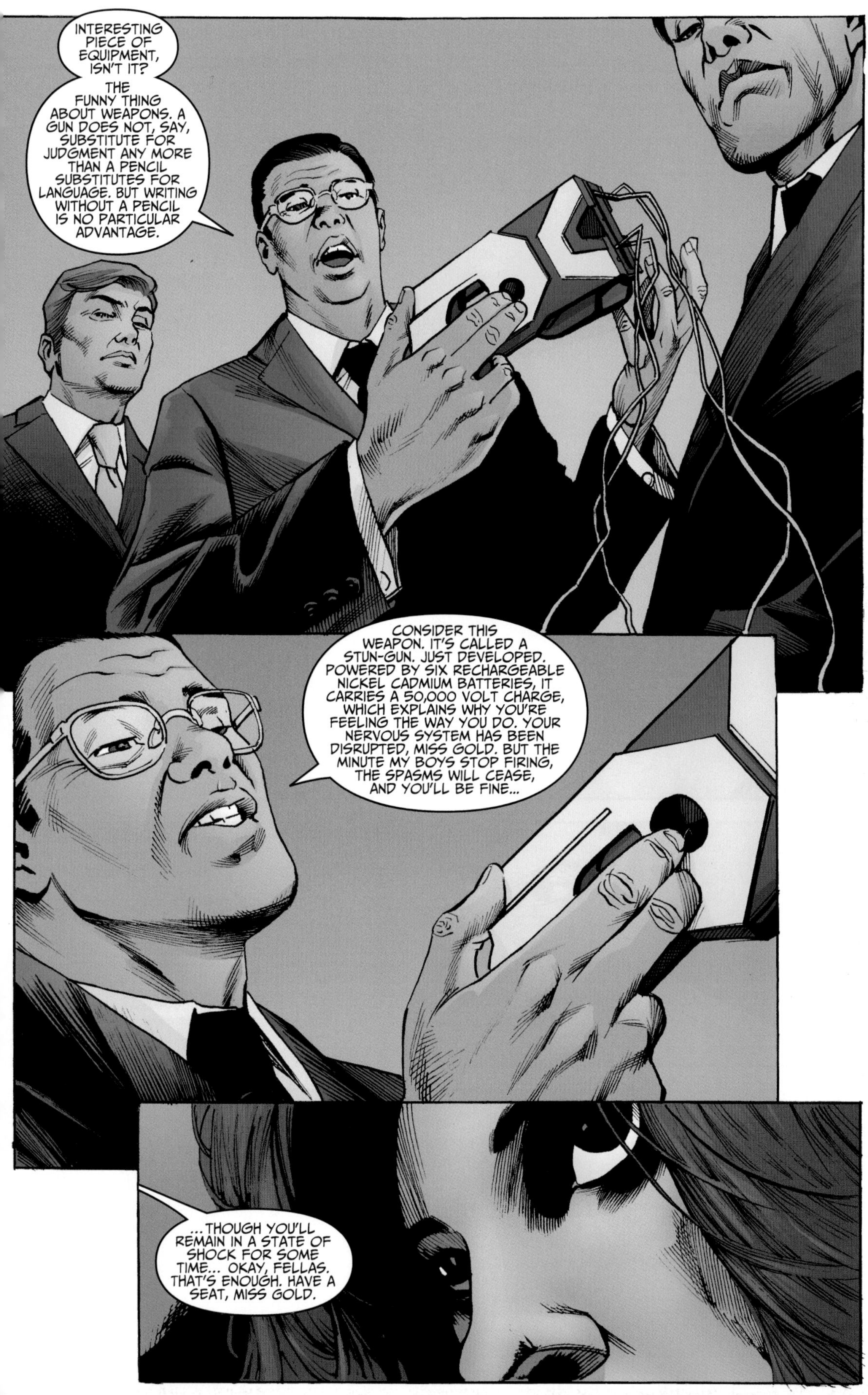
INTERESTING PIECE OF EQUIPMENT, ISN'T IT?
THE FUNNY THING ABOUT WEAPONS. A GUN DOES NOT, SAY, SUBSTITUTE FOR JUDGMENT ANY MORE THAN A PENCIL SUBSTITUTES FOR LANGUAGE. BUT WRITING WITHOUT A PENCIL IS NO PARTICULAR ADVANTAGE.
CONSIDER THIS WEAPON. IT'S CALLED A STUN-GUN. JUST DEVELOPED. POWERED BY SIX RECHARGEABLE NICKEL CADMIUM BATTERIES, IT CARRIES A 50,000 VOLT CHARGE, WHICH EXPLAINS WHY YOU'RE FEELING THE WAY YOU DO. YOUR NERVOUS SYSTEM HAS BEEN DISRUPTED, MISS GOLD. BUT THE MINUTE MY BOYS STOP FIRING, THE SPASMS WILL CEASE, AND YOU'LL BE FINE...
...THOUGH YOU'LL REMAIN IN A STATE OF SHOCK FOR SOME TIME... OKAY, FELLAS. THAT'S ENOUGH. HAVE A SEAT, MISS GOLD.

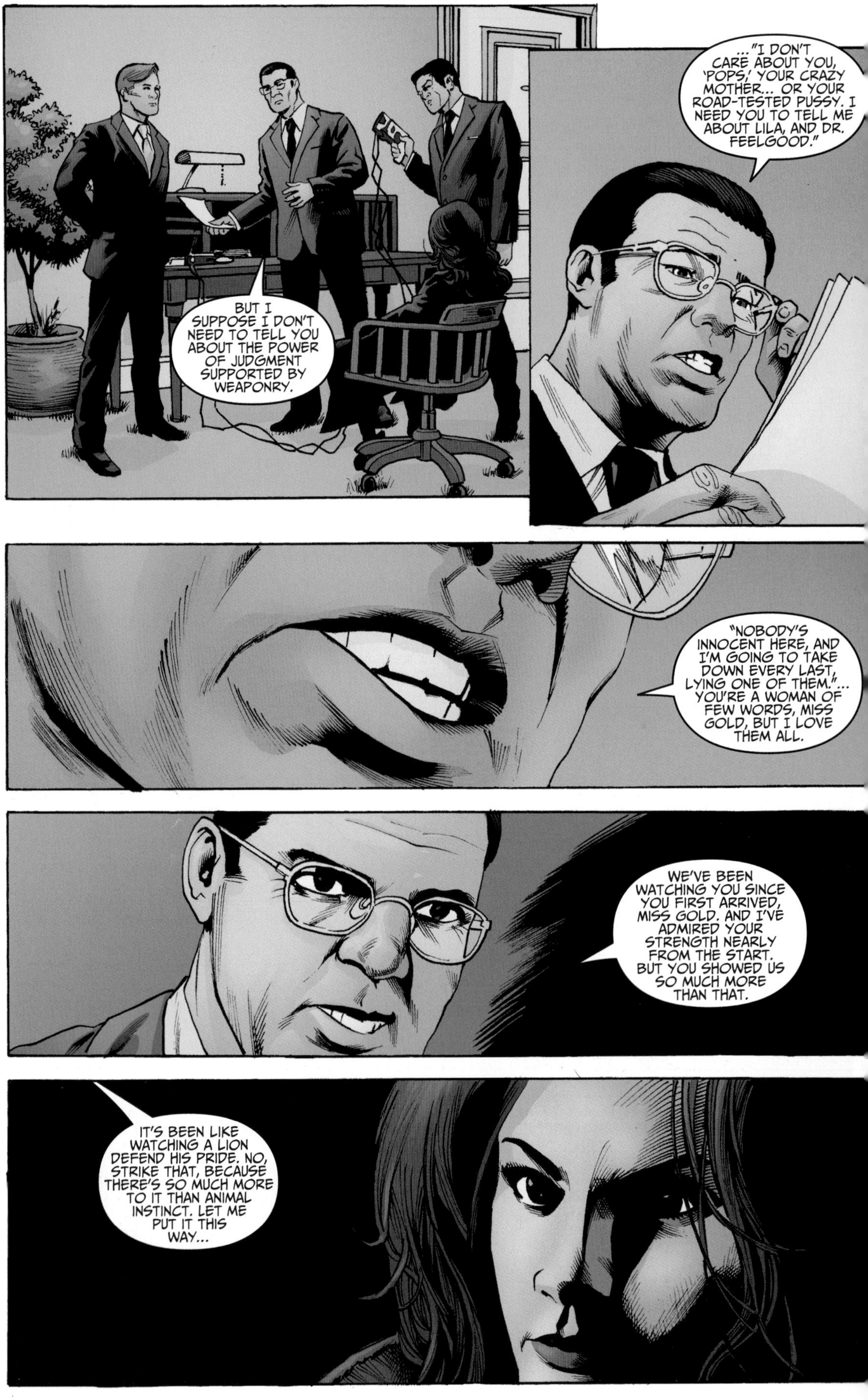
BUT I SUPPOSE I DON'T NEED TO TELL YOU ABOUT THE POWER OF JUDGMENT SUPPORTED BY WEAPONRY.
..."I DON'T CARE ABOUT YOU, 'POPS,' YOUR CRAZY MOTHER... OR YOUR ROAD-TESTED PUSSY. I NEED YOU TO TELL ME ABOUT LILA, AND DR. FEELGOOD."
"NOBODY'S INNOCENT HERE, AND I'M GOING TO TAKE DOWN EVERY LAST, LYING ONE OF THEM."... YOU'RE A WOMAN OF FEW WORDS, MISS GOLD, BUT I LOVE THEM ALL.
WE'VE BEEN WATCHING YOU SINCE YOU FIRST ARRIVED, MISS GOLD. AND I'VE ADMIRED YOUR STRENGTH NEARLY FROM THE START. BUT YOU SHOWED US SO MUCH MORE THAN THAT.
IT'S BEEN LIKE WATCHING A LION DEFEND HIS PRIDE. NO, STRIKE THAT, BECAUSE THERE'S SO MUCH MORE TO IT THAN ANIMAL INSTINCT. LET ME PUT IT THIS WAY...

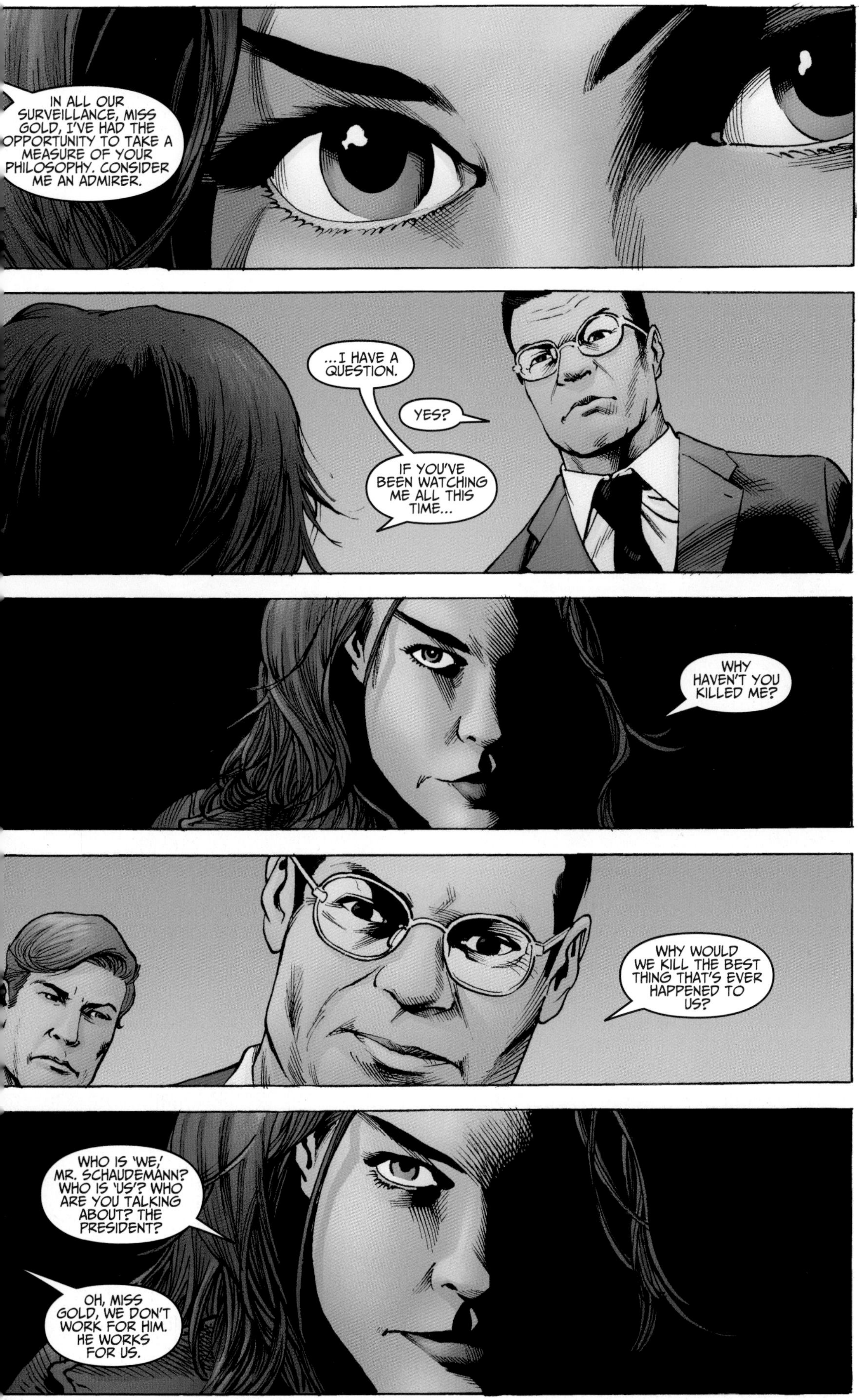
IN ALL OUR SURVEILLANCE, MISS GOLD, I'VE HAD THE OPPORTUNITY TO TAKE A MEASURE OF YOUR PHILOSOPHY. CONSIDER ME AN ADMIRER.
...I HAVE A QUESTION.
YES?
IF YOU'VE BEEN WATCHING ME ALL THIS TIME...
WHY HAVEN'T YOU KILLED ME?
WHY WOULD WE KILL THE BEST THING THAT'S EVER HAPPENED TO US?
WHO IS 'WE,' MR. SCHAUDEMANN? WHO IS 'US'? WHO ARE YOU TALKING ABOUT? THE PRESIDENT?
OH, MISS GOLD, WE DON'T WORK FOR HIM. HE WORKS FOR US.

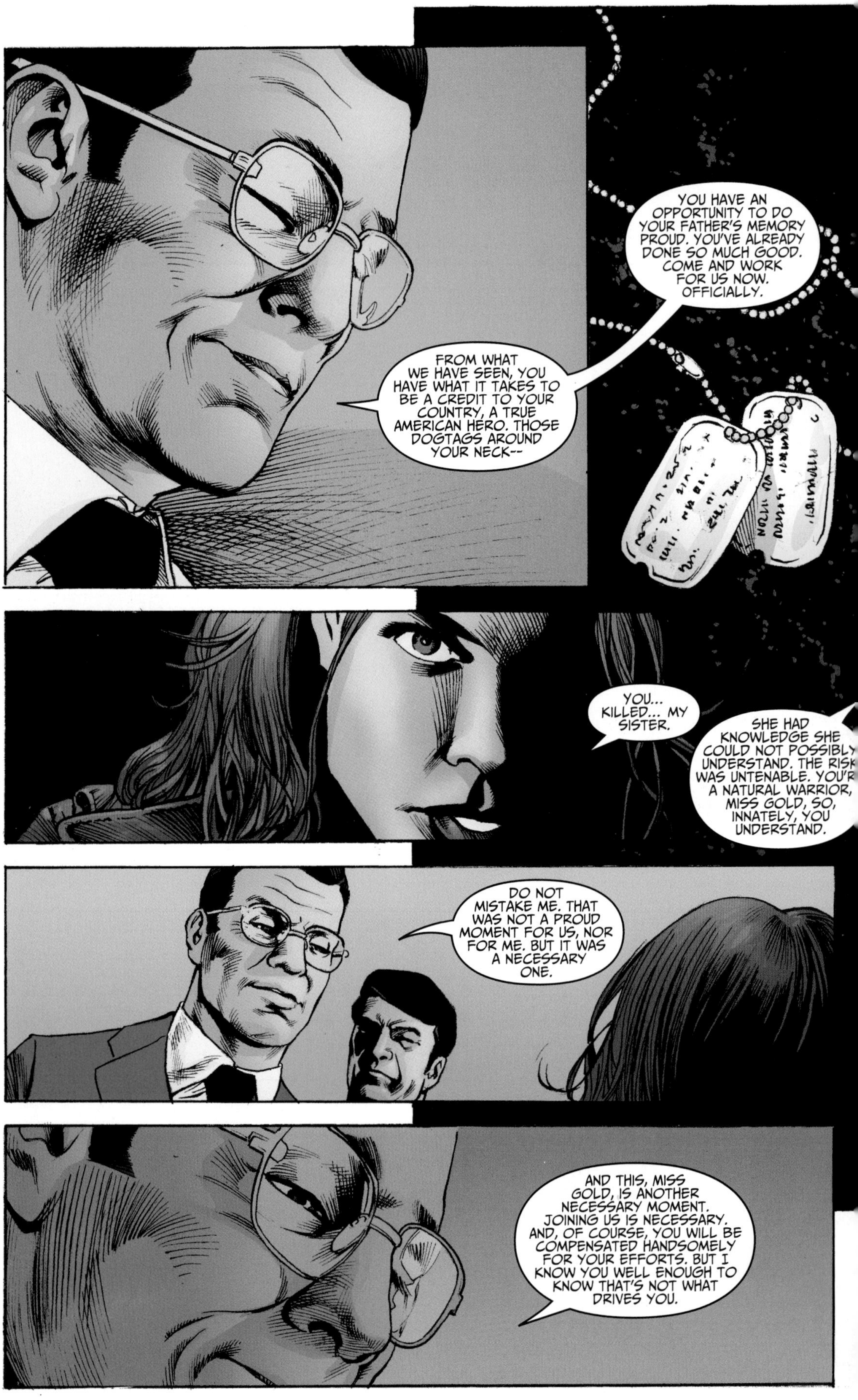
FROM WHAT WE HAVE SEEN, YOU HAVE WHAT IT TAKES TO BE A CREDIT TO YOUR COUNTRY, A TRUE AMERICAN HERO. THOSE DOGTAGS AROUND YOUR NECK--
YOU HAVE AN OPPORTUNITY TO DO YOUR FATHER'S MEMORY PROUD. YOU'VE ALREADY DONE SO MUCH GOOD. COME AND WORK FOR US NOW. OFFICIALLY.
YOU... KILLED... MY SISTER.
SHE HAD KNOWLEDGE SHE COULD NOT POSSIBLY UNDERSTAND. THE RISK WAS UNTENABLE. YOU'RE A NATURAL WARRIOR, MISS GOLD, SO, INNATELY, YOU UNDERSTAND.
DO NOT MISTAKE ME. THAT WAS NOT A PROUD MOMENT FOR US, NOR FOR ME. BUT IT WAS A NECESSARY ONE.
AND THIS, MISS GOLD, IS ANOTHER NECESSARY MOMENT. JOINING US IS NECESSARY. AND, OF COURSE, YOU WILL BE COMPENSATED HANDSOMELY FOR YOUR EFFORTS. BUT I KNOW YOU WELL ENOUGH TO KNOW THAT'S NOT WHAT DRIVES YOU.

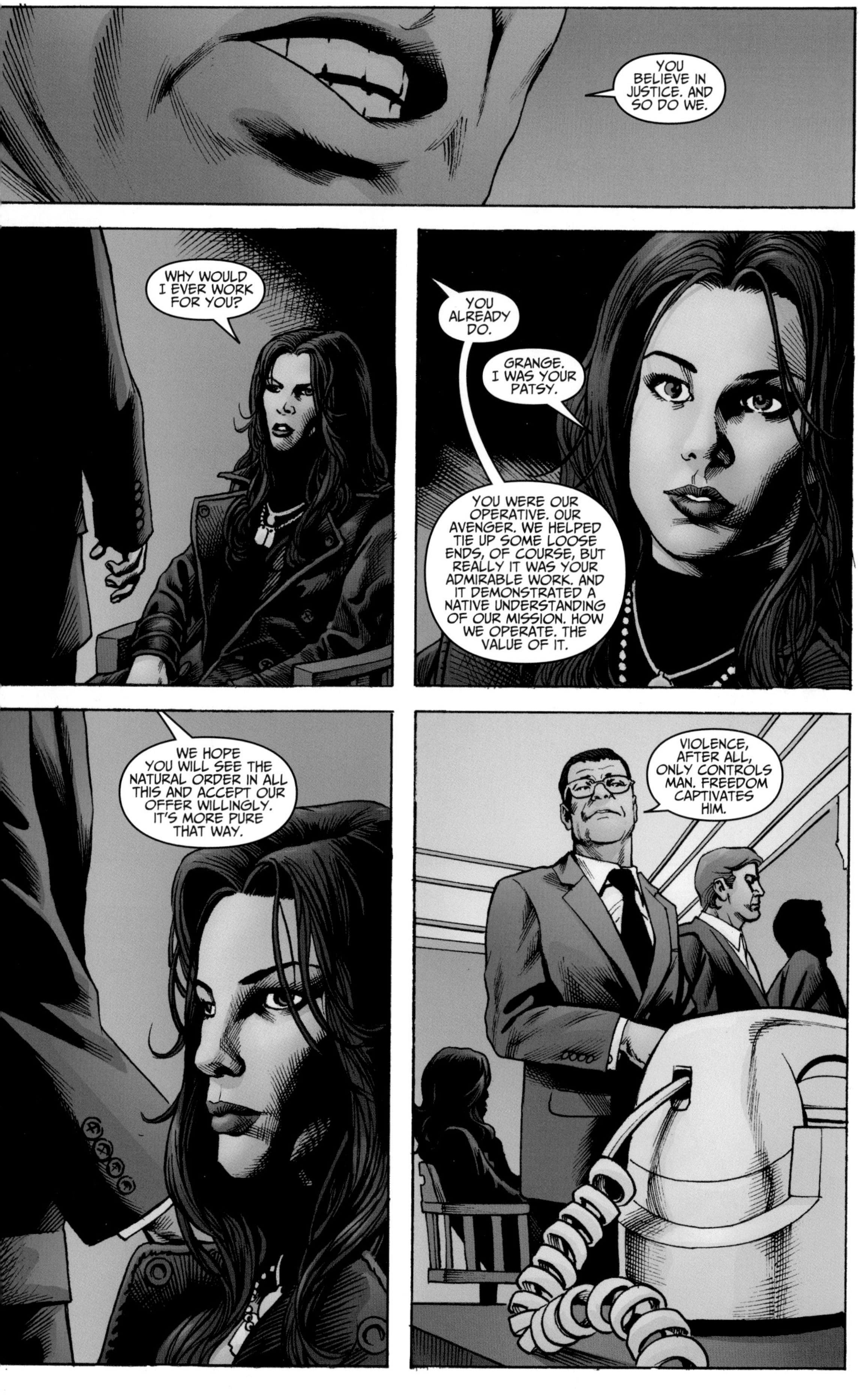
YOU BELIEVE IN JUSTICE. AND SO DO WE.
WHY WOULD I EVER WORK FOR YOU?
YOU ALREADY DO.
GRANGE. I WAS YOUR PATSY.
YOU WERE OUR OPERATIVE. OUR AVENGER. WE HELPED TIE UP SOME LOOSE ENDS, OF COURSE, BUT REALLY IT WAS YOUR ADMIRABLE WORK. AND IT DEMONSTRATED A NATIVE UNDERSTANDING OF OUR MISSION. HOW WE OPERATE. THE VALUE OF IT.
WE HOPE YOU WILL SEE THE NATURAL ORDER IN ALL THIS AND ACCEPT OUR OFFER WILLINGLY. IT'S MORE PURE THAT WAY.
VIOLENCE, AFTER ALL, ONLY CONTROLS MAN. FREEDOM CAPTIVATES HIM.

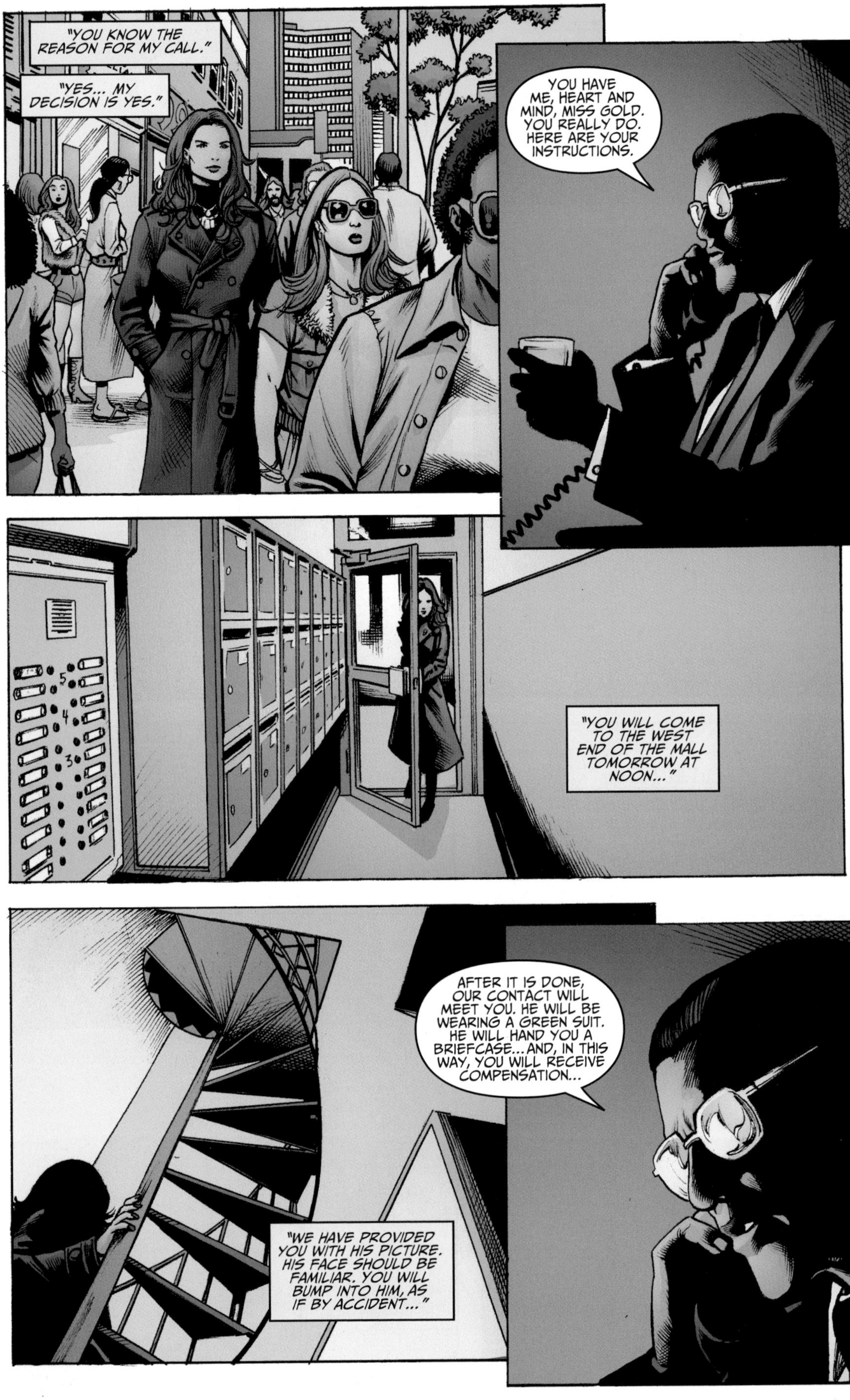
"YOU KNOW THE REASON FOR MY CALL."
"YES... MY DECISION IS YES."
YOU HAVE ME, HEART AND MIND, MISS GOLD. YOU REALLY DO. HERE ARE YOUR INSTRUCTIONS.
"YOU WILL COME TO THE WEST END OF THE MALL TOMORROW AT NOON..."
AFTER IT IS DONE, OUR CONTACT WILL MEET YOU. HE WILL BE WEARING A GREEN SUIT. HE WILL HAND YOU A BRIEFCASE...AND, IN THIS WAY, YOU WILL RECEIVE COMPENSATION...
"WE HAVE PROVIDED YOU WITH HIS PICTURE. HIS FACE SHOULD BE FAMILIAR. YOU WILL BUMP INTO HIM, AS IF BY ACCIDENT..."

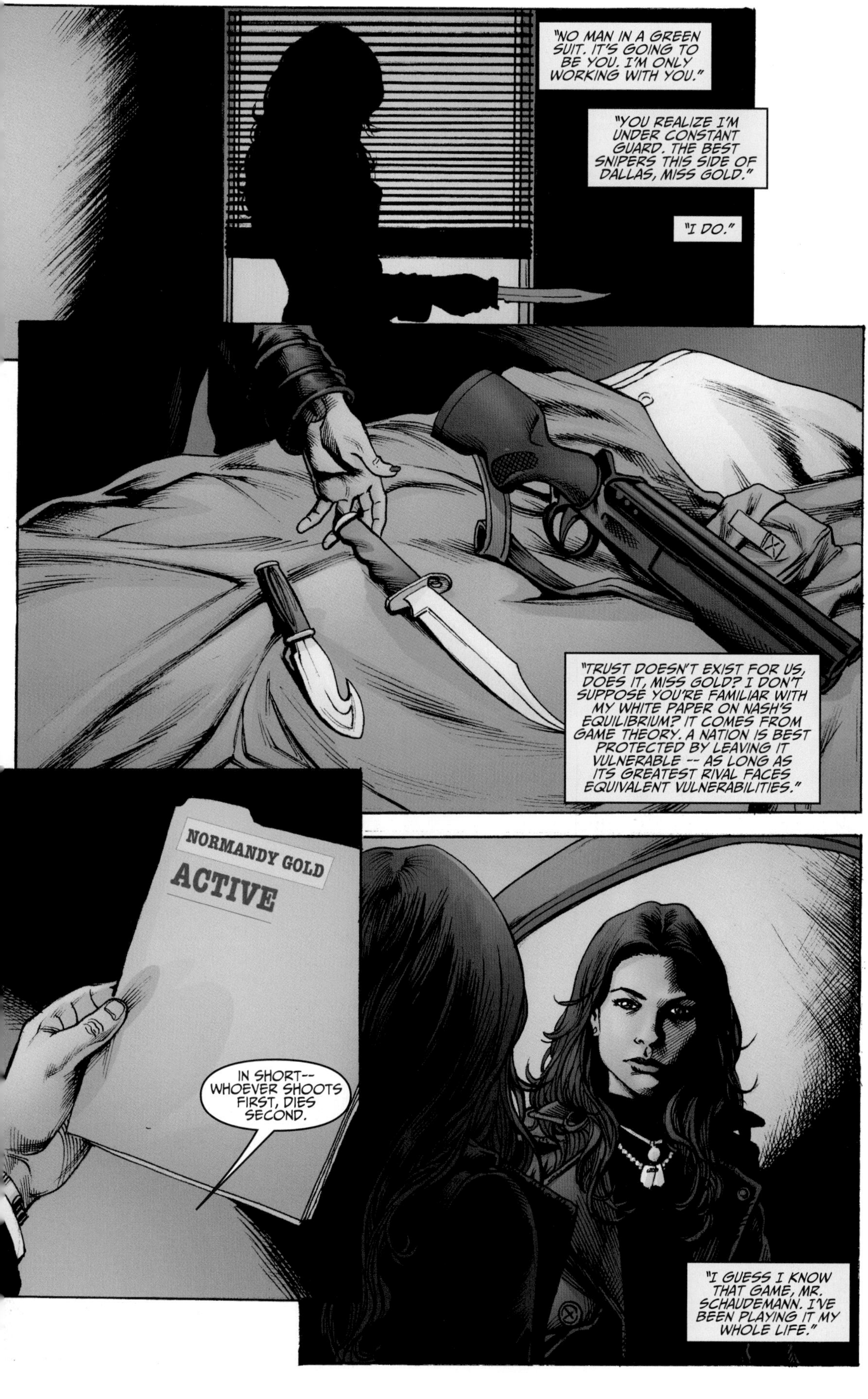
"NO MAN IN A GREEN SUIT. IT'S GOING TO BE YOU. I'M ONLY WORKING WITH YOU."
"YOU REALIZE I'M UNDER CONSTANT GUARD. THE BEST SNIPERS THIS SIDE OF DALLAS, MISS GOLD."
"I DO."
"TRUST DOESN'T EXIST FOR US, DOES IT, MISS GOLD? I DON'T SUPPOSE YOU'RE FAMILIAR WITH MY WHITE PAPER ON NASH'S EQUILIBRIUM? IT COMES FROM GAME THEORY. A NATION IS BEST PROTECTED BY LEAVING IT VULNERABLE -- AS LONG AS ITS GREATEST RIVAL FACES EQUIVALENT VULNERABILITIES."
NORMANDY GOLD
ACTIVE
IN SHORT-- WHOEVER SHOOTS FIRST, DIES SECOND.
"I GUESS I KNOW THAT GAME, MR. SCHAUDEMANN. I'VE BEEN PLAYING IT MY WHOLE LIFE."

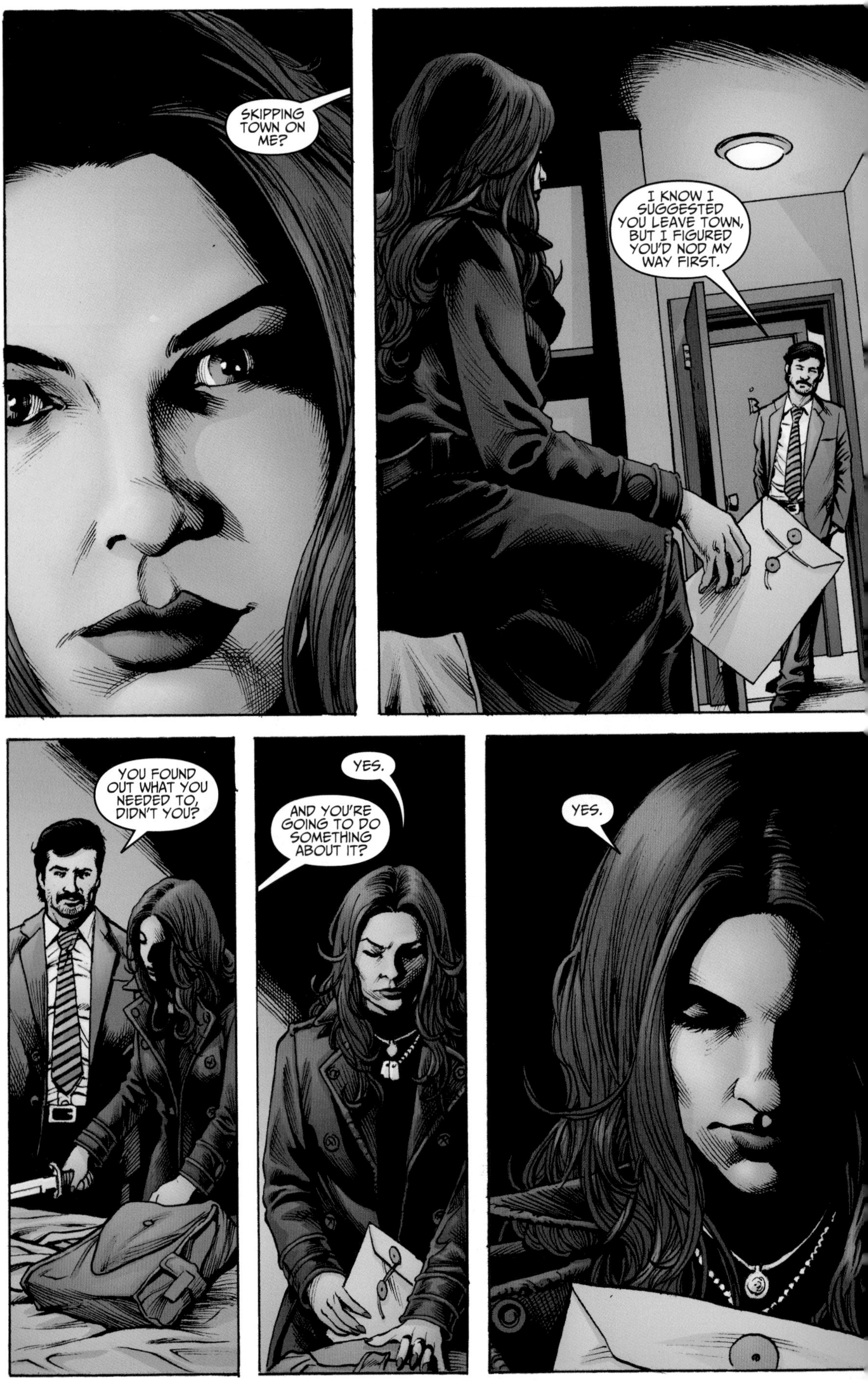
SKIPPING TOWN ON ME?
I KNOW I SUGGESTED YOU LEAVE TOWN, BUT I FIGURED YOU'D NOD MY WAY FIRST.
YOU FOUND OUT WHAT YOU NEEDED TO, DIDN'T YOU?
YES.
AND YOU'RE GOING TO DO SOMETHING ABOUT IT?
YES.

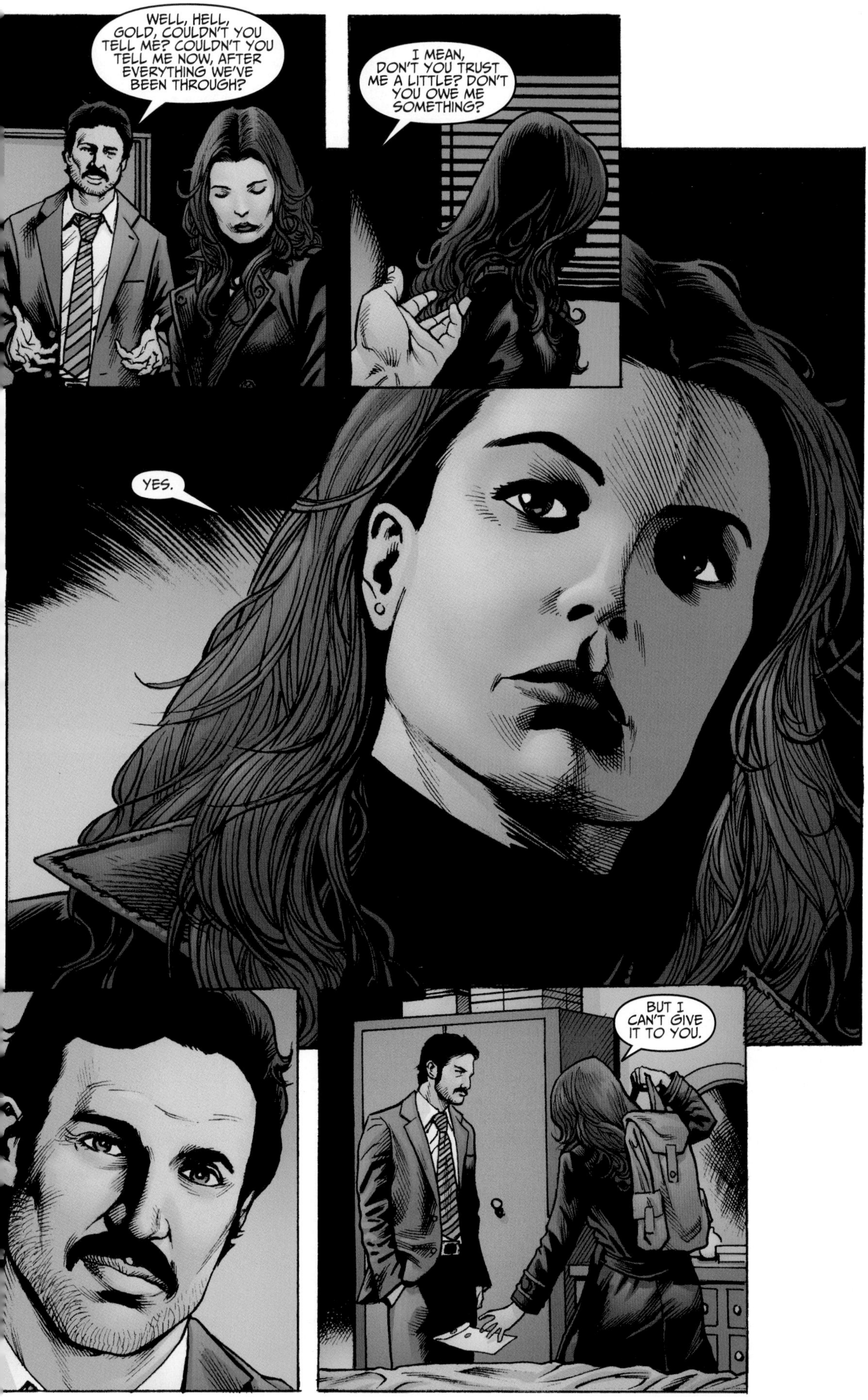
WELL, HELL, GOLD, COULDN'T YOU TELL ME? COULDN'T YOU TELL ME NOW, AFTER EVERYTHING WE'VE BEEN THROUGH?
I MEAN, DON'T YOU TRUST ME A LITTLE? DON'T YOU OWE ME SOMETHING?
YES.
BUT I CAN'T GIVE IT TO YOU.

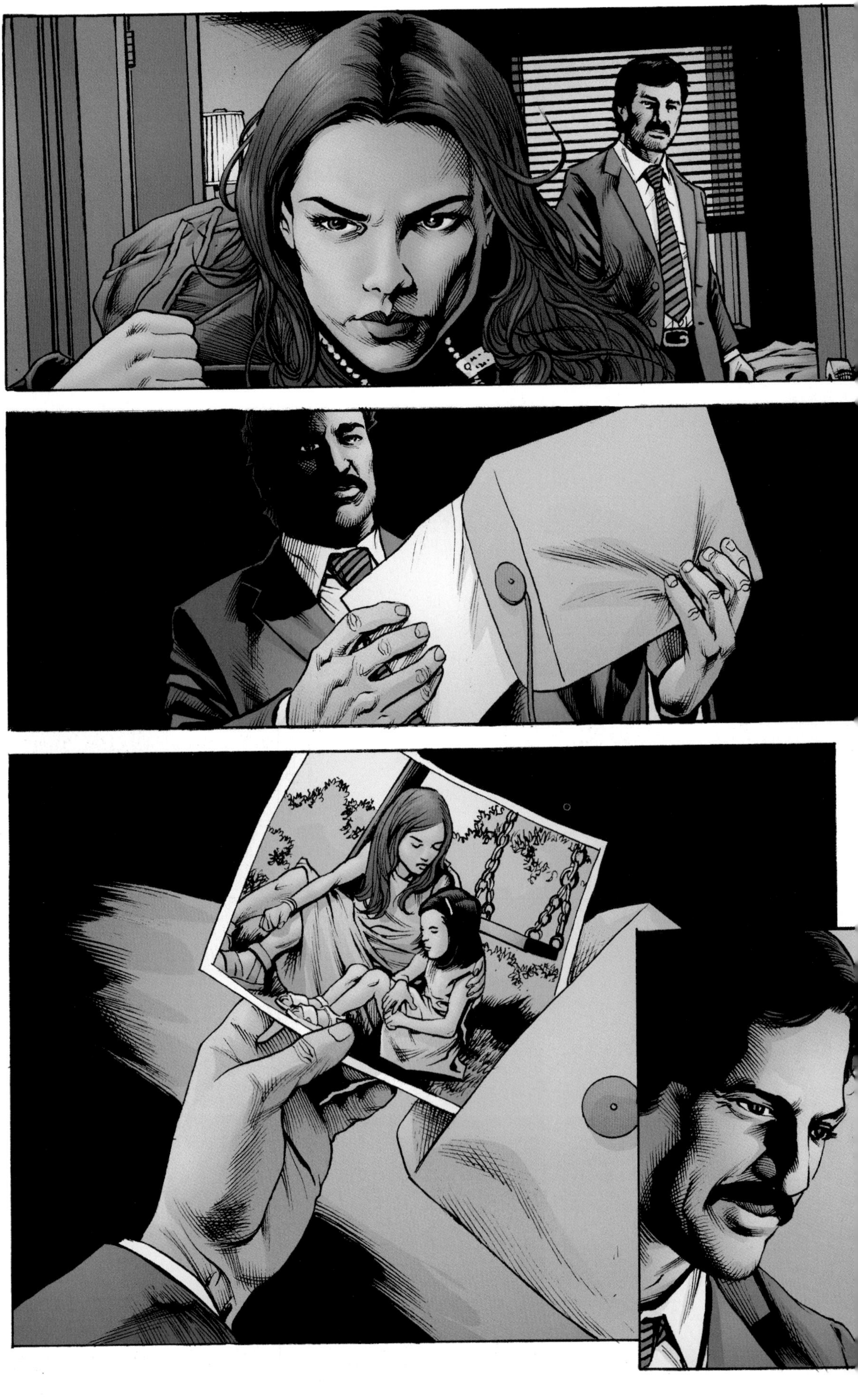

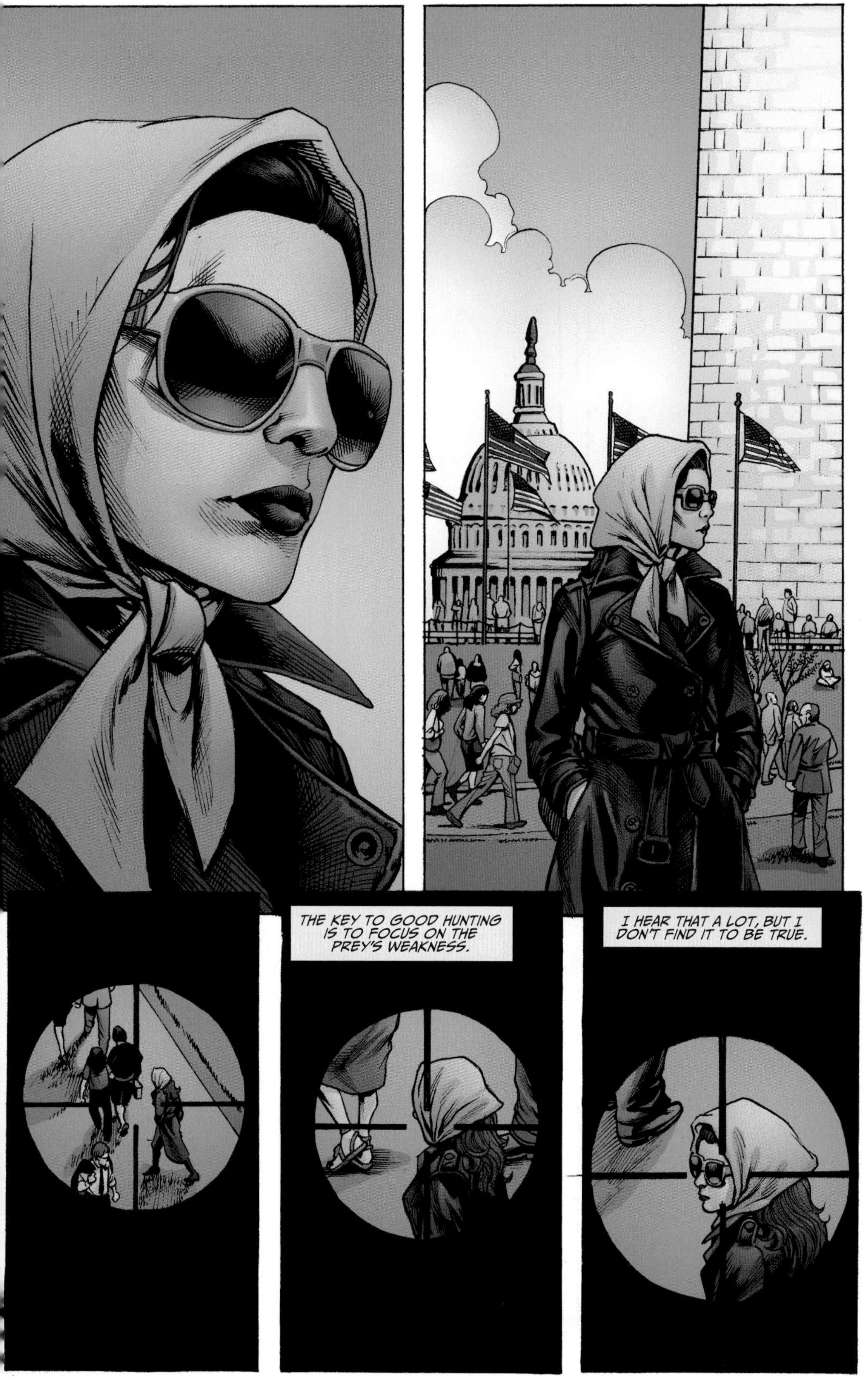
THE KEY TO GOOD HUNTING IS TO FOCUS ON THE PREY'S WEAKNESS.
I HEAR THAT A LOT, BUT I DON'T FIND IT TO BE TRUE.

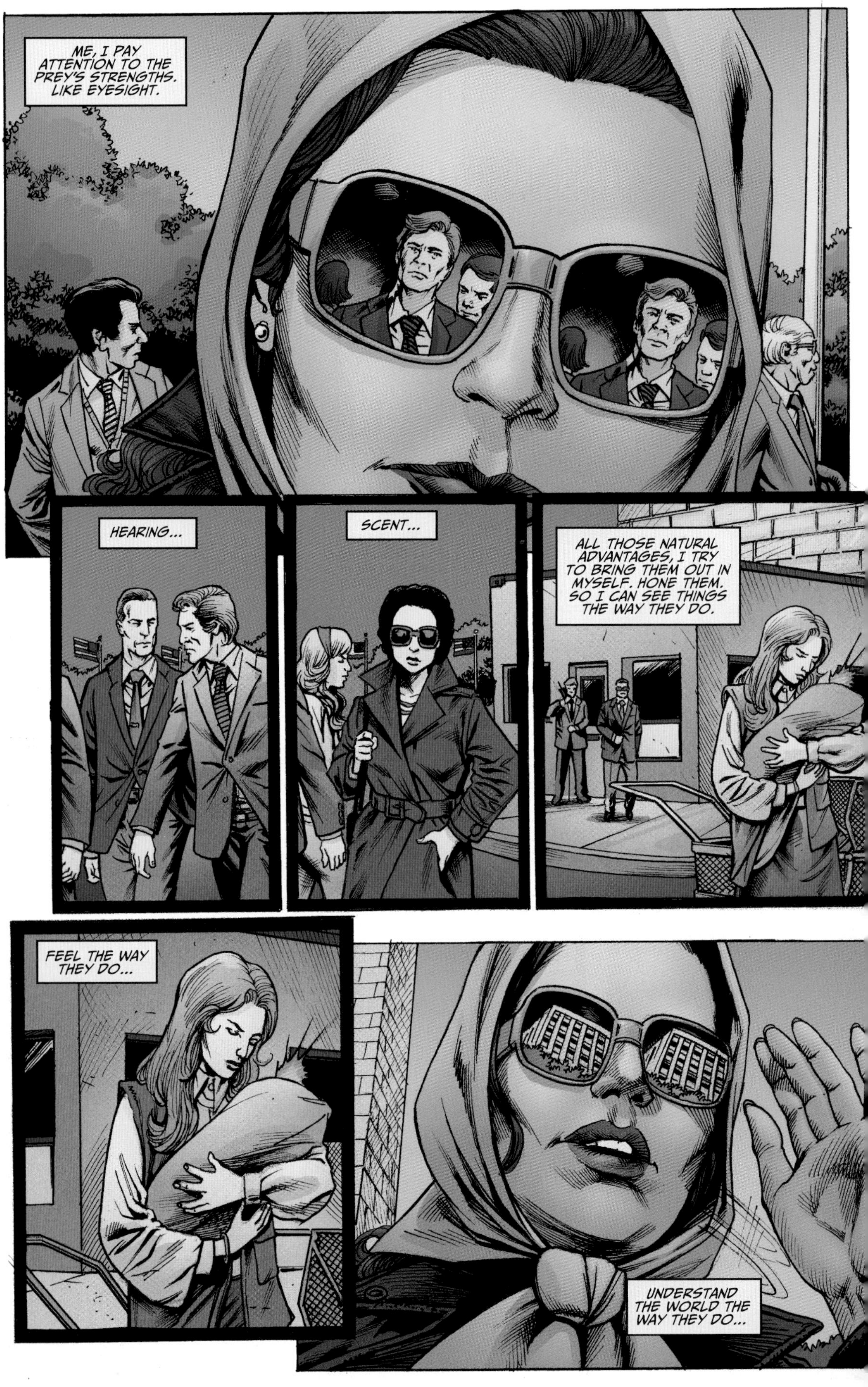
ME, I PAY ATTENTION TO THE PREY'S STRENGTHS. LIKE EYESIGHT.
HEARING...
SCENT...
ALL THOSE NATURAL ADVANTAGES, I TRY TO BRING THEM OUT IN MYSELF. HONE THEM. SO I CAN SEE THINGS THE WAY THEY DO.
FEEL THE WAY THEY DO...
UNDERSTAND THE WORLD THE WAY THEY DO...

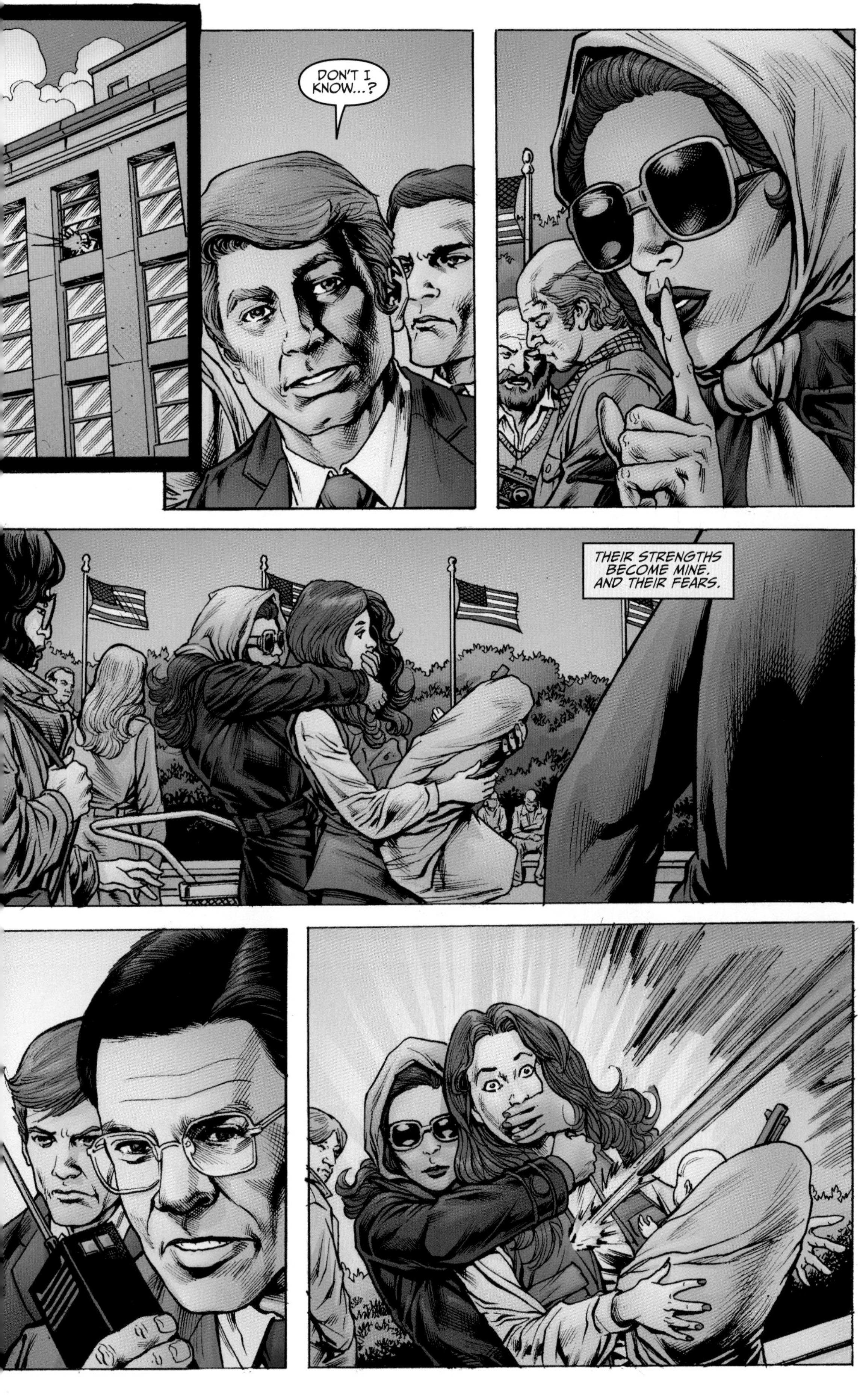
DON'T I KNOW...?
THEIR STRENGTHS BECOME MINE. AND THEIR FEARS.

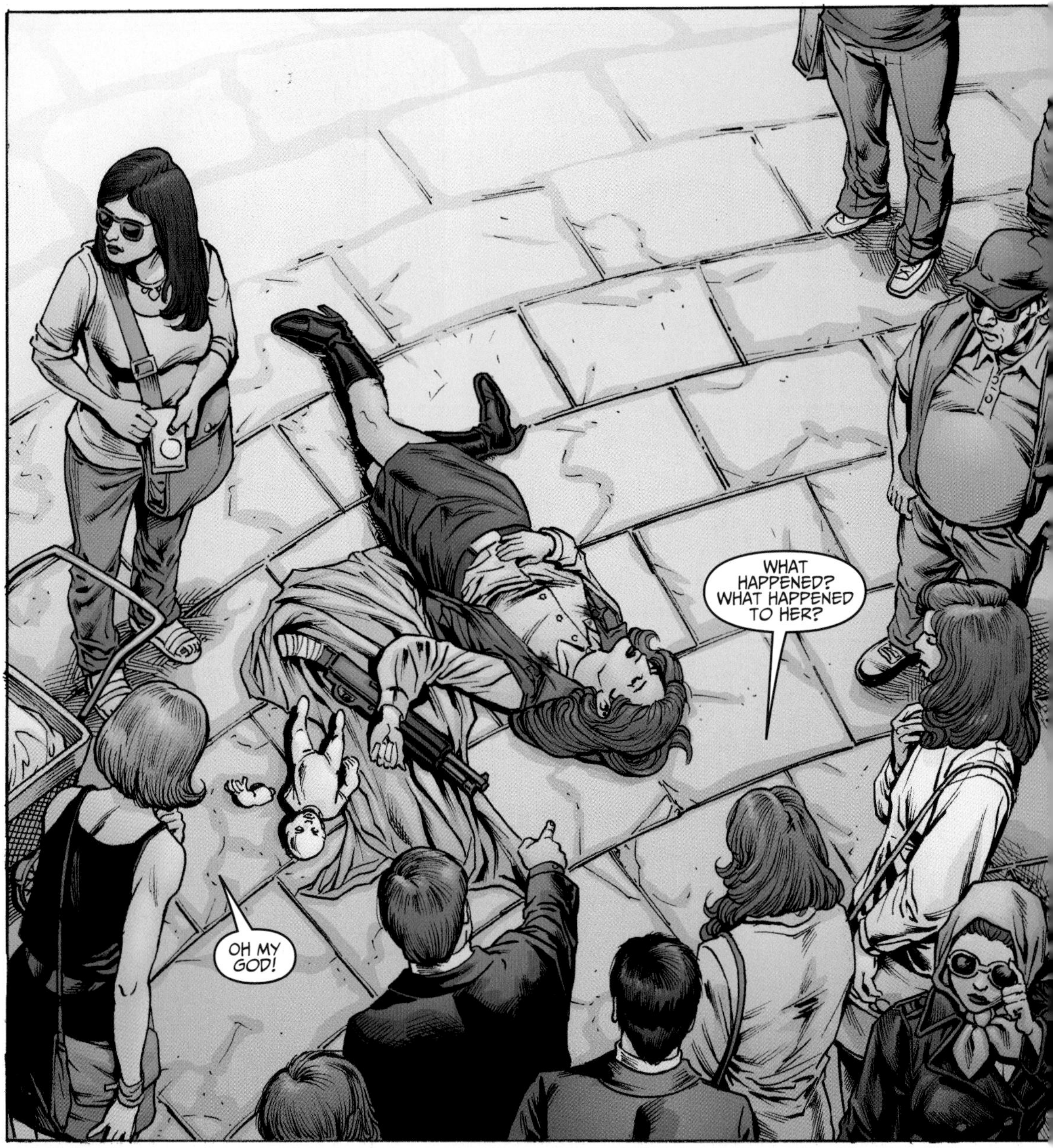
WHAT HAPPENED? WHAT HAPPENED TO HER?
OH MY GOD!

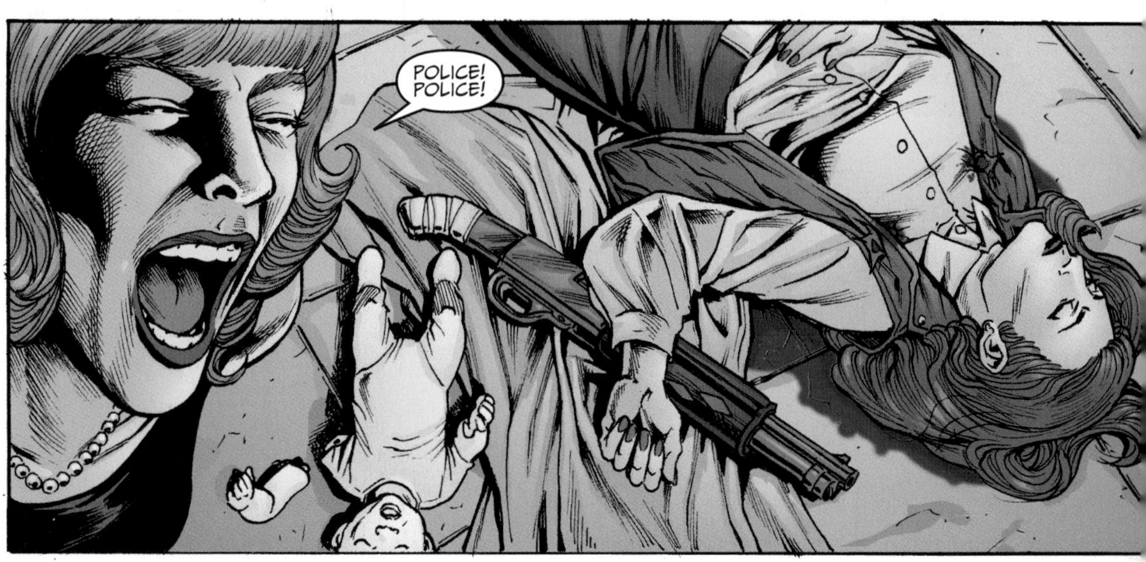
POLICE! POLICE!

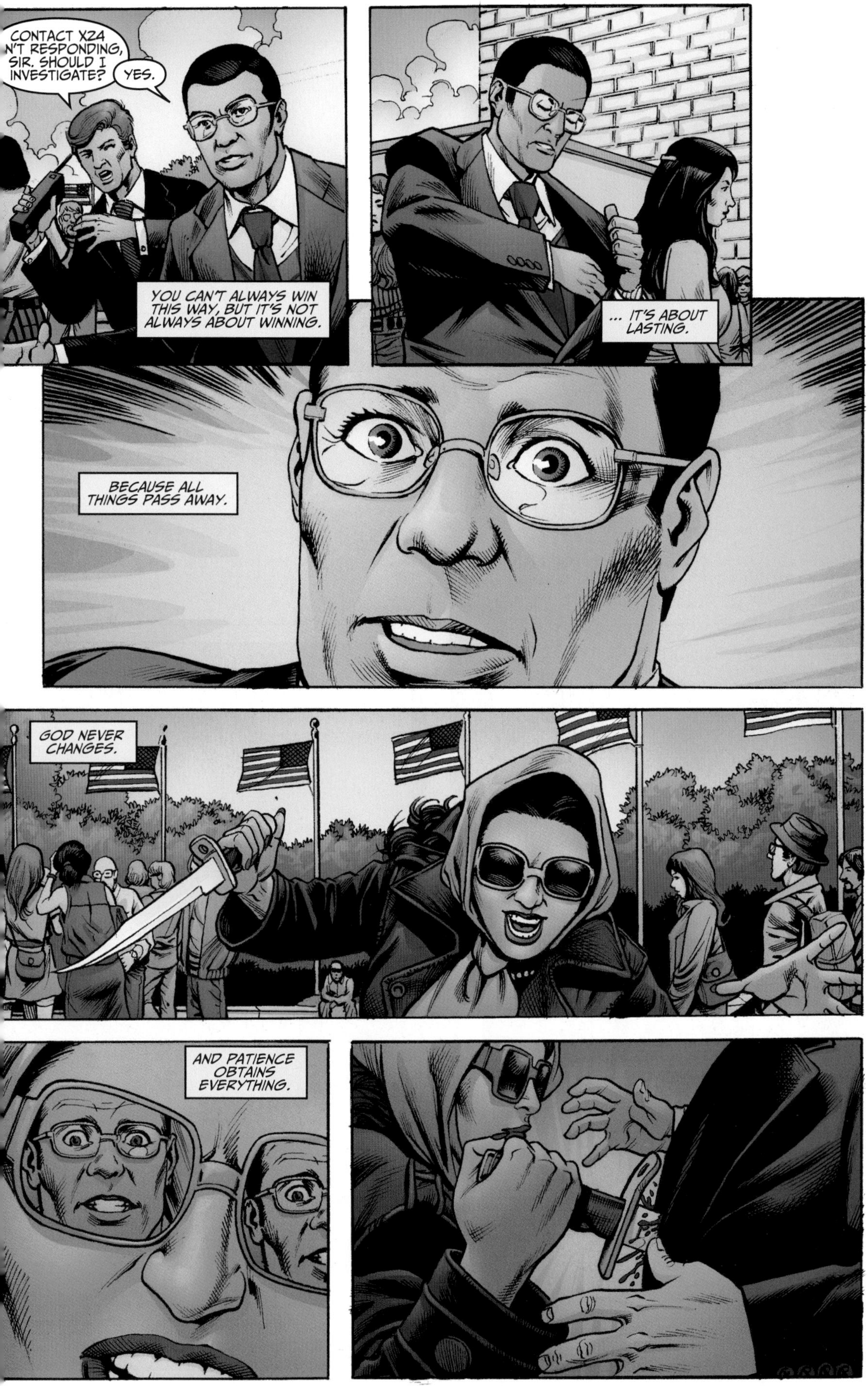
CONTACT X24
N'T RESPONDING,
SIR. SHOULD I
INVESTIGATE?
YES.
YOU CAN'T ALWAYS WIN THIS WAY, BUT IT'S NOT ALWAYS ABOUT WINNING.
... IT'S ABOUT LASTING.
BECAUSE ALL THINGS PASS AWAY.
GOD NEVER CHANGES.
AND PATIENCE OBTAINS EVERYTHING.

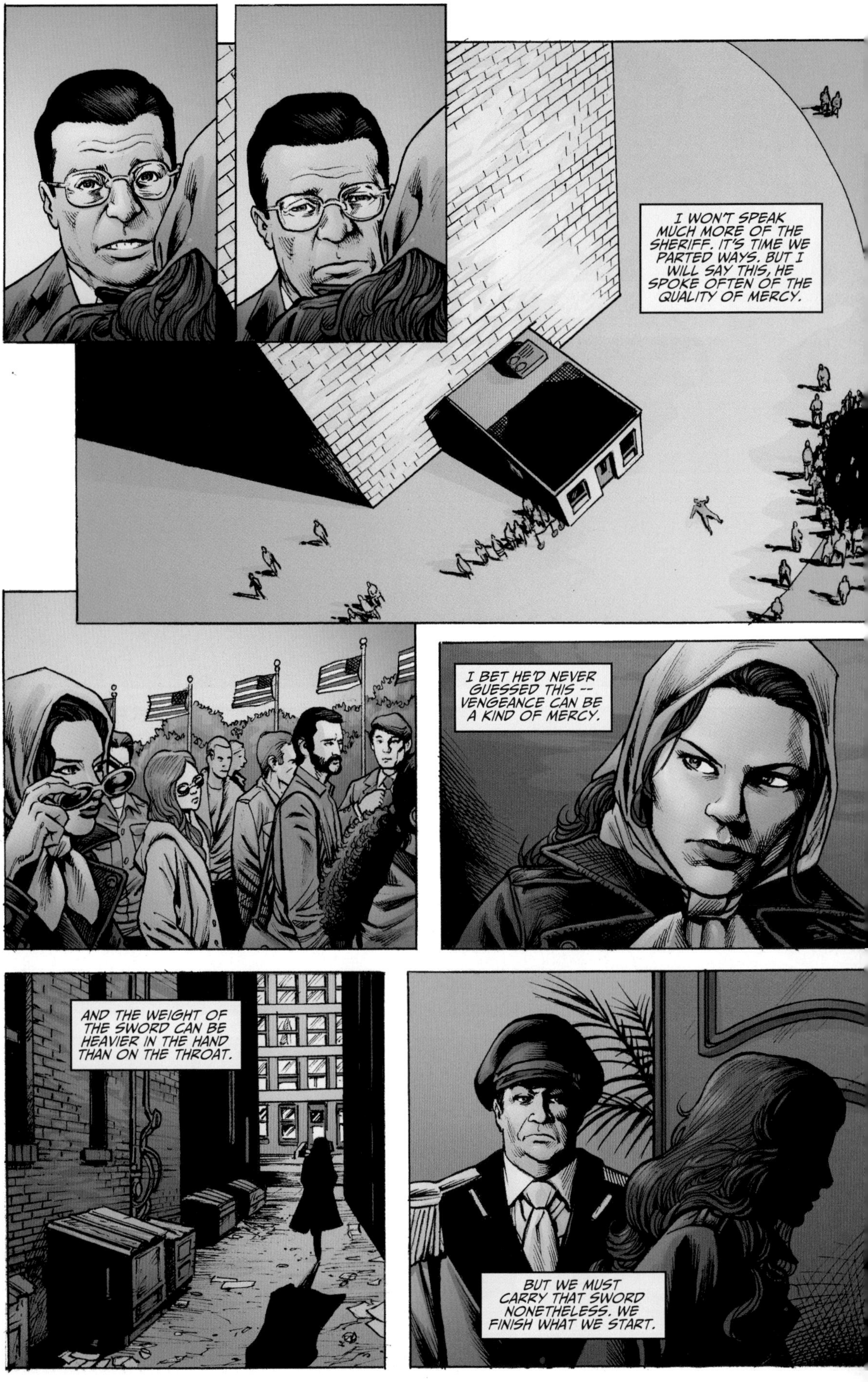
I WON'T SPEAK MUCH MORE OF THE SHERIFF. IT'S TIME WE PARTED WAYS. BUT I WILL SAY THIS, HE SPOKE OFTEN OF THE QUALITY OF MERCY.
I BET HE'D NEVER GUESSED THIS -- VENGEANCE CAN BE A KIND OF MERCY.
AND THE WEIGHT OF THE SWORD CAN BE HEAVIER IN THE HAND THAN ON THE THROAT.
BUT WE MUST CARRY THAT SWORD NONETHELESS. WE FINISH WHAT WE START.

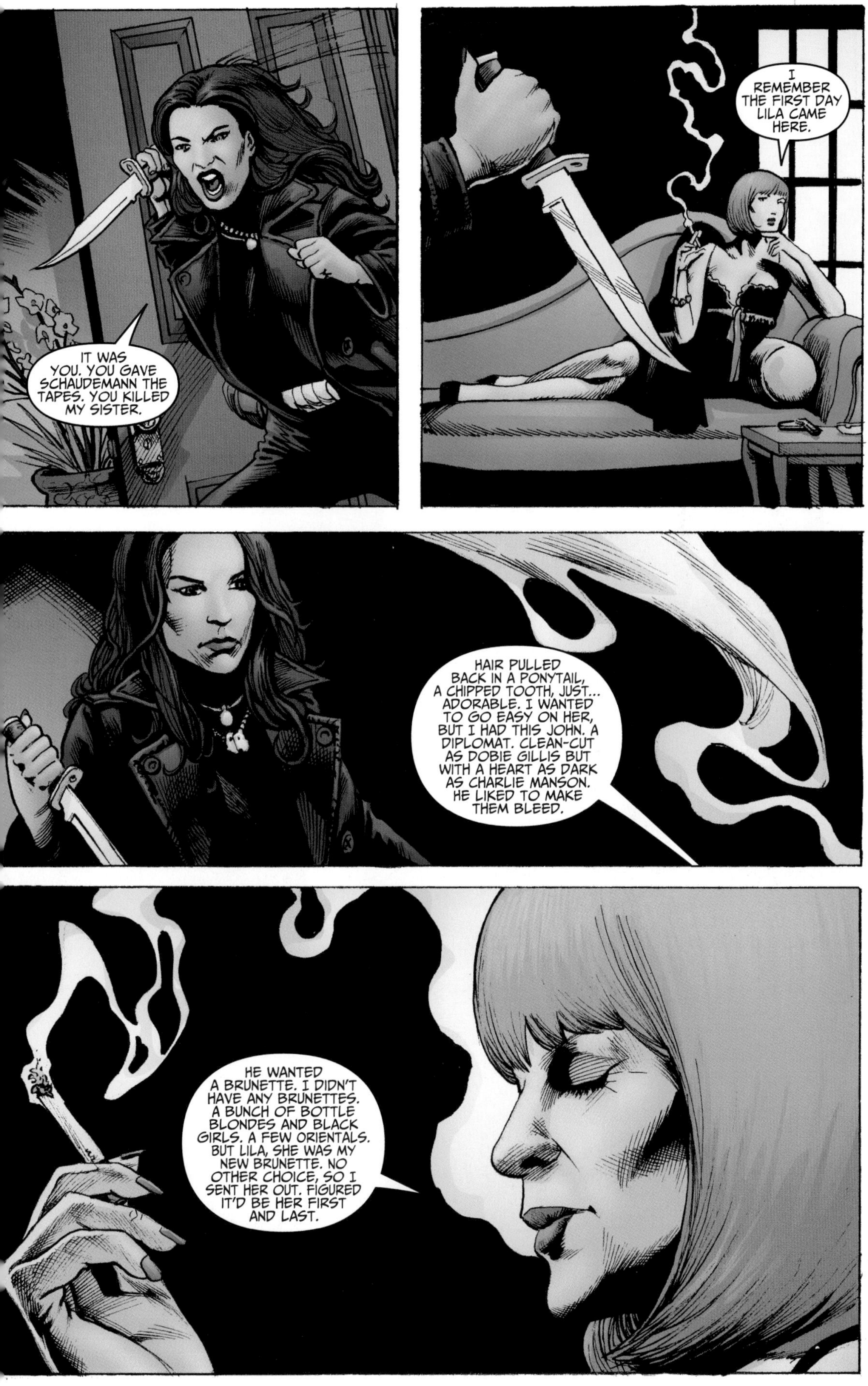
IT WAS YOU. YOU GAVE SCHAUDEMANN THE TAPES. YOU KILLED MY SISTER.
I REMEMBER THE FIRST DAY LILA CAME HERE.
HAIR PULLED BACK IN A PONYTAIL, A CHIPPED TOOTH, JUST... ADORABLE. I WANTED TO GO EASY ON HER, BUT I HAD THIS JOHN. A DIPLOMAT. CLEAN-CUT AS DOBIE GILLIS BUT WITH A HEART AS DARK AS CHARLIE MANSON. HE LIKED TO MAKE THEM BLEED.
HE WANTED A BRUNETTE. I DIDN'T HAVE ANY BRUNETTES. A BUNCH OF BOTTLE BLONDES AND BLACK GIRLS. A FEW ORIENTALS. BUT LILA, SHE WAS MY NEW BRUNETTE. NO OTHER CHOICE, SO I SENT HER OUT. FIGURED IT'D BE HER FIRST AND LAST.

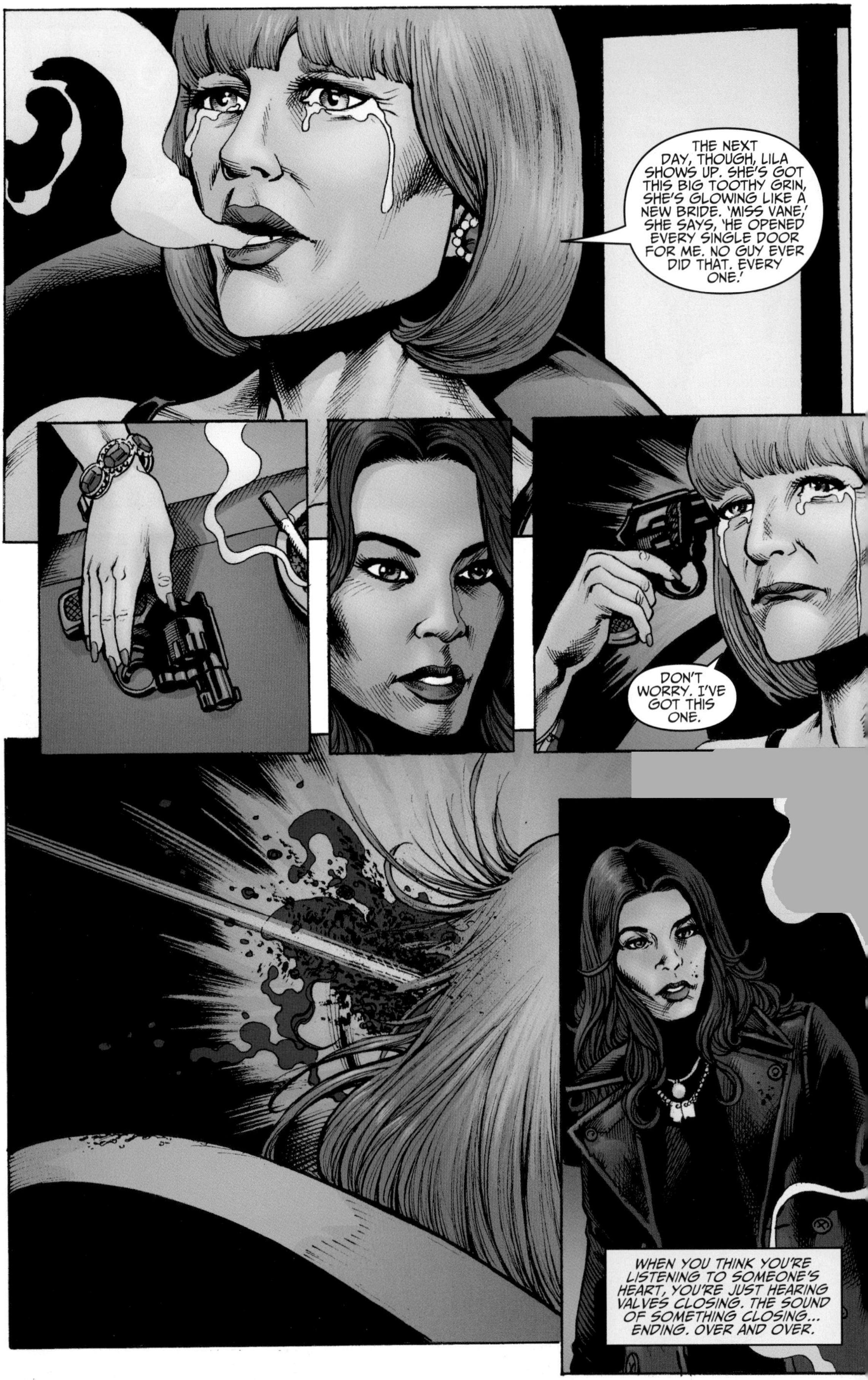
THE NEXT DAY, THOUGH, LILA SHOWS UP. SHE'S GOT THIS BIG TOOTHY GRIN, SHE'S GLOWING LIKE A NEW BRIDE. 'MISS VANE,' SHE SAYS, 'HE OPENED EVERY SINGLE DOOR FOR ME. NO GUY EVER DID THAT. EVERY ONE.'
DON'T WORRY. I'VE GOT THIS ONE.
WHEN YOU THINK YOU'RE LISTENING TO SOMEONE'S HEART, YOU'RE JUST HEARING VALVES CLOSING. THE SOUND OF SOMETHING CLOSING... ENDING. OVER AND OVER.

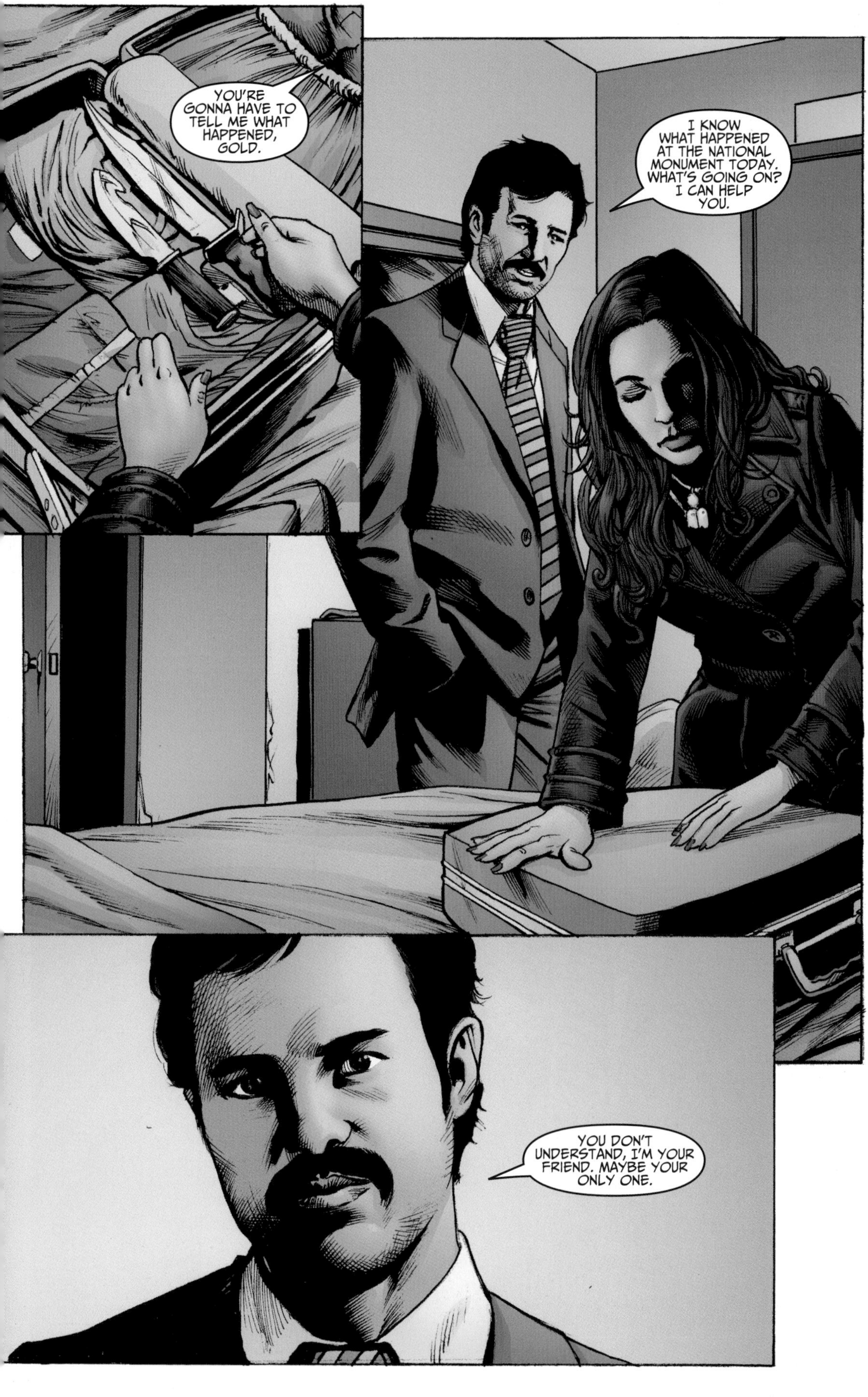
YOU'RE GONNA HAVE TO TELL ME WHAT HAPPENED, GOLD.
I KNOW WHAT HAPPENED AT THE NATIONAL MONUMENT TODAY. WHAT'S GOING ON? I CAN HELP YOU.
YOU DON'T UNDERSTAND, I'M YOUR FRIEND. MAYBE YOUR ONLY ONE.

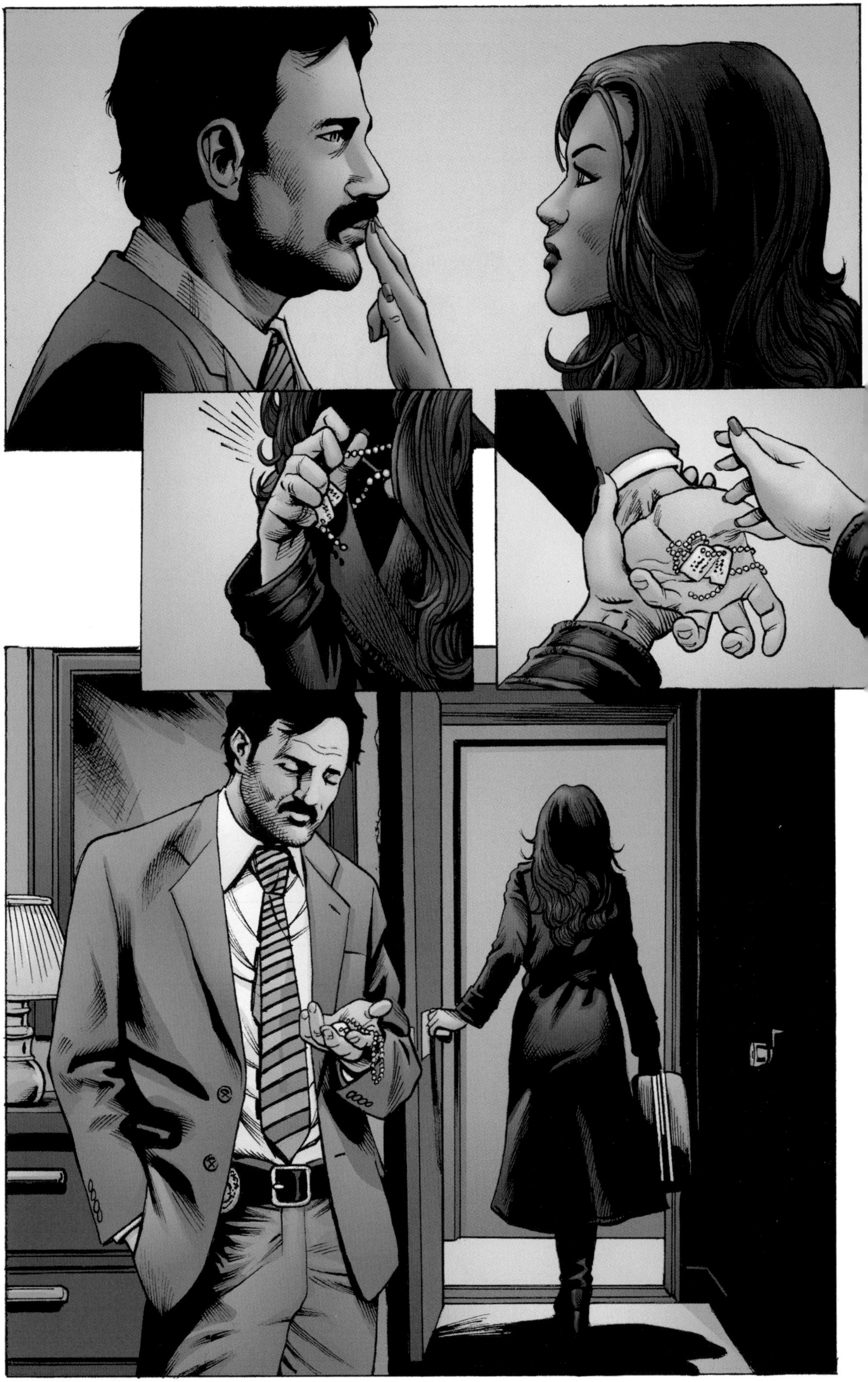

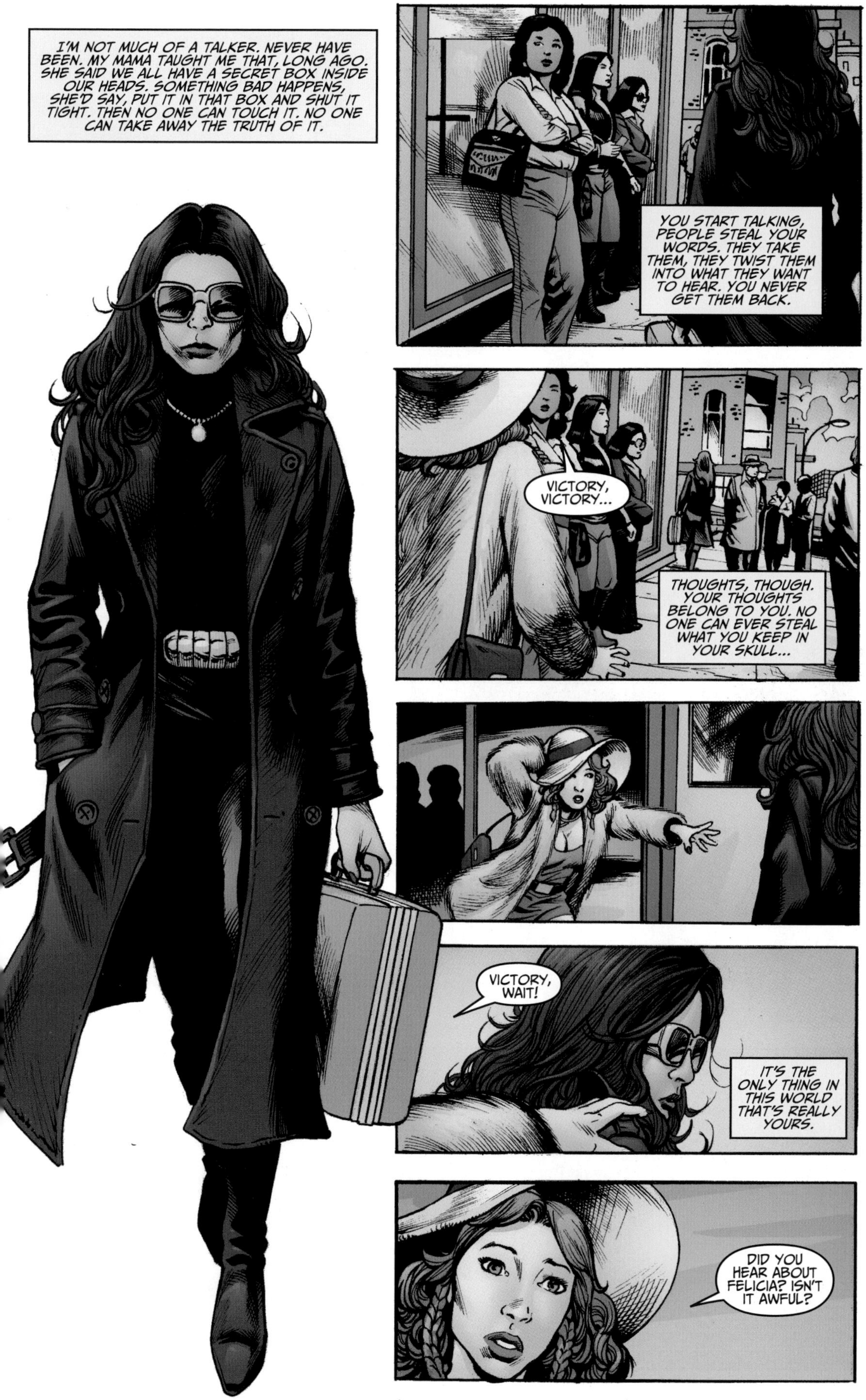
I'M NOT MUCH OF A TALKER. NEVER HAVE BEEN. MY MAMA TAUGHT ME THAT, LONG AGO. SHE SAID WE ALL HAVE A SECRET BOX INSIDE OUR HEADS. SOMETHING BAD HAPPENS, SHE'D SAY, PUT IT IN THAT BOX AND SHUT IT TIGHT. THEN NO ONE CAN TOUCH IT. NO ONE CAN TAKE AWAY THE TRUTH OF IT.
YOU START TALKING, PEOPLE STEAL YOUR WORDS. THEY TAKE THEM, THEY TWIST THEM INTO WHAT THEY WANT TO HEAR. YOU NEVER GET THEM BACK.
VICTORY, VICTORY...
THOUGHTS, THOUGH. YOUR THOUGHTS BELONG TO YOU. NO ONE CAN EVER STEAL WHAT YOU KEEP IN YOUR SKULL...
VICTORY, WAIT!
IT'S THE ONLY THING IN THIS WORLD THAT'S REALLY YOURS.
DID YOU HEAR ABOUT FELICIA? ISN'T IT AWFUL?

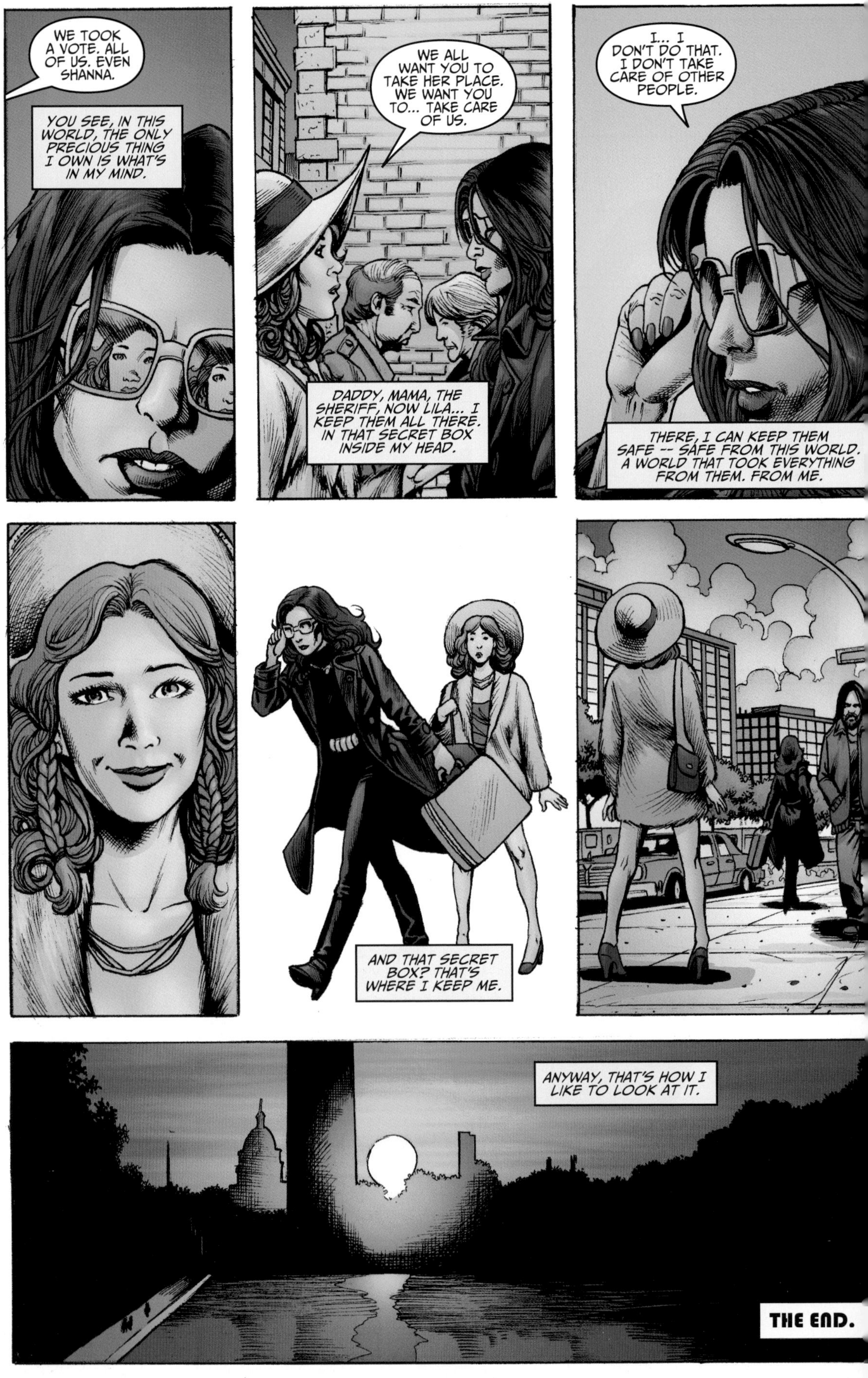
WE TOOK A VOTE. ALL OF US. EVEN SHANNA.
YOU SEE, IN THIS WORLD, THE ONLY PRECIOUS THING I OWN IS WHAT'S IN MY MIND.
WE ALL WANT YOU TO TAKE HER PLACE. WE WANT YOU TO... TAKE CARE OF US.
DADDY, MAMA, THE SHERIFF, NOW LILA... I KEEP THEM ALL THERE. IN THAT SECRET BOX INSIDE MY HEAD.
I... I DON'T DO THAT. I DON'T TAKE CARE OF OTHER PEOPLE.
THERE, I CAN KEEP THEM SAFE -- SAFE FROM THIS WORLD. A WORLD THAT TOOK EVERYTHING FROM THEM. FROM ME.
AND THAT SECRET BOX? THAT'S WHERE I KEEP ME.
ANYWAY, THAT'S HOW I LIKE TO LOOK AT IT.
THE END.

NINE MOVIE MUSES OF NORMANDY GOLD

Normandy Gold was born of our mutual love of 70s movies. The gritty look, the relentless pacing, the deeply flawed heroes and the dizzying unpredictability of films like *The Parallax View*, *Three Days of the Condor*, *All the President's Men* and *The Conversation* resonated with both of us, as did the creeping, this-could-really-happen sense of paranoia they continue to inspire. When we wrote the script for *Normandy*, we wanted to make sure the art would feel not just "70s" but cinematic. So in addition to reference photos of everything from conversation pits to Mel Ramos paintings to group sex at Plato's Retreat and shots of real-life historical figures H.R. Haldeman, Martha Mitchell, and Robert McNamara, we included stills from several different movies to accompany our panel descriptions. In bringing it all to life, the remarkable Steve Scott exceeded our wildest expectations.

Some of the film stills that inspired us are listed below.
Can you spot them?

TAXI DRIVER
ALL THE PRESIDENTS MEN
CARRIE
SHAMPOO
HARDCORE
PRETTY BABY
THE CONVERSATION
DRESSED TO KILL
DEEP THROAT

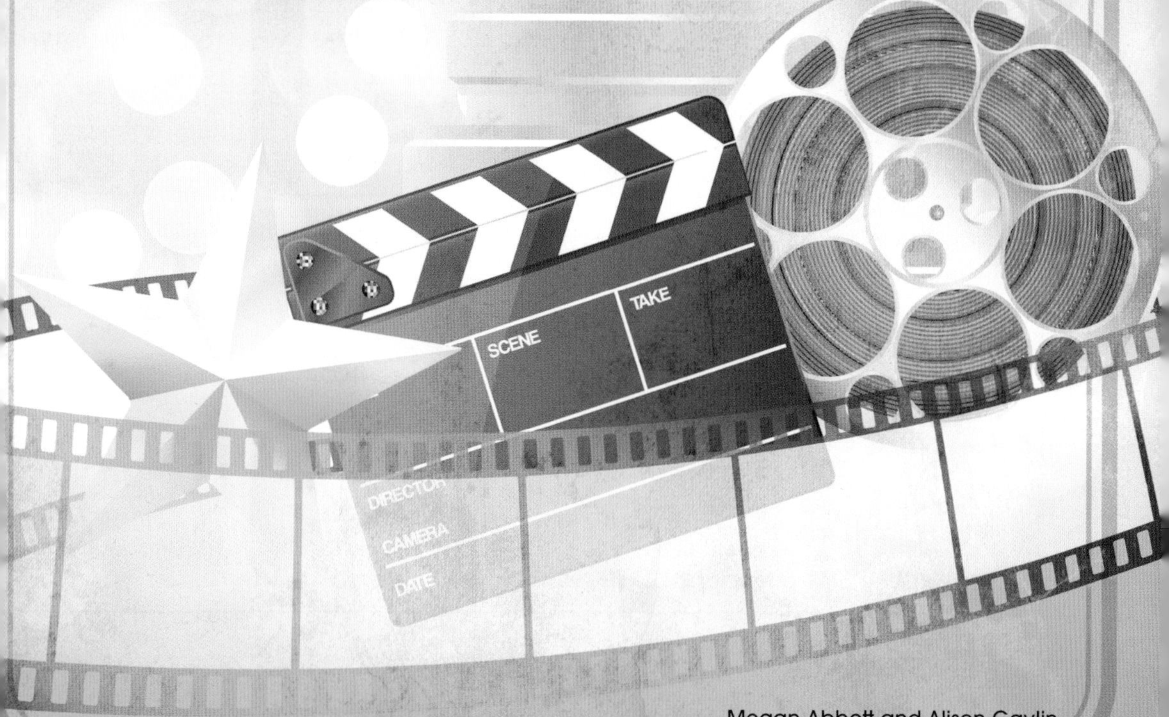
TAKE
SCENE
DIRECTOR
CAMERA
DATE

Megan Abbott and Alison Gaylin

FANTASY CASTING

Many writers envision movie versions of their books, casting favorite actors in each of the roles. But when we wrote *Normandy Gold*, we went one step further and made fantasy casting an actual part of the creative process.

Normandy was born not so much of an era but an era of cinema; we saw it as the best 70s noir thriller that never existed. So when we wrote the script, we often introduced characters by including headshots of the actors we ideally saw portraying them. As you'll see, we did this for nearly every major role. And though we tried to stick to actors from the era, some are clearly not… while others aren't even actors

OUR FANTASY CAST (IN ORDER OF APPEARANCE):

LILA: OLIVIA HUSSEY

DET. PAUL STURGES: MARK RUFFALO

LARA THE RECEPTIONIST: PJ SOLES

CHARITY: JODIE FOSTER

FELICIA VANE: LEE GRANT

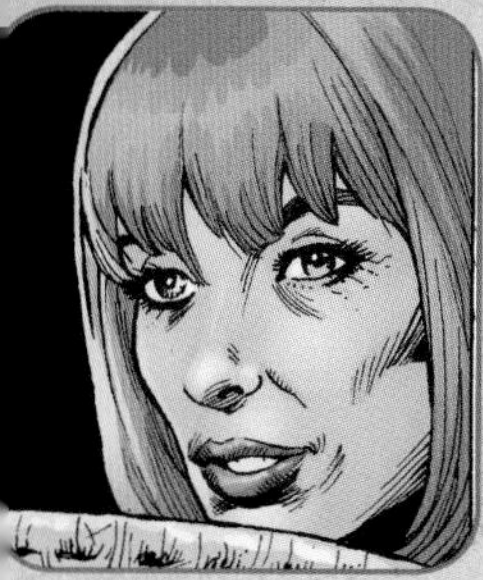
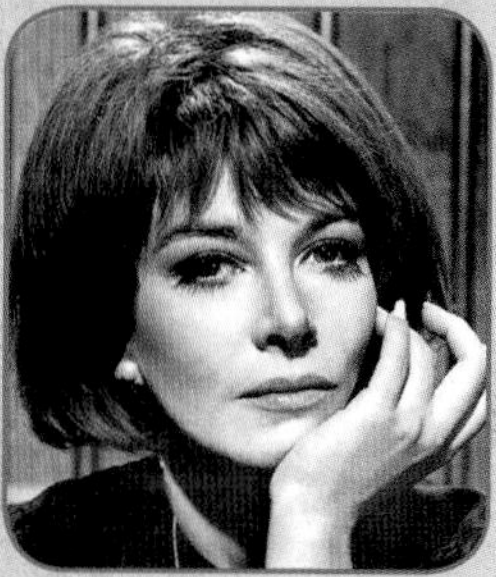

SHANNA: NANCY ALLEN

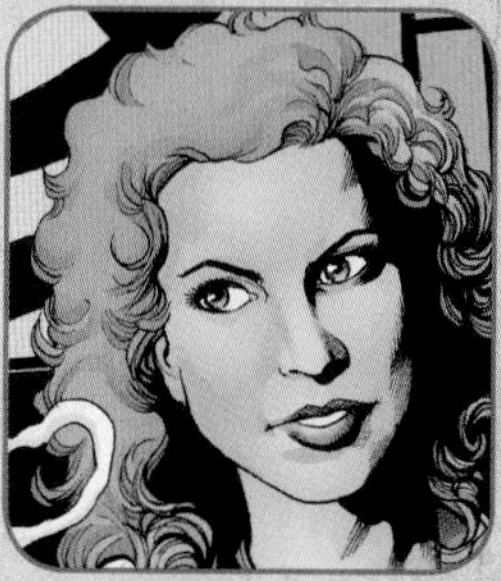
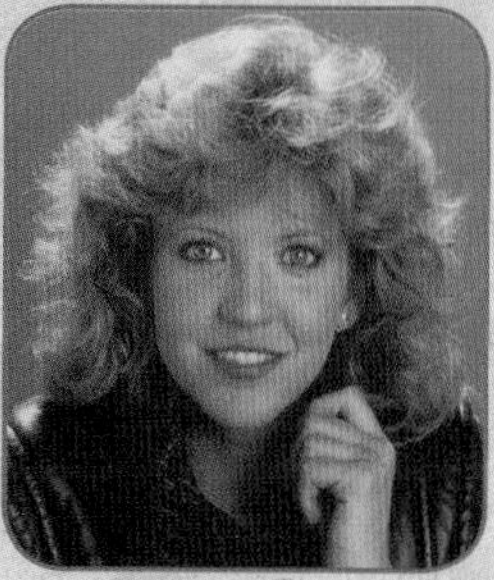

SELWYN GRANGE: ROBERT REDFORD

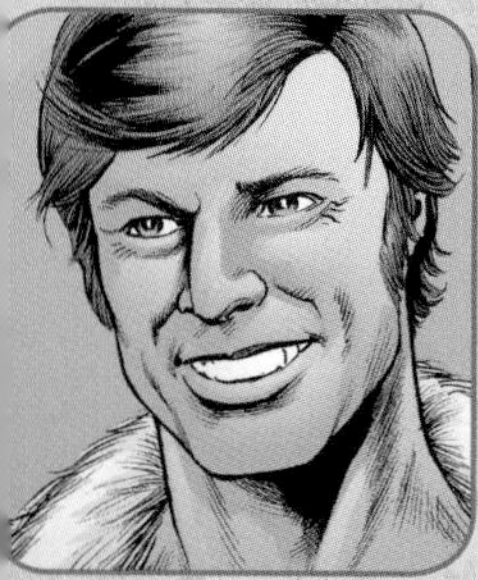
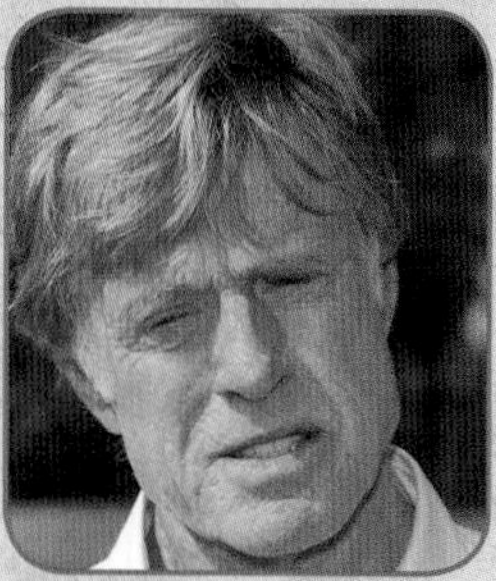

CHIEF JUSTICE (NORMANDY'S LIMO CLIENT): HAL HOLBROOK

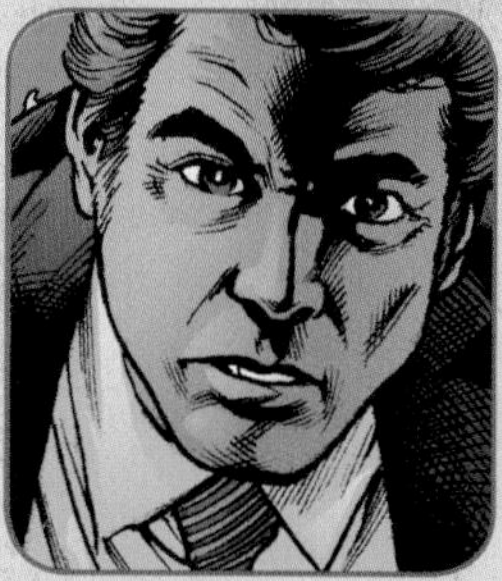
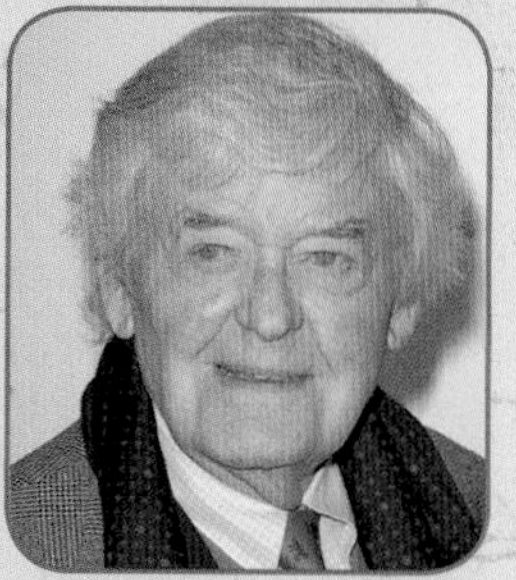

JOHNNY DEEPER: SAM ELLIOTT

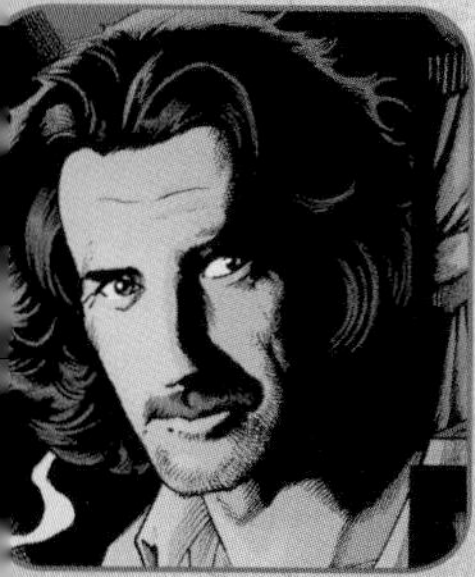
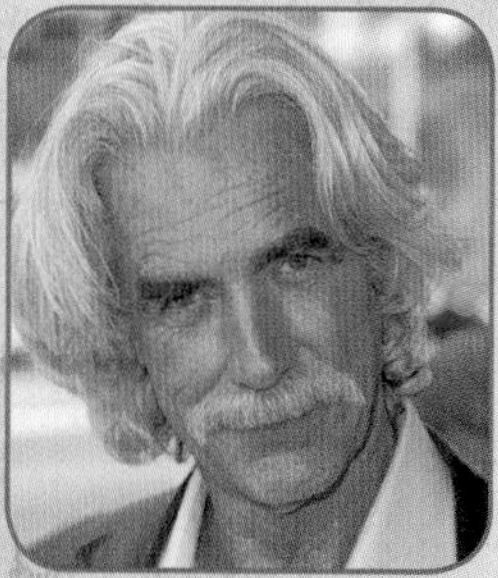

PHILLIPA SALES: MARTHA MITCHELL

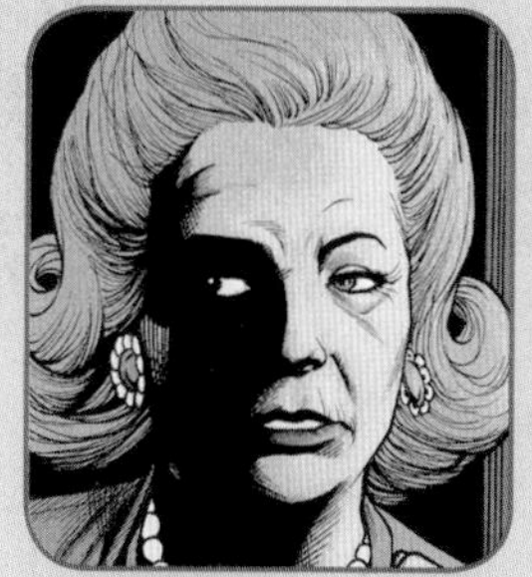
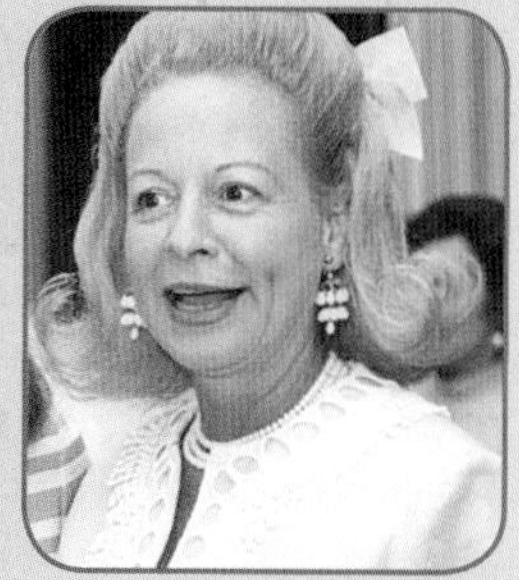

APHRODITE'S HIDEAWAY CLIENT (DESCRIBED IN SCRIPT AS "HARRY REEMS LOOKALIKE"): HARRY REEMS.

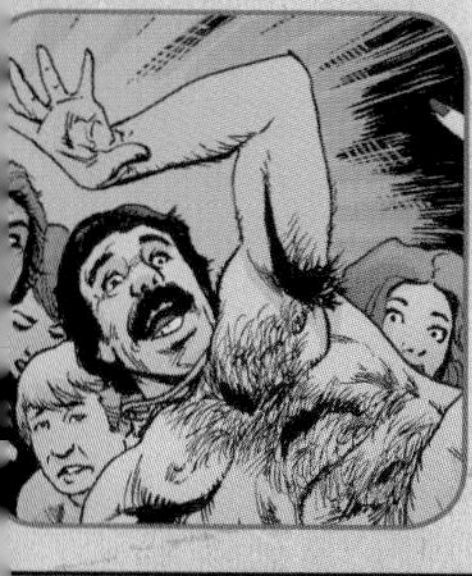
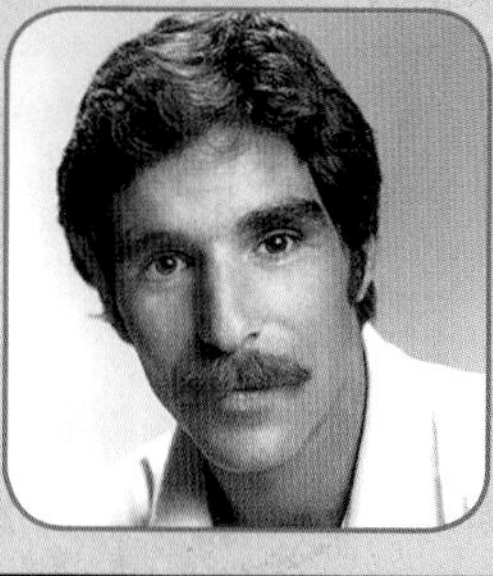

HUGH SCHAUDEMANN: ROBERT MCNAMARA

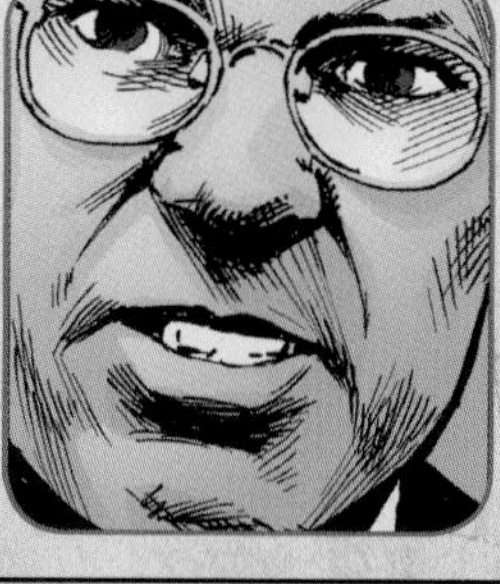
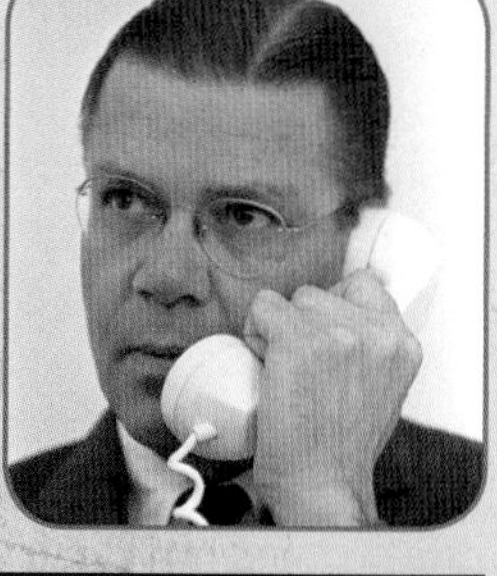

' course, the one role we didn't actually cast was that of Normandy herself. While we discussed numerous actresses that would be perfect for the ırt — Raquel Welch, Pam Grier, Charlize Theron and Beyonce to name a few — we never pinned down a final choice. And we'd love to hear ur opinions. Please tweet any and all casting suggestions to @ComicsTitan, along with the hashtag #NormandyGoldCasting.

Megan Abbott and Alison Gaylin

FILMS, FEARLESSNESS AND FEMALE RAGE

MEGAN ABBOTT AND ALISON GAYLIN TALK
NORMANDY GOLD

Alison Gaylin: As I recall, we first came up with the idea for *Normandy Gold* nearly ten years ago. At the time, we wanted to write something based on our mutual love of 70s political conspiracy movies, but it's kind of surprising how relevant it's become.

Megan Abbott: Isn't it? It appears that abuse of power is evergreen. I think we were also very interested in exploring female rage and vengeance. So many great 70s movies – from *Dirty Harry* to *Taxi Driver* – deal with avenging men and they tend to be portrayed as either bad-ass heroes or darkly glamorous anti-heroes. But what about an avenging woman? Especially one operating in men's arenas, be it prostitution or politics. Normandy's rage was so satisfying to write about because she gets to act on it. That's the other part, of course, that seems very timely now.

AG: Exactly! I think it's important to point out here that Normandy isn't a superhero, or some great detective. She's just a really, really pissed off woman, which as it turns out is a very powerful thing.

It's interesting — we both write crime novels, but while we were writing this, the one thing we kept reminding each other is that Normandy is not an investigator. She has a lot more in common with Lee Marvin in *Point Blank* than she does with say, Angela Lansbury in *Murder, She Wrote*. She doesn't give a damn about the shadow government or who wins the Presidency or whatever dirty deeds are going down behind the scenes. She wants

to find out who killed her sister so that she can kill that person. She is single-minded, which isn't a trait you see that often in female characters. Did we ever want to make her more "likeable"? (I know the answer to this question, but I'm asking you anyway.)

MA: I think we both feel what makes a protagonist likable is when they feel real. And there's something very, very real about Normandy's rage, her sense of loss, her regret, her refusal to perform "femininity" for anyone. She's all drives and action which is thrilling to write about. I think we made a conscious effort to flip that hackneyed gender script and that it would be Sturges, the cop, who would be the one on the sidelines, the thinker, the talker, the conscience. Normandy would be the do-er. And also that she would make mistakes. And that, like any noirish male hero, she would have a self-destructive impulse too. Normandy is, in many ways, willing to go down with the ship, isn't she?

AG: Yes. She is absolutely fearless. And she has such conviction. I found writing her exhilarating. And I think we both have a soft spot for Sturges, whom we envisioned as Mark Ruffalo in *Zodiac*.

I keep coming back to movies here, but movies were so much on our minds when we were writing this script, and one of the many things we've bonded over as friends.

MA: Normandy is fearless, but also with a kind of nihilism, or at least a willingness to enter the

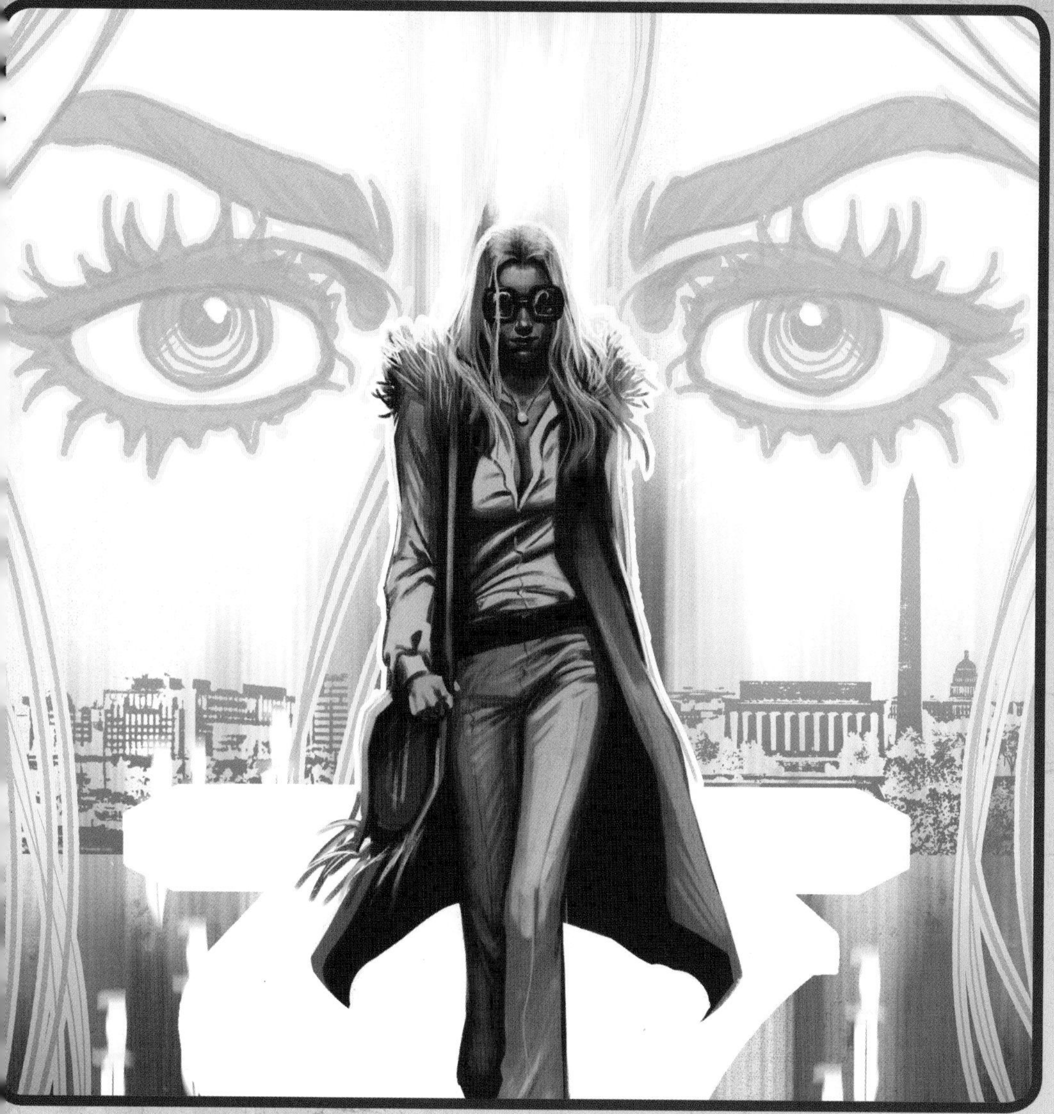

oid if she needs to. Which makes her such a
·omplicated protagonist, which I know we
·oth love.

hose women are hard to find in so many of our avorite 70s movies — they're often women who xist in the corners of the narrative, like Paula rentiss in *Parallax View*, or Season Hubley in *ardcore*. Weirdly — and I'm getting to perhaps ur greatest movie-bonding moment — one f the most fully realized women in these 70s aranoid thrillers is Nancy Allen's character in *ressed to Kill*. And yet Brian De Palma frequently ets a bad rap!

G: Yes! We love our De Palma movies, and ancy Allen is glorious in *Dressed to Kill*. (As a side-note, we also had the pleasure of re-visiting *Body Double* on a big screen at BAM not too long ago, and boy did it hold up.)

MA: So where do you think Normandy goes after the comic's last pages? What happens to her?

AG: I want to say she takes over for Felicia, having found a new sister to care for in Charity. But maybe she and Charity head back out west and enforce the law (or lack of it) in some other small town. What do you think? Whatever she does, the one thing I can say for sure is that Normandy won't be talking much about it.

MA: Haha! Agreed. And in that spirit, let's toast to Normandy and her silences that speak volumes!

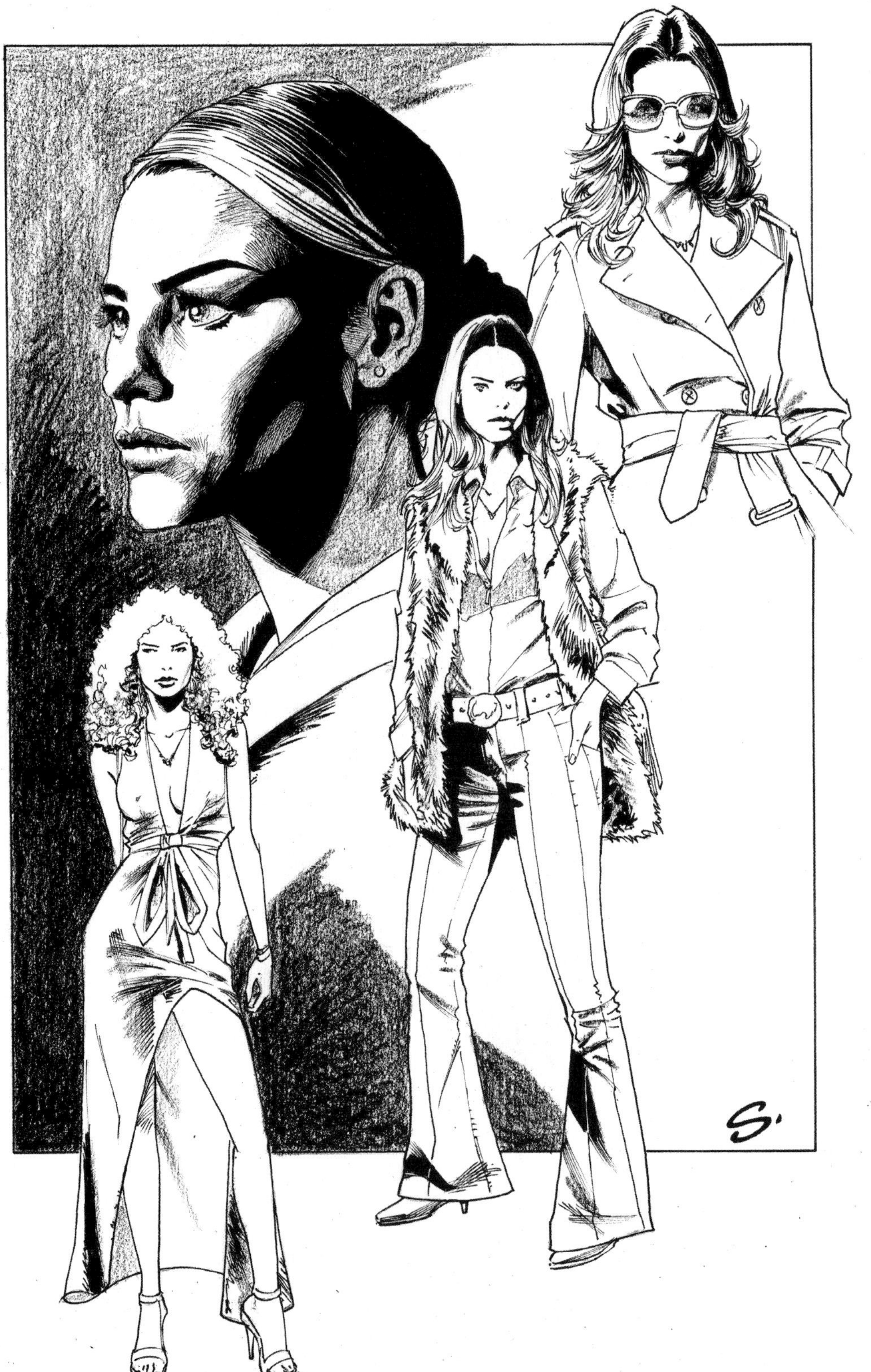
S.

NORMANDY GOLD (by Steve Scott)

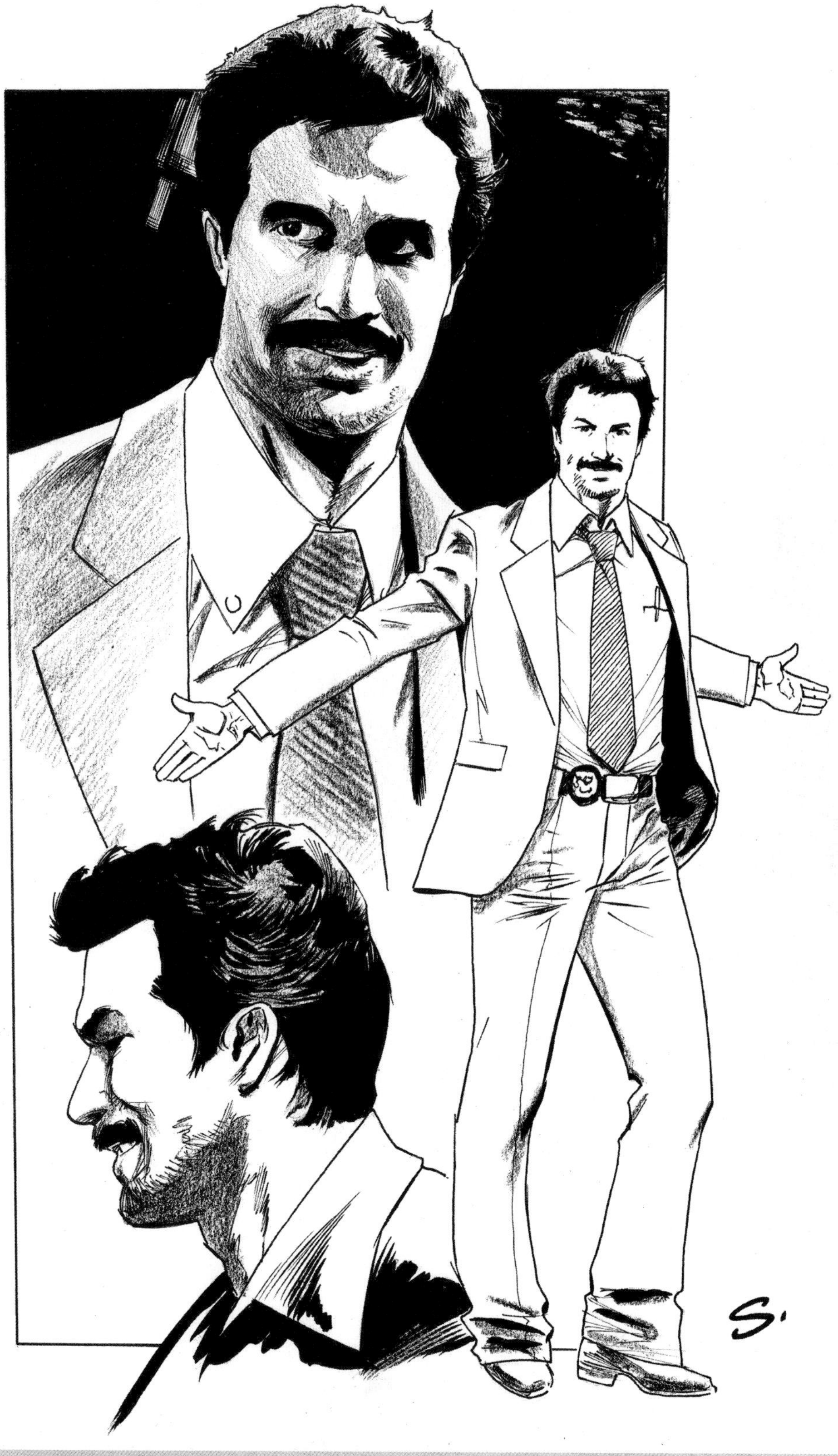
S.

PAUL STURGES (by Steve Scott)

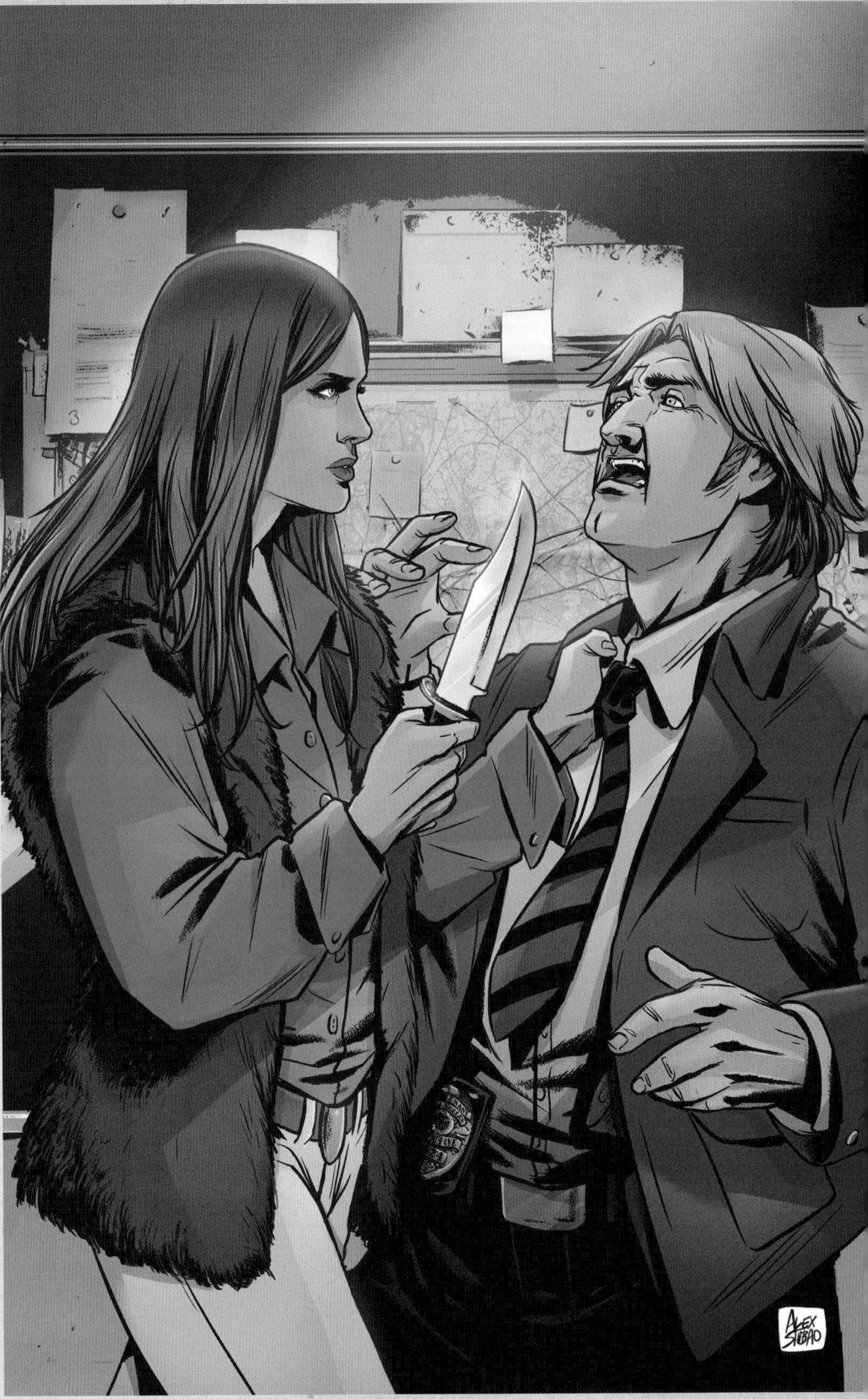
ALEX SHIBAO

ISSUE 1 COVER C BY **ALEX SHIBAO**

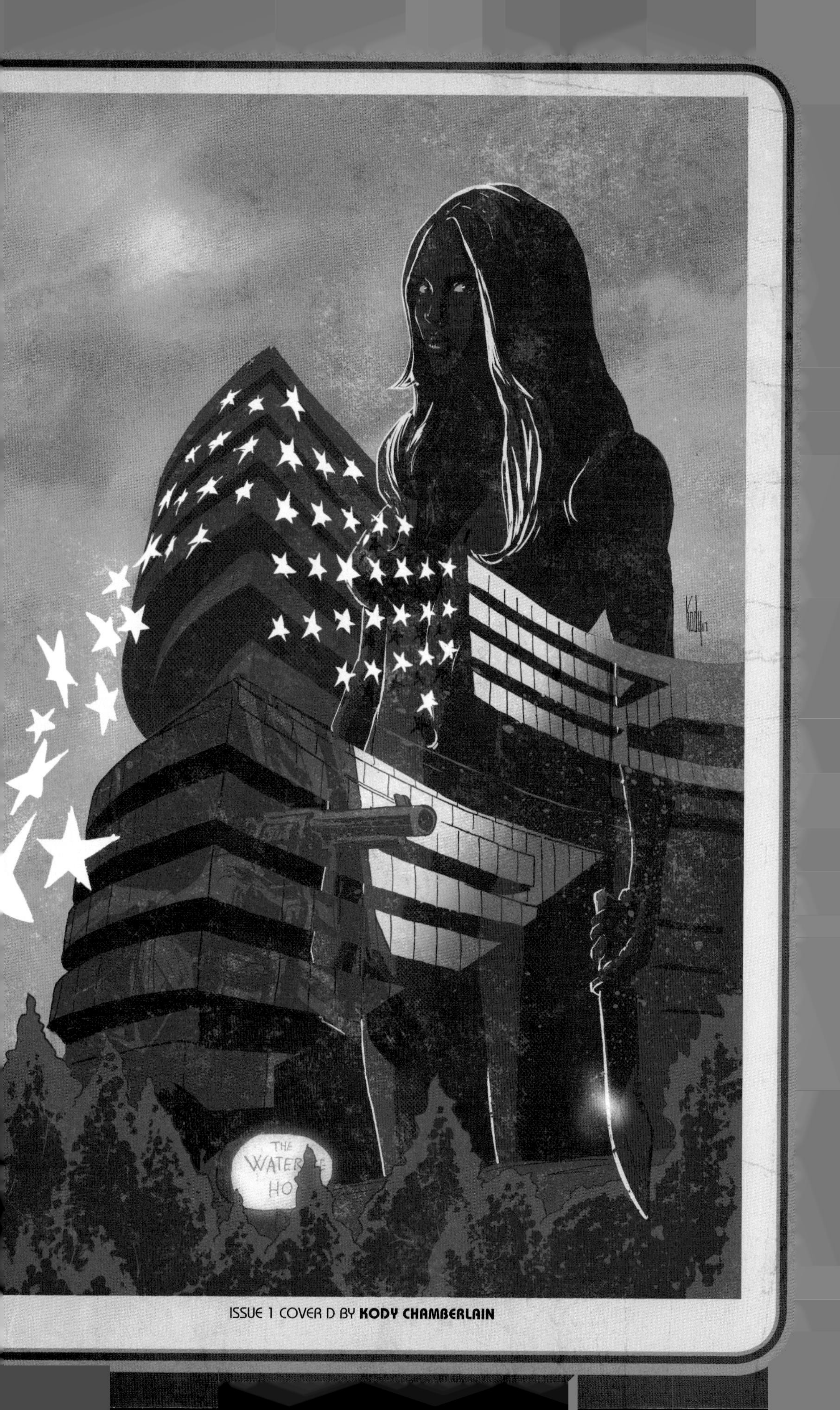
THE
WATER
HO

ISSUE 1 COVER D BY **KODY CHAMBERLAIN**

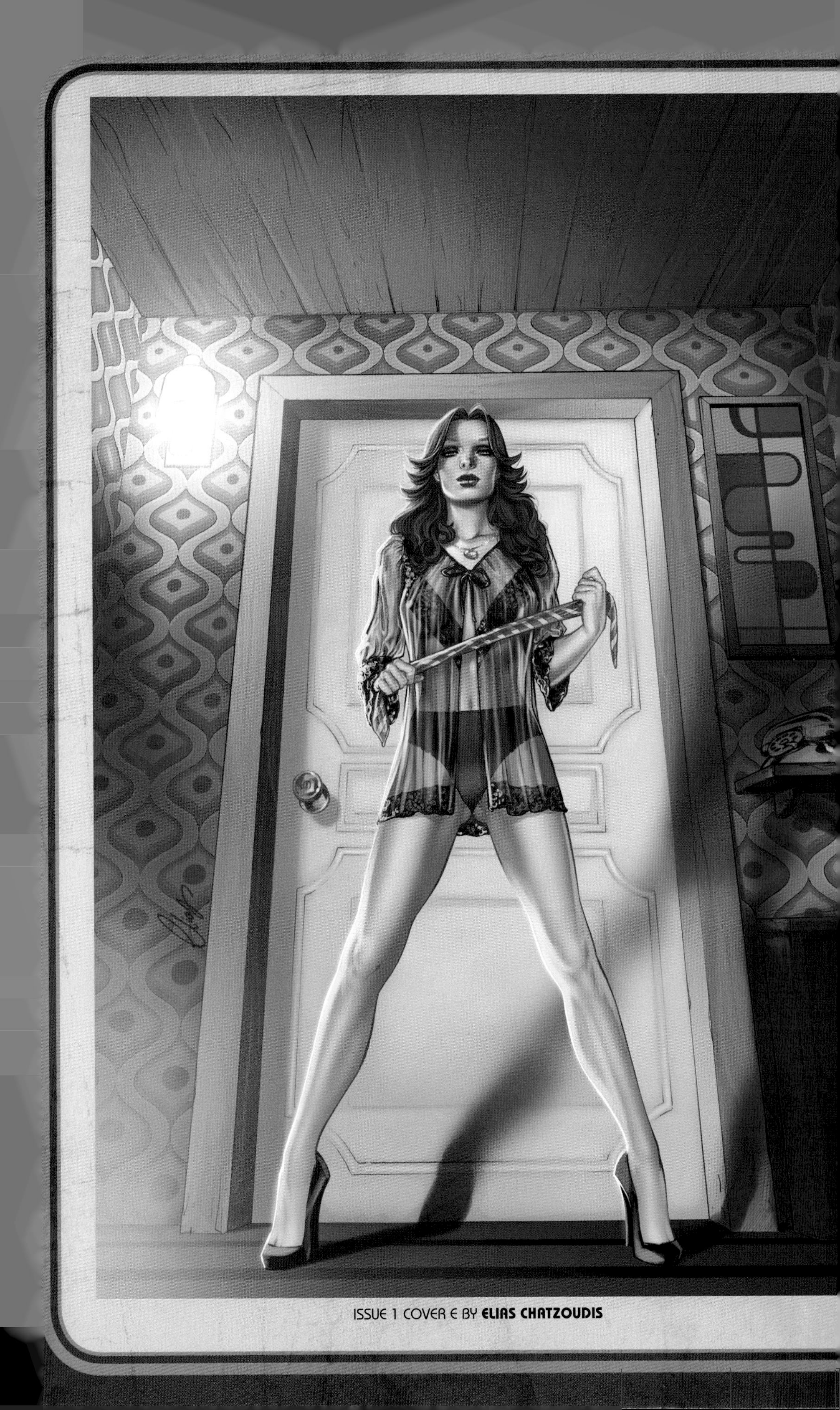

ISSUE 1 COVER E BY **ELIAS CHATZOUDIS**

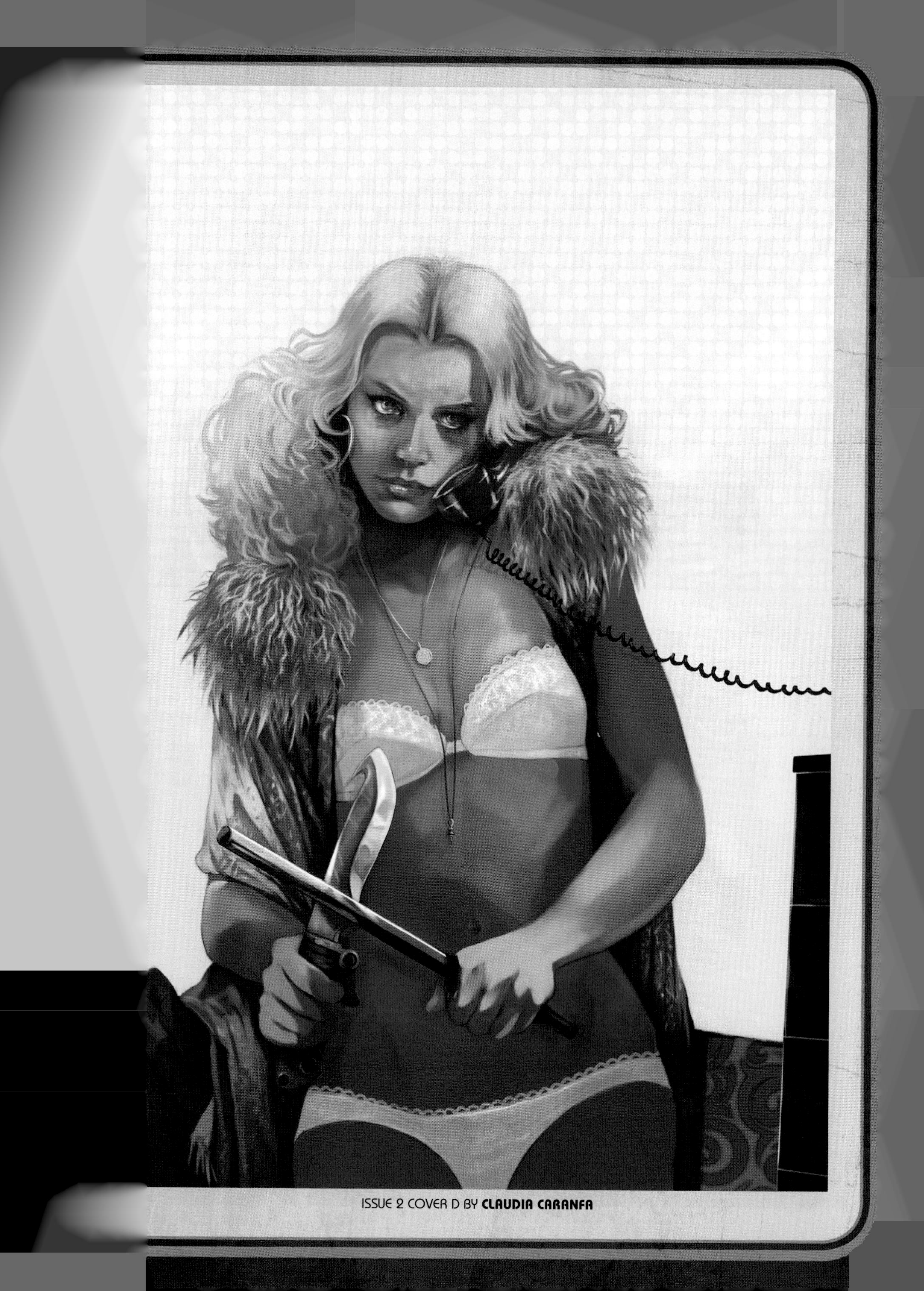

ISSUE 2 COVER D BY **CLAUDIA CARANFA**

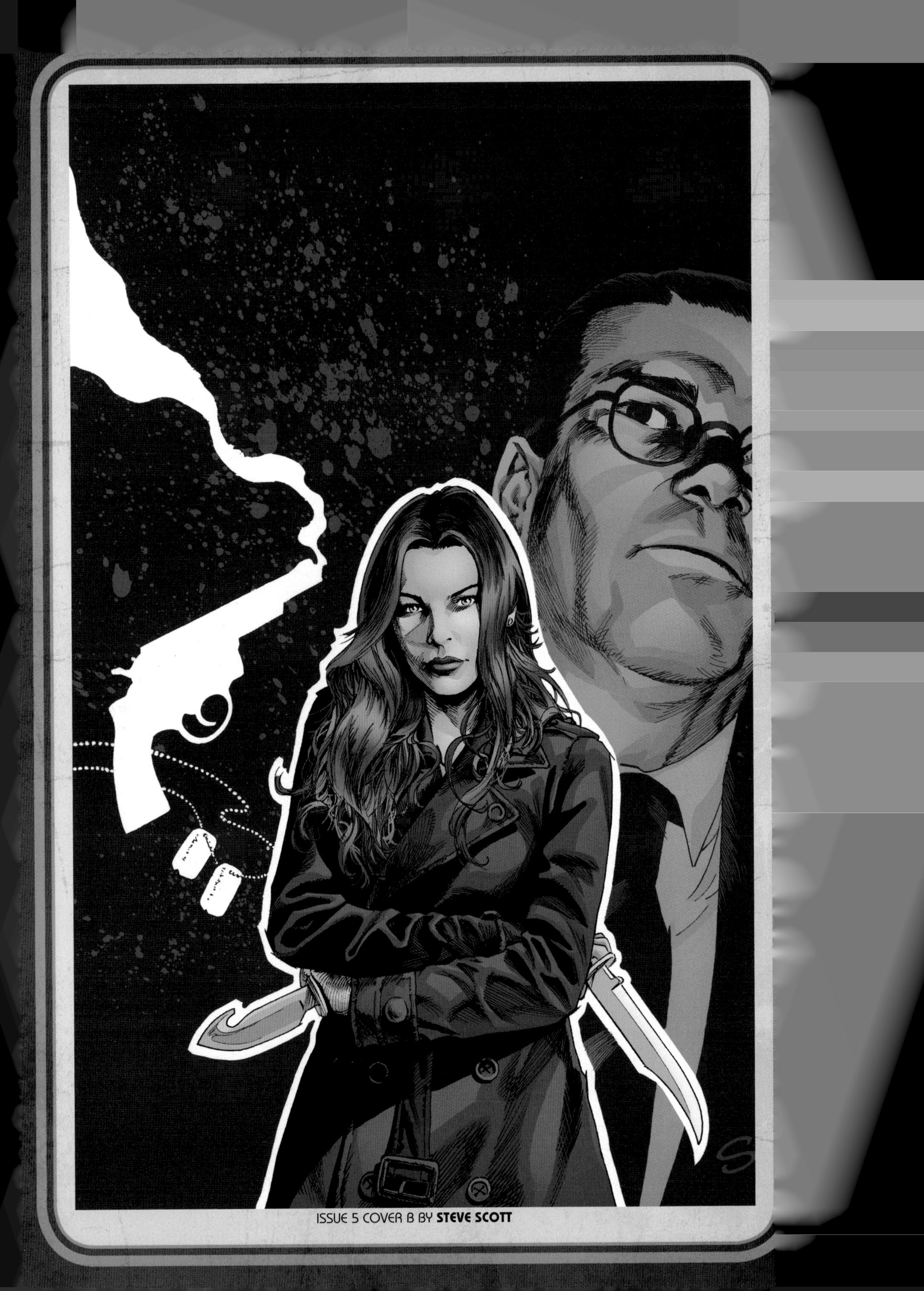

ISSUE 5 COVER B BY **STEVE SCOTT**

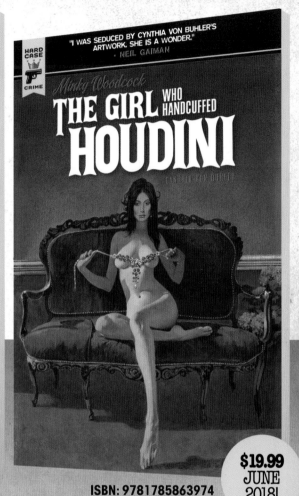

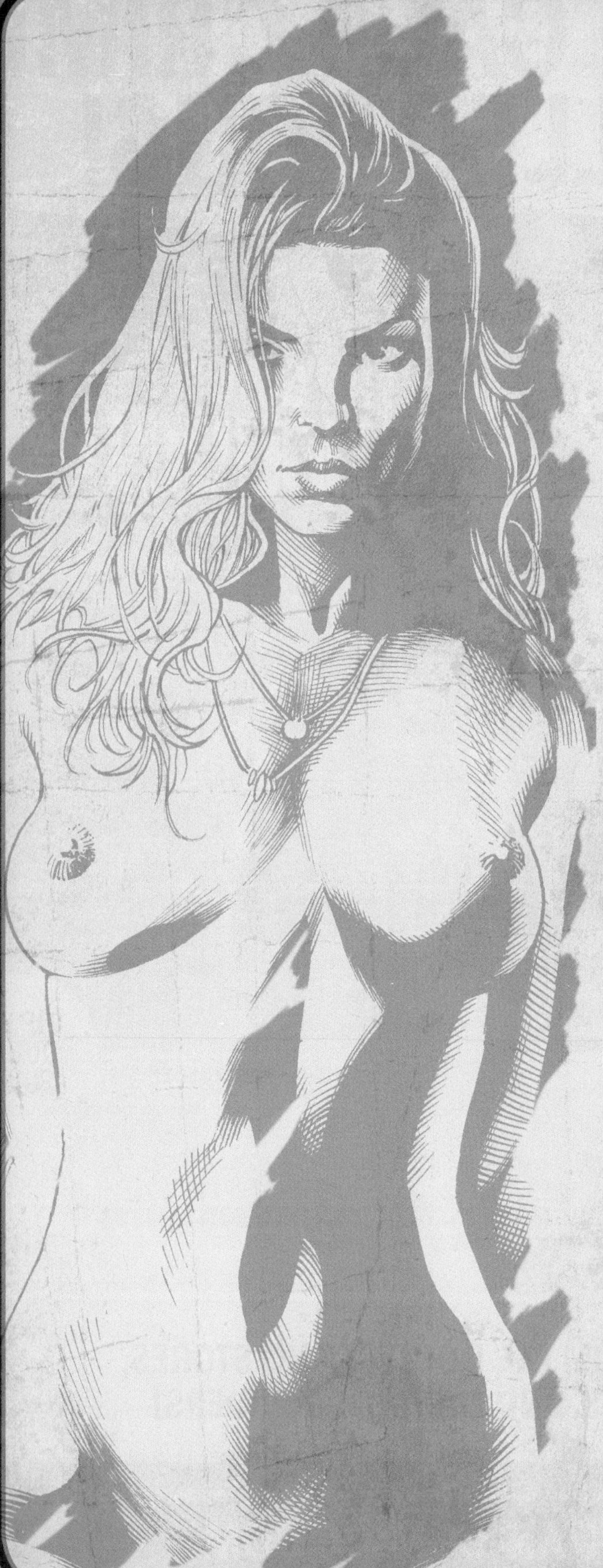

NORMANDY GOLD

CREATOR BIOS

MEGAN ABBOTT

is the Edgar award-winning author of eight novels, including *Dare Me*, *The Fever* and the bestselling *You Will Know Me*. She is currently a staff writer of HBO's new David Simon show, *The Deuce*. Her next novel, *Give Me Your Hand*, comes out in July 2018.

ALISON GAYLIN

is a national and international bestselling author. She has been nominated for the Edgar award three times, most recently for *What Remains of Me*. She is the author of ten books, including the Shamus award-winning *Brenna Spector* suspense series *If I Die Tonight*, out in March 2018 from William Morrow.

STEVE SCOTT

is an American comic book artist who has illustrated such titles as *Batman*, *X-Men Forever*, *JLA*, *Batman Confidential*, *Marvel Adventures Hulk* and many more. An industry veteran, his most recent work includes the adaptation of Neil Gaiman's *The Graveyard Book*.

RODNEY RAMOS

is an American comic book artist whose career has seen him pencil and ink work for the likes of Marvel, DC Comics and Valiant. He has worked on such titles as *Batman*, *Green Lantern*, *Wonder Woman*, *52*, *Countdown*, *X-Men*, *Spider-Man*, *Iron Man* and the critically acclaimed *Transmetropolitan*.

LOVERN KINDZIERSKI

is a Canadian colorist, writer and illustrator, who has worked for every major publisher in the industry. Considered one of comics' most influential colorists, his work has been nominated several times for both Eisner and Harvey awards. Some of his most recognised work includes *Hellblazer*, *Hulk*, *Shame*, *Wolverine* and *Spider-Man*.